From:

....

To:

....

Date:

....

I can do all things through Christ
who strengthens me.

— Philippians 4:13 (NKJV)

STRENGTH FOR TODAY
Daily Devotional

By D. James Kennedy and Jerry Newcombe

Cover and Interior Design by Roark Creative, roarkcreative.com

ISBN: 978-1-929626-45-8

Printed in Canada

Published by:

D. JAMES KENNEDY MINISTRIES

D. James Kennedy Ministries
National Processing Center
P.O. Box 7009
Albert Lea, MN 56007
1-800-988-7884
www.DJames KennedyMinistries.org
letters@djameskennedy.org

STRENGTH *for* TODAY

D. JAMES KENNEDY, PH.D.
& JERRY NEWCOMBE, D.MIN.

D. JAMES KENNEDY MINISTRIES
Advancing Biblical Truth™

A NOTE FROM CO-AUTHOR JERRY NEWCOMBE

Dr. Kennedy said, "We were created by God to do great things, to soar high, and to make an impact upon our world for Him." The Apostle Paul wrote, *"I can do all things through Christ who strengthens me."* It is Christ inside us who gives us our strength.

I trust you will find hope and encouragement for today in these insightful and encouraging devotional readings from Dr. Kennedy. May they inspire you and challenge you to love our Savior more deeply and to seek to walk in the strength He gives us each day, including today.

Soli Deo Gloria

Jerry Newcombe, D. Min.
Fort Lauderdale, Florida
August 2015

This book is dedicated to my granddaughter,
***Elizabeth Lilly Nassif*,**
who is part of a new generation for Christ.

DR. JERRY NEWCOMBE is an on-air personality and senior television producer for D. James Kennedy Ministries. He has written 25 books and co-authored seventeen with Dr. D. James Kennedy, including the best-selling, *What If Jesus Had Never Been Born?*

Mark 10:35-45

SATURDAY, MARCH 19

THE PATH TO GREATNESS

"The Son of Man did not come to be served, but to serve, and to give his life as a ransom for many." —Mark 10:45

The last week of Jesus' life was only a few days away. The cross was near. Would you dare ask Jesus what James and John asked, saying in effect that they wanted the best seats in his kingdom?

James and John forgot that the path to greatness involves service. They wanted power and privilege. They wanted to be served. But that would not be the path for them. They would suffer for following Jesus. They would suffer in ways like he suffered.

These words of Jesus are the theme verses of the book of Mark. They capture the essence of why Jesus came to live among us. He didn't come for greatness; he came to give his life. Serving others was his mission. Others always came first for Jesus. His service culminated at the cross, where he showed his greatest love in laying down his life for us.

Do you find it hard to serve others? Is it hard for you to consider others' needs before your own? How is God calling you to serve? Whom is he calling you to serve? Someone in your family, at work, at school, or in your community? When we're tempted to look for greatness, we need to focus on the cross and remember how Jesus served. Then we need to be willing to lay down our lives as he did.

Holy Father, when we're tempted to want to be great in the eyes of others, steer our eyes back to the cross, where we see the great Son of God serving us through his death. Mold us into his image, we pray. Amen.

MEEKNESS AND MAJESTY

"Hosanna!" "Blessed is he who comes in the name of the Lord!" "Blessed is the coming kingdom. . . ." —Mark 11:9-10

Maybe you have heard or sung the song with this refrain: "Oh, what a mystery—meekness and majesty; bow down and worship, for this is your God!" What an appropriate song to sing during Lent—and especially on Palm Sunday.

On the holy day that Christians call Palm Sunday, Jesus entered Jerusalem riding the colt of a donkey. The Old Testament prophet Zechariah (9:9) had said Israel's king would come in just that way. He rode in to shouts of "Hosanna!"—meaning "Lord, save us!" The crowds took their salvation cry from Psalm 118:25-26. They hoped that their promised Messiah had finally come to overthrow the Romans and renew their kingdom.

Majesty was on display on Palm Sunday. The King of Israel had come, fulfilling the Scriptures.

But there must have been some confusion that day as well. Instead of riding a powerful warhorse, as military leaders did, Jesus rode on a donkey. To some, this must have seemed like a joke. Later in the week, many saw Jesus' kingship that way as cheers turned to jeers and people cried, "Crucify him!" (Mark 15:13). The crowds wanted a king, but not a meek one. For too many, meek meant weak.

As you worship today, remember that Jesus is the King who is worthy of our worship because he is also the humble Servant who gave his life for us.

Jesus, you are our King and our Servant. May we see your glory not only at your triumphal entry but also in your crucifixion. We love you, Lord. Amen.

STRENGTH *for* TODAY

JANUARY 1

You Can Do It

"I can do all things through Christ who strengthens me."
— Philippians 4:13, NKJV

Question for you: What would you do if you knew that you couldn't fail? Probably, it will immediately become clear that we set the bar too low. What most of us do is to do that which is easiest, but not necessarily best.

If I stated the question differently, I would put it this way: What would you attempt if you were given an absolute assurance of success? Well, you have that assurance. The fact of the matter is, you have a guarantee—a guarantee from God. The Apostle Paul, speaking for God, said, "I can do all things through Christ who strengthens me." There is the guarantee, and it is a tremendous one, indeed.

We were created by God to do great things, to soar high, and to make an impact upon our world for Him. In fact, most of the great men and women who have accomplished impressive things in this world have been men and women who have dreamed dreams—big dreams, great visions of what God, by His grace, could do in their lives.

The key to this whole verse is the second part: It is *Christ* inside us who gives us the strength. We may well be able to accomplish great things apart from Christ. But in the long run, they will not be of much heavenly use. But through Christ who strengthens me, I can do all things. Pray that this year God will you use in greater ways than ever before.

Father, at the start of this new year help me to realize that the greatest limitations to my serving You may well come from within. Thank You that with You nothing is impossible. Give me the strength to serve with all my heart…

BY GOD'S STRENGTH, WE CAN
SERVE HIM WITHOUT RESERVATION.

Dreams

"He who had received the five talents went and traded with them and made another five talents."

— Matthew 25:16

At the start of a new year, it is as if we have a blank slate in our lives. We have a new beginning and new opportunities. I suppose everybody has had dreams of a greater life. The problem is that we all as children dreamed dreams and had great visions, but alas, as we grew up, most of those dreams faded away. They are destroyed by that pesky voice in our ear that whispers, "You can't do it." "No, you can't." "You never have, you never could, and you never will."

So like acid rain that falls upon our dreams, they slowly disappear. Our great visions fade, our ambitions corrode, and our future fades entirely because we believed the negative words of the devil: "You can't, you can't, you can't." And so, we invent all kinds of reasons why we can't. We may not want to admit that there is something whispering in our ear, but that is really the problem.

But the Lord has told us in the parable of the talents (Matthew 25) that He wants us to take that with which He has entrusted us, whether great or small, and use it profitably in this life for His glory and others' good.

We should strive to be like the first servant who received five talents and earned five more for his master. In the hustle and bustle of everyday life, it is easy to lose sight of ideas the Lord may have laid on our hearts. Is there some dream He has put in your heart that just won't die? Maybe this is the year to begin pursuing it.

Dear Jesus, I turn over to You the dreams I have. Guide me and use me so that I may accomplish those things You would have me do. Thank You for the opportunity to serve. Lord, give me strength for today to do what pleases You…

BY GOD'S STRENGTH, WE CAN FULFILL HIS PURPOSE FOR OUR LIVES.

JANUARY 3

All Things Through Christ

"...boast in Christ Jesus, and place no trust in the flesh."
— Philippians 3:3

The Apostle Paul said he could endure all circumstances, good or bad, because the Lord strengthened him though it all. Through Christ, he could do all things. I want you to notice what Paul is not talking about—PMA, a modern term for "Positive Mental Attitude," also described as "positive thinking." There is a great difference between positive thinking and what Paul is talking about. Note what Paul did not say: "I can do all things through PMA." One man thought he had seen a sign in an office that said, "I can do all things through coffee and donuts." Not quite.

Let me point out to you that PMA, positive thinking, has many good things about it. It helps people to do a lot of things, but it only goes so far and then it fails because it is really a sin. That I am sure grabs some of you the wrong way. A sin? Yes. The Bible says, *"Cursed is the man who trusts in man and makes flesh his strength, and whose heart departs from the LORD"* (Jeremiah 17:5). To paraphrase: "Cursed is he that trusts in self."

Furthermore, it is really nothing other than trusting in self for your salvation. Paul did not say, "I can do all things because I have complete confidence in myself." Rather, it was Christ who strengthened him. What counts is not positive thinking—it is Christ-thinking—resting upon His strength and not on our own. Then there is no limit to what that can do.

Dear Jesus, forgive me for trusting in me. Forgive me for short-circuiting Your power in my life through unbelief. Give me strength for today to truly trust in You...

BY GOD'S STRENGTH, WE CAN RELY ON HIM AND NOT OURSELVES.

JANUARY 4

Who Are the Real Trouble-Makers

*"When Ahab saw Elijah, Ahab said to him,
'Are you he that troubles Israel?'"*

— 1 Kings 18:17

Sometimes the people of God are accused of causing troubles in this world. The reality is often the very opposite.

We see this in the example that occurs in the great encounter that takes place between Elijah and Ahab. Here was this wicked king, Ahab, who was in some ways a man who had done great things for Israel. But in spite of all of the blessings that he had brought upon the land politically, he was one who was bringing the nation ultimately into total destruction because of his furthering Israel's apostasy. Because of that apostasy, God had caused a three-year drought, which He proclaimed through His servant Elijah.

Now Ahab meets Elijah again and says to him, "Are you he that troubles Israel?" How often down through history has this been the case—where ungodly magistrates or judges or kings have been confronted with the preachers of God, men of righteousness, who have preached the word of God in the midst of an ungodly time—and they have accused them of troubling the nation?

But Elijah said, "I have not troubled Israel, but you and your father's house, in that you have forsaken the commandments of the Lord and you have followed the Baals." Today, we have forgotten the Law of God and forsaken the God of Sinai who gave us the law and the God of Calvary who gave us His Son. The righteous are not the troublers of the land, but the unrighteous. We must pray for a great revival.

Heavenly Father, in this world which calls good evil and evil good, help us to be faithful to You who are truly good. Give us strength for today to do that which You call good...

IN GOD'S STRENGTH, WE STAND FOR
HIM IN A WORLD THAT REJECTS HIM.

Be An Encourager

"But Barnabas took him, and led him to the apostles."
— Acts 9:27

It is a sin to discourage people from using their gifts. Too often, people will pull down others who are trying to use their gifts by a careless word or stinging remark. Such discouragement is a sin.

We should encourage people to use the gifts they have without making unrealistic expectations. What is the point of any accomplishments? The Psalmist gives us the answer to this: *"Not unto us, O Lord, not unto us, but unto Your name give glory"* (Psalm 115:1).

We should encourage each other to use our God-given talents for the glory of God and the advancement of the Christian faith. Some people feel so beaten down by life that they don't use their gifts. That is a great tragedy. Perhaps, you know someone like that who could use some real encouragement.

When the Apostle Paul got converted, many Christians were afraid to have fellowship with him because they thought it could be a trap. But Barnabas encouraged him at a crucial time.

Many believers accomplish only a fraction of what they could. Yet God has given us numerous resources to accomplish great things for His glory. Unfortunately, these resources are often short circuited by wrong thinking and doubts, including heavy discouragement from others, sometimes well-meaning Christians.

Together, we can accomplish many things, and let us be ever mindful to give the Lord the credit for it. Go out and be an encourager.

Lord Jesus Christ, forgive us for sometimes discouraging others. Forgive us also for listening and heeding those discouraging and destructive voices that come, not from,You but from below. Lord, give me strength for today to encourage others for Your sake…

BY GOD'S STRENGTH, WE CAN
ENCOURAGE OTHERS FOR JESUS' SAKE.

JANUARY 6

Despise Not Small Beginnings

"He said to them, 'Go into all the world, and preach the Gospel to every creature.'"

— Mark 16:15

Dr. Kennedy's church (Coral Ridge Presbyterian Church of Fort Lauderdale, Florida) grew exponentially when they learned how to engage in personal evangelism and train others to do the same. Out of that grew Evangelism Explosion (or EE), which is now all over the world.

Here is an update on that ministry: Dr. John Sorenson, Dr. Kennedy's hand-picked successor as the president of EE, told Dr. Kennedy in 2006: "If things stay on track and we do the things that the EE Vice Presidents think we should do, we're going to see 100 million people come to Christ in the first fifteen years of the third Millennium." Dr. Kennedy told John to "hold that thought," and he went off and came back with some papers that he had been studying. He had calculated that in the first 1,500 years of the Church, 100 million people had come to Christ. Then Dr. Kennedy said, "Now you're saying that in fifteen years we are going to see that number of people come to Christ through EE?" John went on to say to the folks at a recent EE banquet, "While we don't take any credit, it's all the work of the Holy Spirit, the truth is, we're going to pass that number. It's not just going to be 100 million, it is going to be 103 or 104 million. Glory to God!"

Whatever you have in your heart to do for the Lord, do it with gladness and with all your heart. Do not despise the day of small beginnings. All great works started very small and humbly.

Heavenly Father, we praise You that You do great things, even with small beginnings. Thank You for the amazing ways You are at work in our world. Lord, give us strength to be world-changers as we share the message of Christ and Him crucified...

BY GOD'S STRENGTH, WE CAN SHARE OUR FAITH WITH OTHERS.

JANUARY 7

Faith vs. Unbelief

"And without faith it is impossible to please God..."
— Hebrews 11:6

One great philosopher said that the greatest theme in all of history, which makes every other theme seem insignificant, is the great contest that has gone on from time immemorial between faith and unbelief. All conflicts in the world are really just variations of this big war.

This contest even happens at a small level each day. For example, you get up in the morning, get dressed, go out, and you meet someone. What do they say? They say, "How are you today?" Faith says, "I am redeemed, saved, justified, and sanctified. I am on my way to Paradise. I am fantastic." But unbelief says, "Oh, pretty good, thank you." But faith knows the answer. "God is doing wonderful things. He is not even finished with me yet. The greatest is yet to come."

So faith and unbelief begin their war every day in your life. Unbelief might try to make us go back to bed for fear of the day that lies before us. But faith realizes that we can do all things through Christ. Paul tells Timothy to stand firm. He tells him, *"For God has not given us the spirit of fear, but of power, and love, and self-control"* (2 Timothy 1:7).

The writer of Hebrews noted that without faith, it is impossible to please God. In this life, unbelief will rob us of many spiritual riches God wants to bestow on us. May He grant us faith to trust Him in all things.

Dear Lord, increase our faith. Give us strength for today to see who You are and what You have done in Christ. Forgive our unbelief. Lord, we do believe—help our unbelief...

BY GOD'S STRENGTH, WE BELIEVE HIM AND HIS PROMISES.

JANUARY 8

God's Guidance for Our Lives

"Trust in the LORD with all your heart, and lean not on your own understanding; in all your ways acknowledge Him, and He will direct your paths."

— Proverbs 3:5-6

The subject of guidance is one that troubles many people's lives. We had a visiting youth minister named Cliff who said that he had dated a girl for a short time. One day she told him that the Lord had told her that they were supposed to get married.

"Isn't that wonderful," she said, "to have such marvelous guidance on such an important matter?" and Cliff replied that it was wonderful indeed, and just as soon as God told him, then he would call for a preacher. Alas, some people I fear are merely trying to feign some kind of an intimate relationship with God that they don't really have, pretending that God is thus audibly speaking with them today.

That is generally not the way we get our guidance in this day in which we live. On the other hand, some people give little thought whatsoever to the matter of guidance at all. They seem not to seek God when it comes to things like where they will live, where they will work, where they will go to church, whom they will marry.

Some hymns teach us well about guidance, such as "He Leadeth Me, O Blessed Thought" or "If Thou But Suffer God To Guide Thee" ("If You Will Only Let God Guide You"). Guidance is not something that we experience merely in the great crises, the crossroads of life, but God says that He is guiding us all of the days of our lives. We are to trust Him and seek Him, and He promises to guide us.

Lord, give me strength for today to seek how I might serve You. Thank You that You do not play games with Your will—hiding it from those who truly desire to fulfill it in their lives. If there is anything holding me back from doing Your will, reveal it to me…

BY GOD'S STRENGTH, WE KNOW WHAT WE SHOULD DO AND WE CAN DO IT.

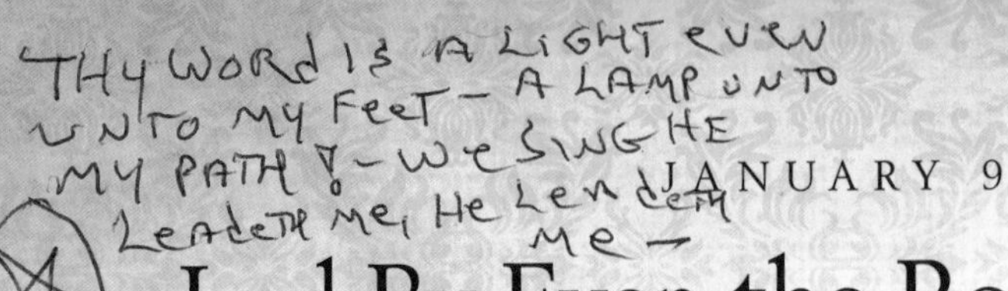

JANUARY 9

Led By Even the Root of a Tree

"...for He who has mercy on them shall lead them, even by the springs of water He shall guide them."

— Isaiah 49:10

How important it is and how blessed we are to follow God's guidance for our lives. You may remember the story of Peter Marshall who was the Chaplain of the Senate some years ago. His life story was made into the film *A Man Called Peter.*

If you recall, as a young man in Scotland, not really knowing what God would have him to do, he was walking across a moor one day and there was dense fog. He could hardly see the ground at all, and then suddenly he tripped and fell flat on his face. When he started to push himself up, one of his hands went right over the edge of the cliff that he would have been looking down into if he could have seen. Then as the fog cleared a little bit he saw, indeed, that he was right on the very edge of a deep precipice that would most certainly have cost him his life if he hadn't tripped over the root of a tree.

He was convinced that in this circumstance God was guiding him and later brought him to America, to Columbia Seminary, where I also studied some time later. Finally, Peter Marshall felt led to the high position of the Chaplaincy of the Senate of the United States.

The Lord guides the steps of the righteous—in this case, it was literally so. We need not fear the future, but only entrust our future to Him.

Dear Father, give us strength for today to seek after You with our whole heart. Thank You that You are sovereign. Help us to not be like a parked car, waiting to be steered. Instead, help us to trust in Your guidance and to put it into practice...

BY GOD'S STRENGTH, WE FOLLOW HIM WHEREVER HE LEADS.

JANUARY 10

The Call of Moses

"Come now therefore, and I will send you to Pharaoh so that you may bring forth My people, the children of Israel, out of Egypt."

— Exodus 3:10

In Exodus 3 and 4, we read of the call of Moses and many things are revealed here. Moses is called by God to go back into Egypt to confront Pharaoh and to bring God's people out of bondage into the promised land. Now I think that this should be more than merely an interesting historical lesson, remembering that all of us have the very same calling resting upon us; not just Moses, not just preachers, but every Christian is called in this same fashion as was Moses. Not as dramatically in most cases, but called nonetheless.

Recall that in the Bible, Egypt represents the world—the lost and fallen world with all of its ungodliness, iniquity, and sin. Pharaoh represents Satan who is the prince of this world. God's people, His elect, are in the world, under the cruel dominion of Satan. We are all called to go and bring out others in order that they might be delivered from the galling bondage of sin—that they might worship and serve the only true God with joy and enter into the promised land, which He has prepared, the heavenly Canaan.

So this is the calling of each one of us. As we think about Moses, let us also think about ourselves and how we are like or unlike him. Just as Moses raised questions and excuses, so do many today. But let us be faithful in order to let the captives know they can be free in Christ.

Lord, give me strength for today that I may be faithful in fulfilling Your purpose in me. Thank You for Your call on my life...

BY HIS STRENGTH,
WE ANSWER HIS CALL.

JANUARY 11

Who Am I To Do This, Lord?

"I will never leave you, nor forsake you."

— Hebrews 13:5

I think I have heard almost every excuse as to why people can't share the Gospel with others. Moses made excuses to wriggle out of His task. He asked God, "Who am I to do this?"

Excuses are as old as the Garden of Eden, when Adam and Eve excused their sin, blaming someone else. But like Moses we have said, and I know that I have said, because I can hear myself echoing in these things: "Who am I that I should do this? Who am I that I should go into the ministry? Who am I that I should go to someone's home and attempt to bring him out of the bondage of sin, into the light everlasting? I am not capable of doing this. I know how strong the power and bondage of Satan and his minions and cohorts are."

No doubt Moses thought, "I tried before and I failed," and he most certainly did.His attempt was a miserable failure. Perhaps you have thought the same. I have. I remember when I first tried here in Fort Lauderdale, and it was a miserable failure, and I was mortified by the attempt and determined that this obviously was something I was incapable of doing. "Who am I? I am obviously not cut out to do this sort of thing, to bring God's people out of Egypt." And the answer that God gives is very simple: "I will be with you, and that is the all sufficient reason."

Lord, give me strength for today to do what is before me and to do it well. Guide me, Oh Thou Great Jehovah. Thank You, Lord, for Your vast kingdom and all the opportunities to serve…

BY HIS STRENGTH,
WE SERVE THE LORD.

JANUARY 12

Who Gets the Credit?

"Not unto us, O LORD, not unto us, but unto Thy name give glory..."
— Psalm115:1 KJV

Chuck Swindoll once pointed out that President Reagan had this saying on a plaque on his desk: "There is no limit to what a man can do or where he can go if he doesn't mind who gets the credit."

In contrast, envy limits itself to that for which we will get the glory. Think of all the times the apostles argued among themselves over one thing—which of them was the greatest? Jesus rebuked them for that and told them that the greatest among them was the servant of all.

If anybody just sits on their God-given gifts because they are concerned that maybe people will not praise them, they are sinning. We should use the talents and opportunities God has gifted us with on a regular basis. If you're concerned about who gets the credit, then remember what we pray in the Lord's Prayer, "... For Thine is...the glory." What is the point of any of our accomplishments? The Psalmist tells us: *"Not unto us, Oh LORD, not unto us, but unto Thy name give glory."* If we live free from the worry of who gets top billing, of who notices us, of how well we are doing by some worldly status criterion, we can do much more work for the Lord.

So whatever task you find at hand, do it with all your might. And do it for God's glory and others' good. God knows what you do, and He will repay you.

Father God, give us strength for today to serve You diligently, even if we aren't always recognized for it here on earth. Thank You, Lord, You who sees all, for being a just God. Let everything we do be truly for Your glory...

BY GOD'S STRENGTH, WE CAN
SERVE ANONYMOUSLY.

JANUARY 13

God's Rules for Sex Are for Our Good

"For the wages of sin is death, but the gift of God is eternal life through Jesus Christ our Lord."

— Romans 6:23

What has the sexual revolution with its promotion of promiscuity brought us? First, there is the spiritual damage. Lust wages war against the soul—many have fallen away from the faith because their lust got the better of them. Then there is the psychological and sociological damage, such as broken hearts and broken homes. Furthermore, today there are more than two dozen sexually transmitted diseases (STDs) that are epidemic in our population.

So maybe God isn't such an ogre after all. And maybe every good gift and every perfect gift does come down from above, and not up from beneath with a hook in it and Satan at the other end of the line.

Probably the basic lie of Satan underlying all of his deceptions is the lie that the laws of God will restrict and narrow and diminish one's life. How many people have sadly learned that just the opposite is true, when their bodies have been vitiated by venereal disease, or their minds have been scrambled by various guilt-induced psychoses or neuroses, and they find only too late that had they followed God's path their lives would have been enriched and ennobled?

The problem is that in America today we have confused love with lust, and these are almost antithetically opposed to each other. The essence of lust is a desire to get something from someone else. Love is the opposite. Love gives.

God of truth, help us never to believe the devil's lies. Help us to trust You fully and to obey Your plan for our lives. Thank You that when we follow You faithfully You give us "none of these diseases." Forgive us for any past sins; give us the strength to avoid them as we move forward…

BY GOD'S STRENGTH, WE KNOW THAT HE HAS GIVEN HIS LAW FOR OUR GOOD.

JANUARY 14

What Will You Hear From Jesus When You Die?

"His master said to him, 'Well done, you good and faithful servant. You have been faithful over a few things. I will make you ruler over many things. Enter the joy of your master.'"

— Matthew 25:21

Those of us in the ministry should take special care to avoid even the hint of scandal, including that involving sex. Not long ago I heard about a friend of mine in the ministry who had fallen into temptation and grievous sin, had scandalized himself, his family, and the church of Christ. He had lost his church and now was in incredible trouble.

Thankfully, he had but a small church, and the scandal never made the daily news or the newspaper. I called him long distance and spoke to him. I don't think I have ever talked to a man who was so crushed. He said, "I… I can't go out of the house. I feel that everybody is looking at me and pointing at me. 'There he is. He's the one.' I don't know what I'm going to do. My life is destroyed. What have I done?"

Then he said something that fell on my ears like a ton of bricks. He said, "Jim, I'll never hear Him say, 'Well done, thou good and faithful servant.'" With that, I choked. I thought that was the saddest thing I've ever heard a human being say.

How about you, my friend? Will you hear those words from Him? May God grant us the grace that moving forward we so live our lives that when we die and stand before Jesus He will look us in the eyes, call us by name, and say, "Well done, you good and faithful servant…"

Lord, give me the strength to obey You and live for You so that when I die, You may say, "Well done, good and faithful servant." Please, lead me not into temptation, but deliver me from the fiery darts of the evil one…

BY GOD'S STRENGTH,
WE CAN FINISH STRONG.

JANUARY 15

Being Faithful In Season and Out

"[King Uzziah] sought after God in the days of Zechariah, the one who instructed him in the fear of the LORD. And in the days that he sought after the LORD, God caused him to succeed."

— 2 Chronicles 26:5

Following God often brings joy and contentment. But the devil is constantly engaged in his one most successful stratagem of reaching his slimy arm out of the pit of Hell and holding some bauble in front of our eyes and turning it this way and that and saying, "Ahhh, will not this bless your life, will not this make you happy, will not this fulfill your wildest dream?" And you say, "Yes," and you bite and there is a hook. Be not deceived.

We are told of King Uzziah in the Old Testament that as long as he sought the Lord, God made him to prosper. And we see that he sought the Lord as long as the prophet Zachariah lived. But tragically there came a time when Zachariah died, and Uzziah no longer sought the Lord. And it shows us the importance of the prophetic office and the proclamation of the Word of God, and how many foolish people there are who suppose that because they have made some progress in the Christian religion that they can now ignore the various ordinances that God has established—they can go their own way and still live a good life. They suppose that the strength is in themselves and it is not there at all. Soon what was there dries up, withers away, and they find themselves totally incapable of withstanding the sin and temptation that they face. We need to be faithful in season and out.

Lord, give me strength for today to recognize those forces in my life that lead me toward You and those that lead me away from You, and to always choose the former and avoid the latter. Help me to choose my friends and associates carefully…

BY GOD'S STRENGTH, WE CAN BE FAITHFUL IN SEASON AND OUT.

Beware of Pride In the Heart

"And as he grew strong, his heart grew more proud, leading to his destruction. Then he acted unfaithfully against the LORD his God, for he entered the temple main hall of the LORD to burn incense on the altar."

— 2 Chronicles 26:16

One day, Judah's King Uzziah transgressed against the Lord God by entering the temple of the Lord to burn incense upon the altar of incense, and God punished him with leprosy. Well, you say that wasn't such a great crime. Or was it? If you understand what was meant by it you would understand that it was. He was not a priest of God. He was not set aside and sanctified unto the priesthood. But he decided that this is what he would do. He should have looked forward to an old age of rest and honor and contentment. But really the problem was that he had everything that he could have desired.

This is what happens to the spoiled kid. This is why we have young people today who come from upper middle class homes, who have two or three cars in their driveways, and yet they are out knocking people in the head. They kill for the joy and excitement of doing it. They rob and take dope for the excitement because they are just bored. They have everything.

Well, Uzziah had everything. He thought that he would be the high priest. He not only usurped the position of the priest, but he usurped the position of the high priest of God. This is the same sin that had caused the kingdom to be wrested from the hands of King Saul. We must guard against the sin of pride in our hearts. As C. S. Lewis once noted, "It is Pride which has been the chief cause of misery in every nation and every family since the world began."

Lord, give me strength for today to follow You humbly. Forgive me for the pride in my heart. Help me to remember that all good things come from You. There is nothing I have that I did not receive. Please replace my pride with gratitude…

BY GOD'S STRENGTH, WE CAN
WALK HUMBLY WITH HIM.

The Problem of Prosperity

"Pride goes before destruction, and a haughty spirit before a fall."
— Proverbs 16:18

There are many people who can withstand the temptations of failure, the temptations of lack or poverty, who have discovered that they could not withstand the perils and temptations of success. How many men and women have you known who did well in their spiritual life and made great progress in studying His word in Sunday School and Bible classes? They were engaged in His work and seeking the Lord; God blessed them and they were marvelously helped, until their pride deceived them into thinking that they accomplished it all on their own.

They began to say in the secret chambers of their hearts the same things that the Israelites had said after they had been delivered from Egypt. They said, *"Our hand is victorious, and the LORD has not done all this"* (Deuteronomy 32:27). And like the bulls of Bashan they kicked out at Jehovah who had delivered them. Therefore, God was angry with them, and He delivered them over to destruction because of their pride.

I have seen people who seem to seek the Lord, but in the end it was apparently with insincere motives. God blesses them, and soon their bank accounts are bulging and their houses are large and their cars and boats are many, and they say in their own hearts, "The Lord has not done all this. No, I did it. It was my talent, my sagacity, my business acumen, that caused this to be done." But God gives grace to the humble, and in due time He will humble the proud.

Lord, give me strength for today to handle the gift of prosperity. Help me to recognize it is Your hand that has helped me. Help me to be generous with all that You have given me. Forgive me for the pride in my heart…

BY GOD'S STRENGTH, WE RECOGNIZE HE IS THE SOURCE OF ALL GOOD THINGS.

JANUARY 18

Don't Forget God

"...then beware lest you forget the LORD who brought you out of the land of Egypt, out of the house of bondage."

— Deuteronomy 6:12

America has been blessed by God, but because of our prosperity we have forgotten Him. We think we don't have to worry; we are not going to have a bitter winter like the Pilgrims had, where half of the population is going to starve. We are not left naked upon the brink of destruction; no, we have much goods laid up for many years. We are strong and self-sufficient. America has been mightily and marvelously helped until she was strong, and America has lifted up her heart in pride and turned her back upon God and kicked against the pricks of His spirit upon their conscience and turned unto sin.

President Lincoln called for a Day of Fasting and Prayer in 1863 and he reminded the nation of how it had forgotten God: "We have been the recipients of the choicest bounties of Heaven. We have been preserved, these many years, in peace and prosperity. We have grown in numbers, wealth and power, as no other nation has ever grown. But we have forgotten God....We have vainly imagined, in the deceitfulness of our hearts, that all these blessings were produced by some superior wisdom and virtue of our own. Intoxicated with unbroken success, we have become too self-sufficient to feel the necessity of redeeming and preserving grace, too proud to pray to the God that made us! It behooves us then, to humble ourselves before the offended Power, to confess our national sins, and to pray for clemency and forgiveness." Amen.

Lord, give me strength for today to recognize Your hand of blessing on us. Forgive me for the pride in my heart that wants to wrest the credit from You to me. As a church and as a nation, give us the gift of repentance and a new Great Awakening...

BY GOD'S STRENGTH AND FROM HIS HAND,
WE HAVE WHAT WE HAVE.

JANUARY 19

He Is Our Righteousness

"God made Him who knew no sin to be sin for us, that we might become the righteousness of God in Him."

— 2 Corinthians 5:21

I am perfect. I have no sin, no guilt, and am in absolutely perfect one-hundred percent obedience to every command of God in thought, word, and deed. That is my righteousness; but, of course, you realize *I didn't live it*—not any of it. In fact, I ran the other way. I violated His commandments in every way.

It was Christ who lived that perfect life, Christ who took away my sin, Christ who gave me His obedience that made me righteous. My righteousness is not my own. It belongs to Christ. But as Paul says, *"by the obedience of One the many will be made righteous"* (Romans 5:19). How are you going to be made righteous before God? "…[B]y the obedience of One the many will be made righteous."

Theologians like to refer to what they call the active and passive obedience of Christ. His active obedience being all He did in obeying His Father through all of His earthly life. This One who could say, *"… for I always do those things that please Him"* (John 8:29). That white robe of obedience was woven day by day out of the pure linen of Christ's perfect obedience with the golden thread of His deity running through it.

His passive obedience was what He endured: the scourge, the thorns, the spikes, the Cross. We get from that passive obedience the word "passion"—the passion of Jesus Christ. Now His active obedience and His passive obedience make up what is known as the righteousness of Christ. He is our righteousness.

Jesus-Tsidkenu, Jesus my righteousness, I praise and thank You today for counting Your righteousness as my own. Thank You, Father, for looking at me through Jesus Christ, as if I had never sinned…

BY GOD' STRENGTH AND THE BLOOD OF JESUS, WE ARE RIGHTEOUS NOW.

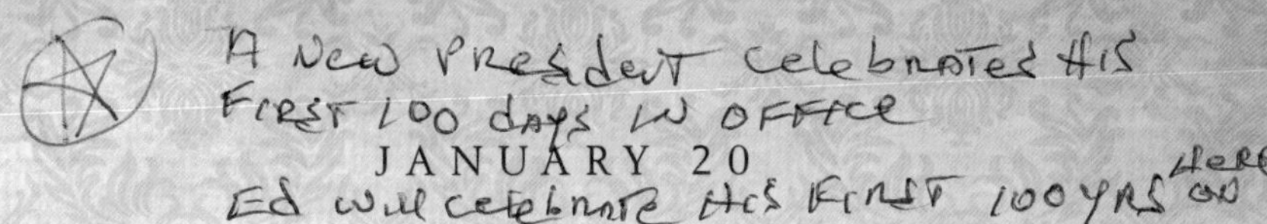

JANUARY 20

Spiritual State of the Union

"...then I will hear from heaven, and will forgive their sin and will heal their land."

— 2 Chronicles 7:14

The "spiritual state of the union"? If it were a patient, it probably would have been pronounced dead on arrival—frozen in ice—no spiritual pulse at all. This is what many think, and this is what many unbelievers find reason to rejoice over. Across our nation we see:

- sexual promiscuity and perversion and rampant abortion;
- television and movies, with all of their terrible demonstrations of every kind and imaginable sin;
- terrorism threatening our lives;
- a scandalous educational system that seems more bent on producing unbelief in God, secularism, and permissiveness than teaching students how to read and write;
- endemic corruption in business corporations;
- the threat of crime, violent or otherwise.

But God gives the solution for a nation gone astray. He says, *"When I shut up the heaven and there is no rain, or when I command the locusts to devour the land, or send pestilence on My people, if My people, who are called by My name, will humble themselves and pray, and seek My face and turn from their wicked ways, then I will hear from heaven, and will forgive their sin and will heal their land"* (2 Chronicles 7:13-14). May God give the grace that enough of His people will seek His face for true positive transformation throughout the land.

Heavenly Father, we have lost our way as a nation. Forgive us for in any way being a part of the problem and not a part of the solution. Lord, give me strength for today to help pave the way toward a true national revival...

BY GOD'S STRENGTH, WE CAN LIVE A LIFE OF PURITY IN AN IMPURE WORLD.

JANUARY 21

An Imputed Righteousness

"For just as through one man's disobedience the many were made sinners, so by the obedience of One the many will be made righteous."
— Romans 5:19

Many today think that they are good enough to make it into heaven. But what they don't reckon with is their actual sinfulness. They are clothed in the filthy rags of their own self-righteousness, but they are too blind to see it.

How about you? You could get hit by a car and killed this very afternoon, and you could find yourself dressed for the worst ultimate, eternal disaster that you have ever even imagined. In what are you dressed? Your righteousness or Christ's? What you have done, or what God has done for you upon the cross?

John Bunyan, who wrote *Pilgrim's Progress*, also wrote *Justification By An Imputed Righteousness*. That is what we believe. That is what Christianity is. It is justification—that by which we are accepted, pardoned, and received into paradise—justification "by an imputed righteousness." Not an inherent righteousness, not one of our own accomplishments of our acquiring, but something which is reckoned to us but belongs to another—the righteousness of Christ.

The great Count von Zinzendorf put it so very well in a familiar hymn:

Jesus, thy blood and righteousness
My beauty are, my glorious dress;
'Midst flaming worlds [in the final judgment] in these arrayed,
With joy shall I lift up my head.

Salvation is by good works—that is, the good works of Jesus who died on behalf of sinners.

Heavenly Father, thank You for dressing me in the white robe of Your Son's imputed righteousness. Thank You, Jesus, that because of Your shed blood, I am clean and spotless without blemish or wrinkle…

BY GOD'S STRENGTH, WE GO
TO CHRIST AND BECOME CLEAN.

The Tragedy of Abortion

"Now the word of the LORD came to me, saying, 'Before I formed you in the womb I knew you; and before you were born I sanctified you, and I ordained you a prophet to the nations.'"

— Jeremiah 1:4-5

Since January 22, 1973, when the Supreme Court gave us abortion on demand through all nine months of pregnancy, America has taken the lives of more than 57 million unborn babies. This is a horrible crime for which we will give an account.

At one time, I was talking with a gentleman who was involved in a suit with an abortion clinic. I suppose we really shouldn't use the term "abortion clinic" because a clinic is someplace you go to get well. Some have used the phrase "abortion chamber." They talk about their hygiene; they talk about the safety factor. Well, I would remind everyone that at least 50 percent of all the people that enter those institutions come out dead. I refer of course to the babies.

This gentleman was talking to the man who sued him and his organization to get them to stop picketing the abortion chamber, and this young man in our church said that he would be glad to stop picketing them if he would just stop killing babies. No way.

Now we have all heard that they are "pro-choice." But there's only one choice provided in such a place—abortion.

The man in our church said that he would stop picketing the abortion center if they would simply provide a table inside the center where he might present the other choice so that people will have a true choice they can make. Of course, he was denied. There is no choice; abortion is murder for money, nothing else. Pray to end abortion.

Dear Lord, thank You for the gift of life. We confess that the land is stained with the blood of the unborn. Forgive us for not doing more to stop this egregious evil in our time. Lord of life, give us the strength to continue working on behalf of life…

IN GOD'S STRENGTH, WE PROVIDE
LIFE-SAVING ALTERNATIVES TO ABORTION.

JANUARY 23

Sticking With It

"To him who overcomes I will give permission to eat of the tree of life, which is in the midst of the Paradise of God."

— Revelation 2:7

Jerry Falwell once said, having worked with Christians in the political arena for some 15 years, that he had learned something. He had learned that when Christians lose, they quit, and when they win, they quit. All politics aside, we need to learn to develop greater perseverance in our service to the Lord.

We live in a world where many people are quite unstable, and they are tossed to and fro with the waves, as James talks about those who are tossed with waves of doctrine. Today, we have a crisis of character, a crisis of integrity. We need men and women who have perseverance or stick-to-it-iveness.

Now a lot of people start off a lot of things well. Even Pliable was able to do that. He started off with Christian in *Pilgrim's Progress* on the way to the Celestial City, and he got just as far as the Slough of Despond. Having fallen in the slough and finding himself up to his neck in mud, he, with great exertion, turned around and crawled back out the side from which he had come and made his way back to the City of Destruction.

Many people start well, but soon they are seen no more. But true grit means that you keep on keeping on. It has much less to do with the size of your muscles or the measurement of your chest, but rather it is a mental or a spiritual attitude. May God give us the grace to be overcomers through Jesus Christ our Lord.

Immortal God, we are so mortal, so weak, and so quick to give up. Thank You that You never give up on us. It is You who keeps us and preserves us so that we may eat of the Tree of Life in Your kingdom…

BY GOD'S STRENGTH, WE CAN OVERCOME AND FINISH WELL.

Babylon the Great

"While he tasted the wine, Belshazzar commanded that they bring in the golden and silver vessels which his father Nebuchadnezzar had taken from the temple which was in Jerusalem, so that the king, and his officials, his wives, and his concubines might drink from them."

— Daniel 5:2

"Babylon the great." The name is significant. It is reminds us of every nation-state that has raised itself against the true God, of every nation that down through the centuries has persecuted the people of God. And King Belshazzar was the avatar, or incarnation of that very spirit of Babylon, which mocked the true God and looked contemptuously upon the rest of the people of this world.

There was never before, and perhaps never since, such a city as "Babylon the great." Its walls were 14 miles on each side and the walls rose to a height of 300 feet into the air, with towers rising higher than that and at their base the walls of Babylon were 187½ feet thick.

Years before, the Babylonians had conquered the Hebrews, carried many of them off to Babylon (including Daniel), raided the temple of its silver and gold and burned it. At this drunken feast, Belshazzar and guests drank from silver goblets from the Lord's temple.

God judged them that very night as the Medes and Persians figured out a way to attack despite those massive walls. Belshazzar learned too late that God will humble the exalted and exalt the humble. God is not mocked.

Everlasting God, we see mockers all around us. May we never be found in the "seat of mockers." May we always honor and revere You as the only true God. Please bring salvation to the mockers before it is too late.

BY GOD'S STRENGTH, WE CAN ENDURE THE MOCKERS.

Is the Bible Reliable?

"Belshazzar the king made a great feast for a thousand of his lords and drank wine before the thousand."

Daniel 5:1

Our text today speaks of Belshazzar the king, and the critics have fastened their talons on these words. For some time, they used to say, "Ah ha. Here again we find one of the many mistakes of the Bible." They would claim there was no such king of Babylon as Belshazzar, and that furthermore the son of Nebuchadnezzar, which Daniel 5:2 says was Belshazzar, is conclusively proved by the monuments to be none other than Nabonidus, and that no Belshazzar is mentioned at all. They delighted to fixate on this passage.

And yet the spades of the archaeologists continued to dig, and need I tell you how the story came out? The Bible has been proven right again and again. Finally the spade of the archaeologist unturned the monuments that brought to our attention the fact that Nabonidus, the son of Nebuchadnezzar, had a son whose name was Belshazzar.

But someone might object that he was not the son, but rather grandson, of Nebuchadnezzar. But the Bible calls him son. Biblical Hebrew has no word for grandson or great grandson or great grandfather or grandfather, but simply refers to one as father, regardless of the number of generations that have intervened. So once again the critics were proven wrong.

As Werner Keller, author of the book, *The Bible As History*, noted in the 1950s: "...as I thought of the skeptical criticism which from the eighteenth century onward would fain have demolished the Bible altogether, there kept hammering in my brain this one sentence: 'The Bible is right after all.'"

God of truth, we thank You for the trustworthiness of Your Word. Thank You for sustaining me and feeding me Your living, holy, and eternal Word everyday...

BY GOD'S STRENGTH AND SUSTAINING POWER, WE ARE UPHELD BY HIS WORD.

JANUARY 26

The Handwriting on the Wall

"Immediately fingers of a man's hand appeared and wrote opposite the lampstand on the plaster of the wall of the king's palace. And the king saw the back of the hand that wrote."

— Daniel 5:5

As noted before, one night, Belshazzar the king of Babylon held a great drunken feast. They brought out the golden vessels and silver goblets which his grandfather Nebuchadnezzar had brought from the temple in Jerusalem before he destroyed it. And so Belshazzar called for the vessels and the goblets of the temple of Jerusalem so that his lords and princes, his women and wives and concubines might drink out of the golden goblets from the temple of Jerusalem. "Where is the God of Jerusalem—where is the God of the Jews?" they might have asked.

But then a detached gigantic hand appeared and wrote inscrutable words on the wall. What did they say? Only Daniel was capable of providing the correct interpretation. Belshazzar had been weighed according to God's righteousness and was found wanting.

Therefore, his kingdom was to be broken apart and given to the Medes and the Persians. While Belshazzar had been drinking from the goblets of Jerusalem, the army of the Medes and Persians had diverted the River Euphrates which flowed from one corner to the other corner of the great city of Babylon and his soldiers had come under that dry river bed. They had thrown open the mighty gates of Babylon, and now the whole hosts of the armies of the Medes and Persians had filled the city. The proud, taunting king died that very night. Babylon the great came to a sudden and final end. It is not wise to taunt the living God.

Lord of the nations, You alone are holy and not to be mocked. We thank You that You do avenge and that Your justice will prevail. In Your mercy and patience, You postpone judgment, but help us to remember that it will come…

BY GOD'S STRENGTH AND IN HIS TIME,
NATIONS AND PEOPLE WILL BE JUDGED.

JANUARY 27

On Avoiding Murmuring

"Do all things without murmuring and disputing…"
— Philippians 2:14

When Paul tells the Philippian Christians to do all things without murmuring, we should remember that just a moment before that he told them to work out their salvation with fear and trembling. Not work *for* your salvation—to work it *out*, for it is God who is working in our hearts.

How are we to work out our own salvation with fear and trembling? Well, he says that we are to do all things without murmuring and disputing. The word murmuring sounds like what it describes. The Scripture in a number of times tells us to avoid murmuring and grumbling.

In John 6:41, we read *"The Jews then murmured about Him, because He said, 'I am the bread which came down from heaven.'"* You can almost hear the muttering, the grumbling, the low tones, the complaining, and the discontent of them. In verse 43, just two verses further, "Jesus therefore answered them, 'Do not murmur among yourselves.'"

In I Corinthians 10:10, Paul cautions, *"Neither murmur, as some of them also murmured and were destroyed by the destroyer."* Twice in that same verse—"neither murmur, as some of those,"—those were the Israelites in the Old Testament wanderings, and they murmured against the Lord, and they were destroyed. They murmured against Moses as well, and they were destroyed. If you know the joy of Christ in your heart, it follows that you will avoid a complaining spirit.

Jesus, Bread of Life, thank You for feeding us and caring for us. Forgive us that we so often complain and murmur. Give us the strength to replace murmuring with thanksgiving…

IN GOD'S STRENGTH,
WE CAN AVOID GROUSING.

Stop Complaining and Strive to Be at Peace With All

"These men are grumblers, complainers, who walk after their own lusts. Their mouths speak arrogant words, and they flatter others to gain profit."
— Jude 16

All sin is ultimately against God, as David said, *"Against You, You only, have I sinned"* (Psalm 51:4). But it is also true that we do sin against one another very often. Paul says we should *"Do all things without murmuring and disputing"* (Philippians 2:14). Yet how much of what goes on in many homes, even Christian homes, involves complaining, grumbling, murmuring, and arguments?

We should be serving God gladly, yielding ourselves to Him happily and cheerfully without murmuring and complaining against one another. How much of that is found in your home? How about the church? Take almost any kind of meeting that goes on in the church, how much of it is spent in murmuring, complaining, and faultfinding?

So we sin against men also in this same way. And whether our relationship to God or one another, we are to do all things without murmuring and complaining. Why? *"…That you may be blameless and harmless, sons of God, without fault, in the midst of a crooked and perverse generation, in which you shine as lights in the world"* (Philippians 2:15). So let us strive to be at peace with all men, as much as it depends on us.

Jehoveh-Shalom, You who are our peace, help us to live in peace without grumbling and fault-finding. Help us today to find the good in others and live in peace with all, as much as it is possible without compromising our core values…

BY GOD'S STRENGTH, WE CAN EXPERIENCE HIS PEACE.

Holding Forth the Word of Life

"...sons of God, without fault, in the midst of a crooked and perverse generation, in which you shine as lights in the world. Hold forth the word of life..."

— Philippians 2:15-16a

Paul tells us that we should bear witness to the world, both by the lives we live and by the word which is the Gospel. This is a twofold duty and responsibility, which is laid upon every Christian, that we are to be witnesses to Him both by our lives and by our lips, that we are to shine and we are to hold forth the word of life.

And so, dear friend, I would ask you, are you doing that? Did you hold forth the word of life to anyone recently? We should ask God to place opportunities in our path in which we might share the good news that has changed our lives. May God grant you the determination to say, "I will indeed determine to be a light in a dark world and hold forth the word of life to a dying world that they may hear the Gospel and be saved."

Paul says, *"...that I may rejoice on the day of Christ that I have not run in vain or labored in vain"* (Philippians 2:16). This is an amazing openness on the part of the apostle. He calls upon them to show a godly life and to hold forth the word of life that he may rejoice in the day of Christ. May God give us the grace that we be faithful followers of Christ, shining as lights and holding forth the word of life, bringing many to the knowledge of the Savior.

Jesus Christ, Light of the world, thank You for being my light and my salvation. May I hold out Your light today, both in my words and by holy living...

BY GOD'S STRENGTH, WE CAN
BE LIGHT IN A DARK WORLD.

Is Your Life An Offering to the Lord?

"For I am already being poured out as a drink offering, and the time of my departure has come."
— 2 Timothy 4:6

God only calls a small percentage of those who follow Christ to be martyrs for Him. Certainly, Paul was one of those.

Paul's last epistle was 2 Timothy, and in the poignant 4th chapter he writes, *"For I am already being poured out as a drink offering, and the time of my departure has come."* He is ready to be offered, the sacrifice is ready to be poured out.

This is now his second imprisonment. He was released after the imprisonment during which he wrote Philippians, then he continued his missionary journeys, probably traveling all the way to Spain. But now he has returned, has once more been captured, taken prisoner and thrown into a dungeon, and this time there is to be no release in this world.

Paul is not afraid of death because Christ has conquered the grave. When he was drawn up out of that prison, led out of the city of Rome down the Appian Way, and the headsman's ax flashed in the Roman sun, the Apostle Paul experienced immortality, and he received the crown of righteousness. We can indeed rejoice that in Christ death has lost its sting. Whether martyred or not, we should live for Christ in such a way that we, too, can look forward to receiving a crown of righteousness.

Lord, give me strength to make my life an offering to You. Help me to avoid carrying a burden You have not given me, but also help me be ready to follow You even unto death…

BY GOD'S STRENGTH, WE ARE A LIVING SACRIFICE.

JANUARY 31

You May Be the Only Bible Many Will Read

"...let your conduct be worthy of the Gospel of Christ..."

— Philippians 1:27

You and I are the clothes that the Gospel wears in this world. How well are we adorning the Gospel in our lives? We are the only Christ that many will see. Are we attracting people to the Savior or are we repelling them from Him? Paul makes it very clear that it is vital that we do the former and not the latter.

Here there is a shift in that first chapter of Philippians—from "I" to "you," from personal testimony to spiritual exhortation. If you go back up the previous verses of the first chapter you will see that Paul has been giving for almost the entirety of this his own personal testimony. You see that he says, "but if I live," "for me to live," and "I shall not be ashamed," and "I know this," and "I am set for the defense of the Gospel." He has been giving his own personal testimony. He knows that the Philippians needed to be encouraged by hearing what was happening with him and his resoluteness in the face of his suffering, his rejoicing in Christ even in prison, but they also needed to be exhorted unto godly living.

Since we may well be the only Bible many people ever "read," it is sobering to consider that some of us may need revision. Someone once said, "Don't be so worried about what other people think of you. Be concerned about what they think of Christ because of you."

Lord, give me the strength to live such a righteous life that people will want to know You and walk with You. My Master and Lord, help me to live a life honoring You in all ways. Help me today to do something kind for someone who does not know You...

BY GOD'S STRENGTH, WE WILL SHOW CHRIST TO OTHERS.

FEBRUARY 1

Never Too Old

"He said, 'O my Lord, send, I pray, by the hand of whomever else You will send.'"

— Exodus 4:13

Some people think they are too old to do something significant in life. But I think of a gentleman who really never did much of anything. He dropped out of school and went to work in a store where he worked for about six months and got fired. That was just a picture of what was to come. He got fired from one job after another. This pattern lasted for decades.

Then one day he got a letter in the mail. It was a letter from Social Security, congratulating him for having reached the end of his working career and included a check. But he refused to quit working.

He was eventually able to buy a small beat-up old building that had been a restaurant and turned it into a decent looking place where he could sell food. What he really liked to do was to cook chicken. So he started selling chicken there, and the people liked it. He had a special recipe—a secret recipe. Finally, his business spread to franchises in other states around the country and around the world.

God blessed Colonel Sanders of Kentucky Fried Chicken, and he succeeded enormously. You're never too old to make a contribution in life. Look at Moses, who may well have thought he was washed up at 40, tended sheep for 40 years, but was then called by God at age 80 to serve the Lord in mighty ways for the next 40 years.

Dear God, thank You that You care about us no matter how old we might be. Thank You that You can use us whatever age we may be. Help us to not sell ourselves short because of age or anything else…

IN GOD'S STRENGTH WE CAN SERVE HIM, WHATEVER CONDITION WE'RE IN.

No Need for Psychics

"…who walks in darkness and has no light? Let him trust in the name of the LORD, and rely upon his God…"

— Isaiah 50:10

Our life on this earth is a pilgrimage. It has a beginning and an end and it is going somewhere, and it is important where we end up. Life is not a meaningless circling about, a meandering here and there with no particular purpose.

God is sovereign and has revealed in His Word how we should live, so that we will not walk in darkness. Many people find life very complicated. This world is a labyrinth with innumerable tunnels leading in every kind of direction. We don't know the future. We don't know where this road will take us.

In one sense, we are forced to live eventually in the future, and yet it is unseen to us. And so the heart of man cries out for guidance, and this is what sends so many people to call psychics on the psychic hotline, or to go to an astrologer or to do all of the various foolish things that people will do indicating their felt need for some kind of guidance. God condemns this kind of divination.

He tells us to trust Him instead. Those who know their God have already experienced Him well in the past and the present. Therefore, we can trust Him with our future. The Bible is infinitely better than tarot guards, crystals, psychics, or any other false substitute to true divine wisdom.

Lord, my Shepherd and Guide, give me strength for today to follow after You and not after any false gods. Help me not to deceive myself by thinking I am following after You in utilizing avenues of guidance that You have clearly forbidden. Lead me by Your powerful hand…

BY GOD'S STRENGTH, WE ARE LED HOME TO HEAVEN.

FEBRUARY 3

Dual Citizenship

"But our citizenship is in heaven, from where also we await for our Savior, the Lord Jesus Christ…"

— Philippians 3:20

We should always remember that we hold a twin citizenship. We have our citizenship in our earthly country, but we also are citizens of a heavenly country, which is far better. Our citizenship is above, Paul tells us. And so we are to live out our citizenship, our conduct, in a way that is honoring and glorifying and adorning of the Gospel of Christ. It should be consistent with the Gospel of Christ.

Therefore, we should remember not to limit our conduct only to the kingdom of heaven of which we are a citizen, but also we are to exercise faithfully all of our responsibilities as citizens of this kingdom here on earth as well. And many Christians will limit themselves only to one and ignore the other, but Paul wants us to be consistent with the Gospel of grace. That is the way our conduct ought to be. We are called to honor and work for the country in which God has placed us, while at the same time help build His kingdom and invest in eternity.

If we are faithful to God's first command—the cultural mandate given at the beginning of creation (Genesis 1:26) to serve as God's vice-regents on earth, and if we are faithful in God's last command to us—the Great Commission of Jesus to go and spread His Gospel then we will fulfill well our dual citizenship.

Lord of heaven and earth, give us strength for today to be worthy citizens of both. Help us to work for Your kingdom, as we live in this world. Help us not to be too comfortable and fond of this world which is temporary…

BY GOD'S STRENGTH, WE CAN FULFILL BOTH THE CULTURAL AND GOSPEL MANDATES.

FEBRUARY 4

Showing Grace to Others

"Only let your conduct be worthy of the Gospel of Christ, that whether or not I come and see you, I may hear of your activities, that you are standing fast in one spirit, with one mind, striving together for the faith of the Gospel."

— Philippians 1:27

As Christians, what should our conduct with others be like? Well we know that we have a Gospel of grace, and therefore, our lives should be gracious.

I think that many people live lives which are unjust and unfair; they take unfair advantage of people in business or they act unlawfully and unjustly. But there are others who would never think of doing a thing like that and they operate on the principle of equity, of doing the fair thing, of being correct and honest in dealing with people—a *quid pro quo*, this for that kind of conduct. However, when somebody crosses them and does not deal with them right, then sometimes these people would deal with them like a judge, and they would punish them in some way for their conduct. But that is not the principle of grace.

You can be less than fair, but you can also be more than fair, and it is in that area that the Gospel is not merely fair, it is far greater, vastly higher than merely fair. It is wonderfully high and that means that we need to learn to deal with people graciously, and that we are going to go the extra mile with them. We are going to treat them lovingly even if they have treated us badly, and in that way our lives will adorn the Gospel and be consistent with the Gospel of Christ.

God of grace and mercy, give me strength for today whereby I may show grace to others. I praise You for Your mercy and Your grace in my life. I pray that You will help me to act and be gracious in my dealings with others. Let me give more than is expected, beyond the call…

IN GOD'S STRENGTH,
WE CAN LIVE GRACIOUSLY.

The Gospel of Peace

"Peace I leave with you. My peace I give to you.
Not as the world gives do I give to you.
Let not your heart be troubled, neither let it be afraid."
— John 14:27

The Gospel of Jesus brings peace to troubled hearts, and so those that are justified have a peace which passes all understanding. Therefore, there should be an element of serenity and peace in our lives that should be seen by others. I think of a description of a man who was described as seeming to float through life and no matter what kind of storms would rage about him as he would pass through them, it did not seem to impact him because he had a wondrous peace that was very attractive to those that saw him. Is your boat easily upset by the waves and the winds around you? If so, I hope that you will remember that if your life is going to be consistent with the Gospel it should demonstrate peacefulness—the peace that passes understanding.

The Gospel is a Gospel that makes peace and reconciles people to God; that is the nature of our Gospel. It is a peace-making Gospel, and we are called upon to be peacemakers. Bill Elliott said that he has known church members that were much more easily identified as troublemakers than peacemakers, and I wonder about you. In your home are you the peacemaker? In your office, or school or workplace, are you a peacemaker or a troublemaker? Are you in church a peacemaker or a troublemaker? Well, God grant that we may demonstrate His peace and also extend it to others.

God of peace, grant me Your peace today so that it will fill me and sustain me and flow out to others. Thank You for Your peace that sets our souls at rest…

IN GOD'S STRENGTH,
WE ARE PEACEFUL.

FEBRUARY 6

"The Mark of the Christian"

"By this all men will know that you are My disciples, if you have love for one another."

— John 13:35

Paul tells us in Philippians 1:27 that we are to live lives *"worthy of the Gospel of Christ."* Included in that notion is that we are to live lives of love. Jesus even said that people will know that you belong to Him if you love one another. As Francis Schaeffer said, love for each other is "the mark of the Christian." How will the world know we belong to Jesus? Because of our love.

Now it is easy to love the lovely, to love the loving, but God loves the God-haters and poured out His life for them. And so we are called upon to show that kind of a loving attitude toward people who may not be the type of persons that the ordinary individual would go out of his way to love.

Someone criticized a Christian leader with the remark that the church (in general) has a lot of kooks in it. The leader replied, "Well, I thank you for that compliment because I think it is true that the church has more of the unfortunate people that are handicapped and people that don't get along well in many social situations than most any other voluntary associative organization. That is a wonderful compliment about the love of Christ being shown, where other people won't put up with those kinds of people." May God give us the grace to show more love, even to the unlovable.

God of love, give me strength for today that I may truly love Your bride, the church. Thank You for loving me. Let Your love so fill my heart that others may also benefit from it. Help me to be more like You and love the unlovable…

IN GOD'S STRENGTH AND BY HIS LOVE,
WE LOVE.

FEBRUARY 7

What Does J-O-Y Spell?

"We are writing these things to you so that our joy may be complete."

— 1 John 1:4

When the king is in residence in his castle, they raise the flag to indicate that fact. One theologian said, "Joy is the flag which is raised over the citadel of the heart to indicate that the King is resident within." Joy is the flag.

Two workmen working in the street in front of a church were watching as the people filed in for Sunday morning service. One of them said to the other, "You know, I've seen a hundred or two hundred people go into that church, and I haven't seen a single smile on any one of their faces." That is tragic indeed.

The Gospel is a Gospel of joy, as well as of grace, peace, and love. At the birth of Christ, the angels said to the shepherds that they brought good tidings of great joy. Paul says in Galatians that the fruit of the Spirit is love, joy… It is the second fruit of the Spirit.

Are our lives typified by joy? In looking at some people's faces you wouldn't think that they had much joy. They seem often to frown and be sullen and unhappy and show little of the joy of Christ in their countenance. Some people seem like the only experience that they have had is an experience of acid indigestion, instead of the transforming wondrous joy of Jesus Christ. If you want to experience more joy, remember this simple formula: J-O-Y means Jesus first, Others second, Yourself last.

Lord, give me strength for today to put Jesus first and others second. God of joy, thank You for giving me so much joy all around me and joy within. Let Your joy overflow unto all the people around me. Thank You for the joy of heaven…

IN GOD'S STRENGTH AND PRESENCE,
THERE IS FULLNESS OF JOY.

FEBRUARY 8

Is There One in Your Church?

"These six things the LORD hates…
one who sows discord among brethren."

— Proverbs 6:16, 19 NKJV

God hates it when people cause needless division. Tragically, such persons exist in many of our churches.

One such lady outed herself in an unusual story I heard around Halloween time. A man was going to a Halloween night party, and he was all dressed up in a devil's suit. He had the whole thing with the horns and the tail and the red suit and everything. And he was driving his little car from one town to the next town where the costume party was going to be held. He ran out of gas, as a lightning storm was about to hit.

Seeing an old country church, he began to walk up the stairs, but hesitated about going in. All of a sudden there was CRASH, lightning struck right behind him and he leapt through the door. With smoke and lightning behind him, people turned around and they all saw the devil standing there.

It scared the daylights out of everybody and in a moment they were all through the windows except for one lady of generous proportions who was too big to get out. And finally she gave up and turned to him, saying, "Now, Mr. Devil, you know that I've been in this church for 45 years, and I've been on your side the whole time." May God help us to have the wisdom with how to deal with those who sow discord among the brethren and to make sure we are not one of them.

Lord, give me strength for today to truly work together with those You have put in my life. Omniscient Lord, You see everything and You see our hearts. Let me not sow discord or division among believers. Give me discernment to test the spirits, to know what is of You...

BY GOD'S STRENGTH,
WE WILL BE UNIFIERS.

Milk or Meat?

"Brothers, I could not speak to you as to spiritual men, but as to worldly, even as to babes in Christ. I have fed you with milk and not with solid food. For to this day you were not able to endure it. Nor are you able now, for you are still worldly."

— 1 Corinthians 3:1-3

At this point in their spiritual lives, the Corinthians should be consuming meat—but instead they are only drinking milk. They are babes in Christ.

It is God's eternal intention for every one of us that we grow to maturity in Jesus Christ. How do we do that? First of all, through the Word of God. One of the ways you can tell if you are born anew is that as a newborn babe you desire the sincere milk of the Word. We are not talking a feeling. We are talking about the knowledge that we are in need of the Word.

May I ask you how much time did you spend in the Word this week? That will tell you whether you are a babe or mature, whether you are spiritual or carnal. Do you study the Word of God? Do you hide the Word of God in your heart? Do you meditate upon that Word in the night seasons? That is absolutely essential. Without it you cannot live. Deprive your newborn physical baby of milk, and that child will die. Our spiritual life desperately needs the milk of the Word that we may grow thereby, and as we grow stronger, we can then feed upon the meat. And you notice that Paul later lamented those could only take milk. They should be taking strong meat. They should be teaching others, but they need to be taught the basic principles of Christianity all over again.

Lord, give me the strength to desire Your Word more. Help me to grow and mature in You. You are the one that causes growth and new leaves and fruit. Let me grow as long as I live…

BY GOD'S STRENGTH,
WE GROW AND MATURE.

Clothed in the Righteousness of Christ

"But when the king came in to see the guests, he saw a man who was not wearing wedding garments."

— Matthew 22:11

The Bible uses the symbol of clothing to teach us about righteousness. Jesus told a parable about a wedding feast where all were given the right robes to wear. But somehow a man slipped through who wasn't dressed properly, and he was thrown out in disgrace. This symbolizes the difference between trusting in Christ or in self for salvation.

Remember that text in Genesis where it all began, that God, seeing the feeble attempts of Adam and Eve to clothe themselves with fig leaves to cover their shame and nakedness after their sin, killed several animals and made coats of skin for them. God clothed them—a foreshadowing of what would yet come. In Isaiah we read, *"For He has clothed me with the garments of salvation, He has covered me with the robe of righteousness"* (Isaiah 61:10).

Isaiah also spoke about those who trust in their own righteousness. Their good works are described as filthy rags in God's sight.

Many times I have talked to people about what their hopes of life eternal rested upon. So many of them say, "Well, I have done this and I have done that, and I have done the other thing." They are looking for something about themselves that will make them acceptable. This astonishing statement in the Scripture, one that amazed Martin Luther and which puts the "amazing" into grace, says that, "His name shall be called Jehovah-*Tsidkenu*" —Jehovah is our righteousness.

Lord, give me strength for today to recognize that it is not by my righteousness, so-called, by which I may be saved. But rather it is through Christ's finished work on the cross. Thank You, Jesus, that You are my righteousness…

BY GOD'S STRENGTH, WE CAN BE DRESSED IN PROPER SPIRITUAL CLOTHING.

FEBRUARY 11

God's Word Hidden in the Heart

"Your word I have hidden in my heart,
that I might not sin against You."
— Psalm 119:11

God's purpose is that we might grow into the stature of the fullness of Jesus Christ. First, we need to regularly read, study, and meditate on God's Word. When we memorize His Word, when we hide it in our heart, that is the best defense against the onslaught of temptation. When was the last time you memorized a verse or passage of Scripture?

Secondly, there is the matter of prayer, as we go to God each day and confess our sins to Christ and ask for His forgiveness and express to Him our gratitude and love, to bring our petitions for whatever our needs may be, to intercede for other people. Such prayers as this should be on the lips of Christians every day.

Thirdly, God has given us the Church. God doesn't need it. I hope you know that. God doesn't need you. He doesn't need me. We desperately need Him. He provided all of this for us, not for Himself (but for us), that we might be taught, and that we might grow and mature in the Christian faith. We will grow more in Christ if we avail ourselves of those special times when we really study the meat of God's Word, e.g., Sunday night services, in-depth Bible studies, and on-line courses in the Word.

God wants us to progress in His Word. Then we will be *"like a tree planted by the waters,"* as described so well in Psalm 1. Our roots will grow deep. The vicissitudes of life will not upset us.

Lord, give me strength for today to spend time hiding Your Word in my heart. I praise You that You are the one who sanctifies me. Thank You that I'm not in charge of my own sanctification. Help me daily to seek You and study Your Word…

BY GOD'S STRENGTH AND BY HIS SPIRIT,
WE ARE SANCTIFIED. AMEN

FEBRUARY 12

Lincoln the Christian

"Therefore, everything you would like men to do to you, do also to them, for this is the Law and the Prophets."

— Matthew 7:12

Abraham Lincoln is everlasting in the memory of his countrymen. He was greatly influenced by the Scriptures. Read any of his speeches, and they virtually drip with the Word of God.

Many Americans actually think the quote, "A house divided against itself cannot stand" was Lincoln's. Not so. Lincoln was simply quoting a Bible verse (Matthew 12:25), which his audience probably recognized. In the 19th century, Americans were far more biblically literate than we are today, unfortunately. Lincoln often studied the Bible and used *Cruden's Concordance* as a study aid.

John G. Nicolay, Lincoln's private secretary, said: "He praised the simplicity of the Gospels. He often declared that the Sermon on the Mount contained the essence of all law and justice, and that the Lord's Prayer was the sublimest composition in human language."

Earlier in his life, Lincoln was not a Christian. But later, after coping with the death of his son, it is reported that Lincoln came to believe in Jesus. He was planning to join the church on Easter Sunday 1865, but was shot on Good Friday.

Lincoln once received a cherished gift—the Holy Bible—given to him by a delegation of black Americans, on September 7, 1864. This is what he said at the time: "In regard to this great book, I have but to say, it is the best gift God has given to men. All the good the Savior gave to the world was communicated through this book. But for it we could not know right from wrong."

Oh Lord, raise up Christian statesmen and women in our time. Help us to elect good and righteous leaders to rule over us that we might dwell in liberty and peace...

FEBRUARY 13

The Importance of Fellowship

"Now you are the body of Christ and members individually."

— 1 Corinthians 12:27

One of the great means of growth is Christian fellowship. We ought to know people who are holier than we are, and we ought to fellowship with them, and our life will be blessed by their presence.

And I hope that you get into a congregation where you can really get to know some other Christians. Remember the old axiom that birds of a feather flock together? This is true in the spiritual realm of spiritual birds as well. They flock together also. And I want to ask you who are the people with whom you spend time fellowshipping? Are they Christians or non-Christians? Whoever they are, they are saying a lot about you and what you are.

If they are Christians, are they more spiritual than you are? You know, sometimes people say, "Well, I can't stand this holier-than-thou attitude." Well, nobody likes a holier-than-thou attitude, but what most of these people know is that though that is repugnant, there is such a thing as a holier-than-thou fact. In case you don't know it, there are a whole lot of people in some of our churches that are "holier-than-thou."

Now you may think I am talking about you. I am talking about any one of us. Holier-than-I. Holier-than-thou fact is true, because sanctification is different in all. Some of us are at this stage. Some of us are at that stage. Do you have friends that you fellowship with that are more holy than you are? You should have. They will draw you upward and encourage you and build you up.

Lord, give me strength for today to build stronger relationships with those in the Body of Christ. Thank You for adopting me into the world's largest family. Thank You that as iron sharpens iron, so we can learn from our brothers and sisters in You…

BY GOD'S STRENGTH, WE ALL PLAY
A PART IN THE BODY OF CHRIST.

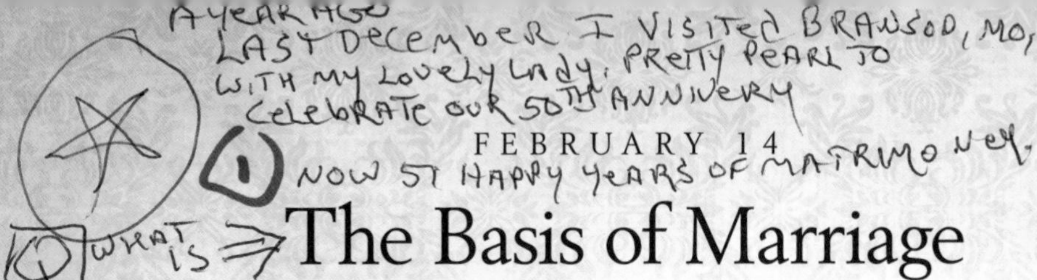

FEBRUARY 14

The Basis of Marriage

"If I speak with the tongues of men and of angels, and have not love, I have become as sounding brass or a clanging cymbal."

— 1 Corinthians 13:1

What is a marriage based upon? Many erroneously think that love is the foundation of any true marriage. Furthermore, they erroneously define love as a feeling. It is there, mysteriously, and then, some months later it is gone and the plaintive cry goes up: "Alas, I don't love him (or her) anymore." So, what is there to do, but get a divorce?

A marriage is not based on any *feeling* of love. This feeling of love is like a mysterious bird of paradise. We do not know where it comes from, why it comes to some, and why it leaves. But this mysterious bird of paradise flaps its wings, floats down on two people and they are "in love." It is a glorious, marvelous, wonderful thing. And so they get married. Two years later, they wake up one morning and decide that the bird has flown away. No one knows why. It is utterly mysterious. But it is gone. So, they must get divorced and then wander through life, waiting and hoping that once more that bird will descend from the skies upon their hearts. That is the secular view of marriage. The consequences have been devastating.

A marriage is actually built upon *commitment*. Feelings come and go. Feelings of love can proceed from that commitment. But feelings are not the foundation of a stable marriage. Until we understand this, there is little chance that our marriage will succeed. Marriage is a lifetime commitment to another person: "'til death do us part."

Lord, give us strength to live out (if so called) a Christ-centered marriage and to champion monogamy in this twisted and perverse generation…

IN GOD'S STRENGTH, WE CAN SHOW THE WORLD WHAT MARRIAGE SHOULD BE.

The Unstoppable Evangelist

"Nor do I count my life of value to myself, so that I may joyfully finish my course and the ministry which I have received from the Lord Jesus, to testify to the Gospel of the grace of God."

— Acts 20:24

I once heard about an unstoppable evangelist from Africa. In order for him to not be able to spread the Gospel, the Muslims cut off his feet just about at the ankle bone. He is not able to walk at all. An African missionary showed me a picture of this man, which I showed to my family.

He was sitting on a donkey, and I asked the question, "Does this man walk on those stubs?" "No, he can't do that. He crawls." And then I focused my attention on his knees. If you have ever seen a big, old oak tree, with thick bark with crevices all over. That is what that man's knees looked like.

I remember a number of weeks later it was raining on one Thursday night when our family goes out and shares the Gospel with others. It was raining, and I said to my daughter, "Are you going out tonight in this rain?"

And she said, "If that man can crawl on his knees, I can go out in my car in the rain."

We should not allow obstacles to prevent our service for Christ.

Often when people don't want to do something, they will offer up any number of excuses to try to wriggle out of their responsibilities. But when we consider that Jesus voluntarily suffered so horribly for us, then we should pray for the ability to follow through on our obligations.

May God give us grace to be sold out for Him—like the man with no feet.

Lord, give me strength for today to spread Your Word. Forgive me for allowing petty obstacles to keep me from doing what You have called me to do. Please, bless richly those who suffer for You who never shrink back from their Christian duty…

BY GOD'S STRENGTH, WE CAN SERVE HIM DESPITE SETBACKS.

A Limitation to Growth

"What does it profit, my brothers, if a man says he has faith but has no works?"

— James 2:14

Jesus is Lord, and if you're submitted to Him, He should be Lord of all your life. Are you willing to obey the Lord in all sorts of areas, but one particular one? It may be that because we are holding back in this area, we have reached a spiritual plateau, a limit to our growth in Christ.

We grow in grace by our obedience, because as God tells us various things that He wants us to do, we are confronted with a decision, and it is a decision either to be obedient or to be disobedient. And if we obey God, then He pours out grace upon grace and blesses us yet more abundantly. If we disobey Him, we have the experience of a person rising up and hitting the ceiling and coming back down, then trying to rise again and hitting the ceiling and coming back down because of those acts of disobedience.

May I ask you this: What is it that God has told you to do in His Word that you have refused to do? That is as far as you will grow spiritually. That is your ceiling. That determines the size of your room for growth and improvement. So obedience to what we already know works a tremendous blessing. We don't necessarily understand what that blessing is until we obey. Sometimes obedience precedes understanding. But in retrospect, we realize what a glorious, wonderful adventure to which Christ has called us.

Abba Father, I ask You today to show me any area in which I am not obeying You. Bring to my attention anything that hinders my growth and short-circuits any blessing You have for me…

BY GOD'S STRENGTH, WE CAN OVERCOME ANY OBSTACLE TO OUR GROWTH.

Two Caterpillars

"But we all, seeing the glory of the Lord with unveiled faces, as in a mirror, are being transformed into the same image from glory to glory by the Spirit of the Lord."

— 2 Corinthians 3:18

One thing about the leading of God's Spirit to grasp is that it isn't always easy or comfortable. What Paul experienced was running into one wall after another, one obstacle after another as God led him, so he could later say, *"For the love of Christ constrains us"* (2 Corinthians 5:14).

I know that certainly in my life it hasn't been a matter of being carried on a wave of happy circumstances, but it has been confronting one obstacle after another in an effort to transcend the limitations which circumstances seem to place on my life, because I have had the deep conviction that God has been leading me all along.

You remember the two caterpillars that were crawling in the muck and the mud, talking about whatever caterpillars talk to each other about in the muck and the mud. All of a sudden a large gorgeous butterfly came flitting down out of the sky right over their heads and went on up and up and up and disappeared altogether. And one of the caterpillars turned to the other one and said, "Boy, you'd never get me up in one of those things." And what do you know, a short time later he is one!

And so it is with the Christian life. What looks so threatening from below is glorious when you experience it through obedience. He created us that we may come to the measure of the fullness of the stature of Jesus Christ.

Dear Heavenly Father, I do want to soar and to be right in the center of Your will. Increase my trust in You, for I often wonder how much Your best is going to hurt. Free me from my earth-boundedness.

IN GOD'S STRENGTH, WE CAN LIVE FROM GLORY TO GLORY.

The School of Life

*"Trust in the Lord with all your heart,
and lean not on your own understanding…"*
— Proverbs 3:5

Recently, a church staff member and I were walking down one of the back halls of the church when he spotted something unusual on the floor. He picked up a rather strange looking object and said, "What in the world is this?" As we turned it over and over, he finally realized what it was and what to do with it.

Life is like that. Before we can really know what we ought to do with it, we need to know what it is and what it is for. A lot of people don't really know. In fact, I checked, and probably could give you seventy-five to a hundred definitions by different writers of what life is:

- "Life is a bowl of cherries," said one—until you get to the pits.
- Or, "Life," said Shakespeare, "is a stage [a theater] and every man and woman merely players, full of sound and fury signifying nothing."
- Life is . . . How would you finish that sentence?

I believe the Bible teaches that life is a school. Some of you might be a little unhappy to hear that because you didn't care much for school; you would rather think of it as a seventy-year recess. But the Bible teaches, I am confident, that life is a school. In fact, we are told in the Great Commission of Christ—the central command as to what we are to do—to go out and make disciples of all nations. And the ultimate lesson is that we learn to trust Him.

Lord, give me strength for today that I might learn to trust You more. Thank You for Your patience with me and Your steadfast love. Help me to pass the test in Your school, as You teach me to trust You more…

IN GOD'S STRENGTH AND LOVE,
OUR TRUST IN HIM GROWS.

FEBRUARY 19

Trusting God in All Things

"Cast all your care upon Him, because He cares for you."

— 1 Peter 5:7

A man once discovered the lesson that it is important to trust in the Lord in all circumstances. He was in great distress. He had done everything he could, but nothing was working out right. At length he said that in prayer he climbed the great marble staircase that ascended up through the clouds. When he finally arrived at the very throne room of God, he found that the huge brass doors were closed and locked. Though he beat upon them until his knuckles were raw, he sank to his knees, exhausted, at which time he heard a whisper that seemed to seep under the door saying, "Trust Me. Trust Me."

There is the lesson, my friends. God is simply saying to us in every different course in life, "Trust Me." Whether we are talking about the schools of this world, whether we are talking about business or ministry or relationships. Whatever it may be, God is saying, "Trust Me."

Many modern unbelievers look out into the vastness of the universe and ask the question: Is the universe friendly? I can't vouch for the universe. Surely the jungle is red in tooth and claw and there are many dangerous things in this fallen universe, but one thing I know beyond any peradventure of a doubt, and that is that He who created it is far beyond friendly. He loves us with an everlasting love, and He has promised He will take care of us.

Lord, my Shepherd, give me strength for today to trust in You with all my heart and lean not on my own understanding. Thank You for guiding, leading, and loving me. On the sad and difficult days, let me remember what You have done for me in the past…

BY GOD'S STRENGTH AND LOVE,
WE CAN BE ASSURED OF HIS CARE.

AMEN

FEBRUARY 20

Slow Learners

"Suddenly a great storm arose on the sea, so that the boat was covered with the waves. But He was asleep."

— Matthew 8:24

Since their name in Greek means "students," the disciples spent time with Jesus learning from Him. If you will, they had been enrolled in the school of Christ. But they were slow learners. One time when they were on the Sea of Galilee, the disciples were overwhelmed by a sudden storm. Jesus was asleep. Matthew 8 tells us: *"His disciples went to Him and awoke Him, saying, 'Lord, save us! We are perishing!' He replied, 'Why are you fearful, O you of little faith?'"*(Matthew 8:25-26a). He solved that problem instantly by rebuking the wind and the waves, which obeyed Him.

The disciples had been through Storms 101. But it was in the daytime, then, when they went out to sea, and Jesus was with them. Being weary, He was asleep in the stern when a great storm arose. But now in this more advanced class (Storms 201) Jesus was absent, and it was darkest night. They indeed were filled with distress—and well might they be.

But Mark would have us understand that Jesus, though high in a mountain miles away, was praying for them, as the Great Intercessor. He was watching them in the midst of the lake in their distress in rowing.

They had already been through Storms 101, as described above, and they didn't do well. In fact, they came close to flunking altogether. At best they might have gotten a C minus. How are you doing in the School of Christ's Discipleship? He has proven that we can trust Him in all things.

Jesus Christ, Lord even of the storms, pilot me over the tempestuous seas of life. Though the waves roll and there are treacherous rocks below, Jesus Savior, pilot me...

BY GOD'S STRENGTH, WE MAKE IT THROUGH THE STORMS OF LIFE.

FEBRUARY 21

Jesus, Man of Miracles

"They were all amazed, and they glorified God and were filled with fear, saying, 'We have seen wonderful things today.'"

— Luke 5:26

Jesus often caused people to wonder because of His miracles. In fact, "miracle" comes from the word *mirare*, meaning "to cause wonder." Jesus was a man of miracles. We read that He went about doing good. What were His works? We know that carpenters build things with wood and nails. Preachers preach sermons. As to Jesus, His works were miracles.

Fred Melden said, "He [the Miracle Man] came to us by a miracle and left us by a miracle." He was raised from the dead by a miracle, and everywhere He went there was one continuous stream of miracles. John tells that if all the things Jesus had done were written in a book all the world could not hold it. There are thirty-three miracles recorded in the Gospels. He lived to about thirty-three years of age, but the miracles are all recorded in a three-year period. But these were just a small token of the miracles He did.

He was a man of miracles. He was so full of goodness that the demons fled before Him. He was so full of life that death fled before Him. We read in the Scriptures the reactions to Christ were continually one of wonder and amazement and astonishment. We read, "They were terrified and frightened."..."They marveled."... "They were all amazed."

Of course, His greatest miracle is the transformation He can bring to a human soul. For that miracle in my heart, I will ever be grateful.

Lord, give me strength for today that I might reflect well the great miracle You have worked in my heart—changing me from the inside out. God of the miraculous, thank You for all the signs and wonders that show forth Your power. Thank You for supernaturally intervening in my life without me even knowing it...

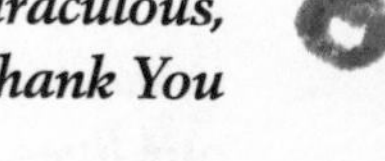

BY GOD'S STRENGTH AND POWER,
ALL IS POSSIBLE.

FEBRUARY 22

Washington the Christian

*"I will praise the name of God with a song,
and will magnify Him with thanksgiving."*
— Psalm 69:30

Some people question the Christianity of George Washington, but the facts speak for themselves. He was a vestryman in good standing in the Episcopal Church at a time when their doctrine conformed closely to evangelical teaching. He was well-known for his godly disposition and his fervent prayer life, for instance, when he was spotted kneeling in prayer at Valley Forge.

His prayers were answered as God sovereignly helped the fledgling nation in its struggle against the most powerful nation on earth. So much so that Washington wrote this to Thomas Nelson, Jr. in a letter dated August 20, 1778: "The hand of Providence has been so conspicuous in all this, that he must be worse than an infidel that lacks faith, and more than wicked, that has not gratitude enough to acknowledge his obligations."

When Washington was inaugurated in 1789 in New York City, he got down on his knees and kissed the Bible. Then he led the entire Senate and House of Representatives to an Episcopal church for a two-hour worship service.

When Washington left office, he penned a lengthy Farewell Address, considered one of the greatest messages in American history. Listen to what he said about the place of religion in our national life: "Of all the dispositions and habits which lead to political prosperity, religion and morality are indispensable supports. In vain would that man claim the tribute of patriotism, who should labor to subvert these great pillars of human happiness."

Lord, give us strength to preserve this great nation You have given us. Help us to learn from some of our nation's founders to put You and Your Word first in our lives...

BY GOD'S STRENGTH, WE CAN
RESTORE THIS NATION.

FEBRUARY 23

The Temptation to Quit

"And let us not grow weary in doing good, for in due season we shall reap, if we do not give up."

— Galatians 6:9

The temptation to quit is a very powerful temptation, because unlike some other temptations it does not take any effort to quit. To quit, one does not have to do anything. He just stops, sits down, and gives up.

Quitting is just a matter of stopping our fight with entropy, which is always tending to push everything down and bring it into chaos and disorder.

We need to realize that we quit through discouragement because we lose hope—we lose the hope of success. The great missionary, William Carey, said that no great enterprise could ever be carried out without hope of success. The Bible says, *"So now abide faith, hope, and love, these three"* (1 Corinthians 13:13). Faith looks to the past and anchors itself in the promises of God. Hope looks to the future and inevitably flows out of that faith in the promises of God—the promises that say we can do all things through Christ who strengthens us (Philippians 4:13). We shall reap in the future, if we do not give up hope (Galatians 6:9).

Having faith in the promises of God and hope for a victorious future, we are enabled to live a life of love in the present. Hope is a powerful motivating factor, and it is that which is guaranteed by God when He says we can do all things through Christ. Therefore, we need to take Him at His Word and believe in Him, so we don't lose heart and give up.

Lord, give me the strength not to lose heart and give up. Give me the ability to persevere despite the obstacles. Thank You that You can do the impossible. Thank You that I can do all things through Christ who gives me strength…

BY GOD'S STRENGTH, WE CAN PERSEVERE TO THE END.

FEBRUARY 24

Remembering God's Presence in Our Lives

"For He has said: 'I will never leave you, nor forsake you.'"

—Hebrews 13:5

How often it is with us, that in the midst of our distresses and troubles, we think God is far away—that Christ is far away—and we seem to be all on our own without any resources or help. Sometimes we despair; we are terrified. But Christ is watching us. Whatever problem we are in, though Christ may seem far away, He is there, watching, and He is willing and able to come to our need.

Oftentimes it seems He comes in the very last moment. When the disciples experienced a storm one night on the Sea of Galilee, He allowed them to expend their energies until finally they were at the end of themselves. He proved again that man's extremity is God's opportunity.

I have had my share of problems and distresses on the water, also. One incident could have been a terrible disaster when a little child was in a boat I was driving. But in God's mercy, the most that was lost were material possessions—not life or limb. What to my mind was certain total disaster, God, in His gracious providence oversaw and allowed the boat to land right on top of a tree, which lowered it gently into the thick under-brush below.

I have often thought about how God was with me, even when I didn't think He was. When He seemed to be far away, and I was out in the middle of a lake, completely helpless, totally beyond my ability to do anything about the situation, I found that God helped.

Oh God, Help of the helpless, abide with me. So often we do not see Your hand that leads us home. Help us to remember in the darkness what You have shown us in the light. Let us trust that You see us when we do not see You.

BY GOD'S STRENGTH, WE WILL MAKE IT THROUGH LIFE.

FEBRUARY 25

The God of 11:59 P.M.

"He saw them straining at rowing, for the wind was against them. About the fourth watch of the night He came to them, walking on the sea."

— Mark 6:48

God's timing is perfect. But sometimes, we may feel that Christ seems far away. Let me assure you He is watching you and is able to come to your aid. It may not be nearly as soon as you would like, but life is a school, and we have to be left to learn the lessons. I believe life's great central lesson is to learn to trust Him.

As we know, when the disciples were on the Sea of Galilee one night, at Jesus' instructions, a storm arose suddenly. Sometimes it seems in life that the winds which seem to be fair for others are contrary to us. It doesn't matter whether you are in a course on storms, economics, sicknesses or hospitals—whatever it may be, that is the course laid out for you in this world by God.

Finally, in the last watch of the night, Jesus came to the disciples walking on the water. No doubt they had been praying for Him to come. But suddenly He appeared in His most astonishing way—walking on the waves, which for them were so troublesome, but for Him they simply provided the pavement for His feet.

The disciples were terrified. They thought they had seen a ghost, a *phantasma* (as the Greek word is), a phantom. And then Jesus spoke to them. He said, *"It is I. Do not be afraid"* (Matthew 14:27). Although it may seem God is late, He is never late, even if He may be the God of 11:59 P.M.

My Savior and my God, thank You for always being there for me. Thank You for all the times You stepped in and cleared up a situation for me. Thank You that Your timing is always perfect…

IN GOD'S STRENGTH,
WE CAN WAIT UPON HIM.

FEBRUARY 26

The Real Super Bowl

"Woe unto the inhabitants of the earth and the sea! For the devil has come down to you in great wrath, because he knows that his time is short."

— Revelation 12:12

Every year millions of Americans eagerly await the Super Bowl. This is when the two most successful and powerful teams in the country meet together for a final conflict, for the championship of the world, preceded by a long competition leading up to the final event.

But when you think about it, there is a real Super Bowl, which is of far greater consequence than any football game. I am talking about a supernatural bowl in which there are two teams in this world that are involved in a contest for the championship of the world, for the dominion of the world.

So in this "Super Bowl" it is Christians vs. the dragons, and many people don't know what the outcome is going to be. There are those in our country today who join Satan's team, really believing they are winning and are going to have the victory, receiving from below the success they are seeking in this world. It is a bowl that should indeed cause great interest, because not merely is there a trophy or ring involved, but the entire conquest and dominion of the world is at stake. This Super Bowl is described in the book of Revelation. Thank God we are on the winning side. As the hymn notes, "So from the beginning the fight we were winning."

Lord, give me strength for today to serve You, knowing that You have conquered the evil one. Though his "craft and power are great and armed with cruel hate," You defeated Him, Jesus, on the cross and in Your resurrection. Renew my spirit to serve You with joy…

BY GOD'S STRENGTH, WE KNOW WE ARE ON THE WINNING SIDE.

FEBRUARY 27

The Secret to Walking on Water

"Peter answered Him and said, 'Lord, if it is You, bid me come to You on the water.'"

— Matthew 14:28

As we know, one night when the disciples were on the Sea of Galilee and Jesus was not present, a storm came up. They were afraid and even thought they saw a ghost. It was Jesus, walking on the water. Then, impetuous Peter said, "If it is you, let me walk on the water to You." And Jesus said, "Come."

Peter, climbing up the gunnel of the ship, steps down upon the water, no doubt very hesitantly. Holding on to the side, he pushes himself away and begins to walk upon the waves, coming to Christ. What an extraordinary experience. Other than Jesus Christ, he is the only other human being I have ever heard of who actually walked upon water.

Now, we may tend to smile at Peter because of the fearfulness that came upon him and his sinking into the waves. But, let us not forget that Peter did walk a number of steps upon the water. How about you? How many steps have you walked on water?

Then Peter took his eyes off Jesus and looked at the boisterous sea. He saw the effects of it in the waves that were dashing about him. And when he took his eyes off of Jesus and looked at the waves, he began instantly to sink.

How many times have you or I lain upon our beds at night microscopically examining the waves and wondering why we were sinking? If you would learn to walk on water, then don't look at the waves, look at Jesus.

Lord Jesus, thank You for holding us up in life, even through difficult storms. Help us to focus on You and not the wind and waves. Give us the grace to keep our eyes on You through the storms of life…

BY GOD'S STRENGTH,
WE CAN "WALK ON WATER."

Fix Your Eyes on Jesus

"Let us look to Jesus, the author and finisher of our faith..."
— Hebrews 12:2

In the early days of my pastoring, I had the pleasure of witnessing to a young man in his twenties, who finally accepted Christ. He was growing in the Lord. The very week after he joined the church, he made the central headlines of the newspaper. The FBI was looking for him for some kind of fraudulent activity he had been involved in before.

In fact, when they found him, he was so overwhelmed by this experience he had a mental breakdown. I visited him in Broward Hospital's mental ward. When I went into his room, he was like a caged lion. He hardly seemed aware of my presence. He was pacing back and forth across the room, mumbling to himself, moaning, bewailing, and gesturing about what was going to happen to him. He was possibly facing twenty years in prison.

After some time, he quieted down as I read the Scripture to him about how Peter had looked at the waves and had begun to sink. I said to him, "You are looking at the waves, and you are sinking into total mental depression and agony of spirit. Lift up your eyes to Jesus. Fix your eyes upon Him. Look upon Him. Look unto Him."

Gradually, all of his anxiety and distress just seemed to drain away. He sat down in a chair and began to look at me with eyes that obviously were quite full of understanding. He was restored. Later, the charges against him were dropped. Though your problems seem insurmountable, fix your eyes on Jesus.

Jesus Christ, give me strength for today to focus on You. Forgive me for too often focusing on the problems of life, but not You. If ever I should start to sink, let me say with Peter, "Lord, save me." Thank You that You have overcome the world...

BY GOD'S STRENGTH, WE CAN
KEEP OUR EYES ON JESUS.

Faith That Overcomes

"For by thee I have run through a troop: by my God have I leaped over a wall…"

— 2 Samuel 22:30 KJV

Despite all his flaws, King David knew God, and he once made the above declaration. Specifically, I would like to talk to you about troop running and wall leaping—not a practice most of us are involved in every day.

Of course, these are just poetic expressions for us today, though they were very real for David. He did both. He ran through a troop with his sword shining in the sun, rescued his wife and children, who had been kidnapped by the Amalekites, and brought them home again. By faith he had leaped over a wall, when his enemies had tried to keep him out of Jerusalem. He did these things.

We probably don't, but as I said, they are poetic expressions; they are figures of speech of the kinds of problems we all have right here in the twenty-first century. I don't know what your troubles are now. I don't know what walls are keeping you from accomplishing the goals you have set for yourself. I don't know what walls are separating you from others in your home—loved ones, or neighbors, or fellow workers. I don't know what kind of opposition you have that seems to form itself as an armed troop against you, but these represent a whole host of various kinds of obstacles that we all face. David is telling us here, and God is showing us, that we can overcome these problems.

Lord, give me strength for today to accomplish what You would have me do. Thank You that by Your grace and Your help, we can accomplish wonderful things. And let us be quick to give You all the praise and glory…

BY HIS STRENGTH, WE CAN OVERCOME THE OBSTACLES WE FACE TODAY.

MARCH 1

Never Too Old to Serve the Lord

"…older women should be…teachers of good things, that they may teach the young women to love their husbands, to love their children…"

—Titus 2:3-4

God can use you whatever your age. I think of a railroad conductor, who worked until he was sixty-five. Because of his job, he didn't get to spend much time in church. When he retired, he wanted to serve the Lord full time. He decided that he was going to invite people to church.

He went around to houses, knocked on doors, gave some kind of literature, and invited people to come to his church. After he died, it was discovered that he had brought 867 people into that church—after he retired.

Are you too old to do anything? I think not. In fact, retired people have more time than most working people. They could use their talents and their energy to serve the Lord and make a great impact.

I think of some people so old that they can do nothing but lie in bed or sit in a wheelchair all day. But if they still have their faculties, they can do something very significant. They can pray. They can pray for their family, for the church, for the pastor, for the country, for the state government, and so on. They can end up having a huge impact for the kingdom through this act of service.

Paul notes that the older women are to teach the younger ones in the church. Could it be, as we see many Americans getting older and older, we have lost sight of their potential service in God's kingdom? As long as we are in the world, we are in His service.

Our Savior and God, we make ourselves available today to do that which You would have us do. Give us compassion for those who are needy, spiritually or otherwise…

LORD, GIVE ME STRENGTH FOR TODAY TO SERVE YOU WITH ALL MY HEART, NO MATTER MY AGE.

MARCH 2

Three Means of God's Guidance

*"The meek will He guide in judgment,
and the meek He will teach His way."*
— Psalm 25:9

There is a story about a ship that was sailing down the coast, and it had to turn into the port. But it was a black night, overcast, no moon, no stars, only a few lights at that time along the shore. How was the captain ever going to find the port? A friend was with him, and he had no idea in that day how in the world this captain was ever going to find his way into that port and into the bay without just running the ship right aground.

And the captain said, in this case it was very simple. "You see that red light over there and that one there and that one there?" He said, "Those lights will eventually line up in a straight line, and at that point I turn 180 degrees to the starboard and sail right into the port."

That reminds us that there are at least three ways that God does guide the humble of heart. The first of which is by the Scripture, and there is much guidance in the Scripture for us. It is, we should always remember, the only infallible guidance that we have. Then there is guidance through circumstances, and there is guidance through the Holy Spirit. Now certainly the Holy Spirit's guidance would be completely adequate, but since we have fallen into sin—though He is broadcasting properly—our receptors are dented and marred and distorted and there is so much static we don't hear clearly. But Scripture is our infallible guide.

Lord, we would be so lost without Your Word. We thank You for the light it daily sheds on our way. Help us to take our guidance from You always. Lord, give me strength for today to follow You where You choose to lead me…

BY GOD'S STRENGTH AND BY HIS SPIRIT,
WE ARE NEVER WITHOUT COUNSEL.

MARCH 3

We Reflect What We Are

"Finally, brothers, whatever things are true, whatever things are honest, whatever things are just, whatever things are pure, whatever things are lovely, whatever things are of good report, if there is any virtue, and if there is any praise, think on these things."

— Philippians 4:8

The author William Thackeray once said: "The world is a looking glass and gives back to every man the reflection of his own face."

Some people never learn that lesson. They are miserable, and their life is a failure because they never learned that simple truth. I know individuals who have been through one job after another, after another, after another. Why? Because of "those folks over there," that's why. Those "no-good, low-down, malicious, gossiping, hateful people." They are going to find when they move to a new job that the people there are just the same.

The mirror of the world is a mirror that reflects quite accurately a picture of ourselves. Thackeray continued "Frown at it, and it will in turn look sourly upon you; laugh at it and with it, and it is a jolly, compassionate boomerang."

As we think in our hearts, so our faces reflect and so our words embody our thoughts. The Apostle Paul said in Philippians 4:8 that we should focus on the good things. May I ask you: How much time did you spend reflecting on those things this past week? We probably take it very lightly and then wonder why things are so difficult in the world.

God of grace and beauty, fill my heart and mind with loveliness. Make me a beautiful person that I might reflect Your beauty to the people I meet today…

BY GOD'S STRENGTH, WE CAN FOCUS OUR MINDS ON THE LOVELY AND PURE.

Making Friends

"A man who has friends must show himself friendly."
— Proverbs 18:24

Some people may wonder why they have so few friends. But the Bible says to have friends, you must be a friend.

Dale Carnegie in his famous book *How To Win Friends and Influence People* said this: "Why should people be interested in you unless you are first interested in them?"

A well-known maxim puts it this way:

I went out to find a friend,
but could not find one there.
I went out to be a friend,
and friends were everywhere.

Carnegie said that the greatest lesson he ever learned about human relations, he learned in his youth from a dog named "Tippy," a little yellow-haired dog with a stub tail. When Tippy would see him coming, he would run up to him, his short stubby tail wagging so hard that his whole body was wagging. He would lick his hands and run around his ankles and want to be petted. He was so genuinely friendly to Carnegie that he just could not possibly keep from petting that little dog. Tippy knew a great lesson, a great secret about relationships. He had no lack of friends because he showed himself friendly.

Show yourself friendly; think about others. Instead, we are so eager to go out and wigwag people into being impressed with us, thinking they will then be our friends. People couldn't care less about that.

It is good to make friends, especially those whom we can build up in Christ. As iron sharpens iron, so one man sharpens another.

Triune God, You who created us for fellowship with You and with each other, I thank You today for my friends. Help me to be a good friend to those You have placed in my life…

BY GOD'S STRENGTH, WE CAN
BE A GOOD FRIEND TODAY.

MARCH 5

Think About Others

"For I have no one like-minded, who will sincerely care for your state."
— Philippians 2:20

If you really want to stand out, think about others instead of just yourself. Most people do the opposite.

Years ago, a telephone company made a detailed study of telephone conversations to find out which word is the most frequently used. It is the same word that is most used in daily conversations. It is the word "I." It was used 3,990 times in 500 telephone conversations. "I." "I." "I." "I." "I." People think about themselves morning, noon, and after dinner, too, said Dale Carnegie.

On an airplane one time I sat next to a tennis pro. We had a very interesting conversation. I talked at length about her tennis, and she was very interested. Then I changed the subject and boom—her interest rate dropped to zero, instantly. I switched the subject back to her and immediately the dial went up to 100 again. She reminded me of "Edith," a lady someone described as "a small country bounded on the north, east, south and west by Edith."

There is not too great a market out there for your complaints. Someone said that you and I will discover that about 50 percent of the people don't care what is wrong with you and the other 50 percent think you are getting what you deserve anyway.

In Christ, we are called to a life of unselfishness. Instead of "looking out for number one," we are told to put others' interest ahead of our own. May God free us from our selfishness.

Self-existing God, You made us for Yourself and You made us to make life better for each other. Help me today to take the focus off myself and my problems and to focus on the people You put in my path…

IN GOD'S STRENGTH, WE
CAN FOCUS ON OTHERS.

MARCH 6

The Secret Rockefeller Learned

"Let each of you look not only to your own interests, but also to the interests of others."

— Philippians 2:4

Did you ever hear of the great lesson learned by John D. Rockefeller, Sr., founder of the Rockefeller dynasty? By the time he was 33, he had become a millionaire. By the age of 53, he had become the world's first billionaire. He was the richest man in all the world. But Drs. S. E. McMillan and David E. Stern, in their book *None of These Diseases*, say that Rockefeller had traded his happiness and his health for his wealth.

Rockefeller had developed a condition called Alopecia, and as a result lost all of his hair. He looked like a mummy. Although he made a million dollars a week, a biographer says that he enjoyed absolutely nothing. He had lost his appetite and his sleep.

Then one night he realized that he was going to die soon, and he couldn't take his wealth with him. That hit him like a bolt right out of the blue. He became totally depressed and overwhelmed. But then he had a brilliant idea.

Being a practical man, the next morning he got up and began to put his idea into practice. He started giving away money systematically. This focus on others caused a major turnaround. He eventually lived to 97.

He was living a happy life because he had simply made a discovery of that which Jesus told us long ago: *"It is more blessed to give than to receive"* (Acts 20:35). Rockefeller had learned to think of someone else other than just himself.

Father God, Giver of all gifts, give me strength for today to live a generous life today and to give of myself. Let Your generosity inspire me to also give generously to others…

BY GOD'S STRENGTH,
WE CAN BE GENEROUS.

MARCH 7

Christ Frees Us from Selfishness

"For even the Son of Man came not to be served, but to serve, and to give His life as a ransom for many."

— Mark 10:45

Instinctively, we know we should not be selfish. There is a problem, however, in doing that. Think about others? Forget yourself? If people are basically self-centered, how can they do that?

There is only one answer to that question, my friends. When we receive Christ into our lives and hearts, we die to self; we are crucified with Christ and we find the God who provides all of our needs.

The reason people can't forget themselves is because they are so needy. They are such pitiful, weak, temporal creatures, and yet Christ comes and meets all of these needs. Christ has promised to supply all of our needs out of His riches in glory. Therefore, because we have the guarantee that Christ is going to take care of us, we don't have to manipulate them to do that because Christ has freely and graciously offered to do it for us Himself. We can begin to think differently of other people.

Because of selfishness and pride, we are always putting other people down. Yet every person has good points and bad points, and generally we tend to see the bad points. Author J. K. Morley said this: "I can complain because rosebushes have thorns or rejoice because thorn bushes have roses. It's all [in] how you look at it." Now think of your husband or wife or boss as that "bush." Which do you do? Do you complain because bosses or wives or husbands have thorns, or do you rejoice because they have roses as well?

Jehoveh-Jireh, we thank You for supplying all our needs and providing for everything we need for body and soul. Help us to be helpful to others and to focus on the good in them…

IN GOD'S STRENGTH, WE CAN SEE THE GOOD IN OTHERS.

MARCH 8

On the Law of Karma

"For Christ also has once suffered for sins, the just for the unjust, so that He might bring us to God…"

— 1 Peter 3:18

There are religions, like Hinduism, whose followers talk about "karma." The Hindus believe that salvation is wrought through karma; that all one has to do is reflect up to the gods, and the gods reflect it back to us and we get what we deserve—tit for tat, quid pro quo, something for something.

But that does not wash since every one of us is a sinner. If everything we have ever said, thought, or done that is wrong reflected up to God, it would come down upon us like a safe falling out of a window of a tall building.

Thank God, however, He takes all of that ill thinking and all of those unkind words to Himself, and all of our sin upon Himself. He goes to a Cross and there He dies in our place. He shines back upon us the soft beam of His love. It is no reflection of what we have done; it is a reflection of what He is, of His smiling face, of His willingness to accept us—not because of our success, but because He has given His Son to die for us.

If we will trust in Jesus Christ, He will receive us just as we are—with all of our moles and warts and imperfections, all of our sins and transgressions—by His grace. God operates, not by karma, but by grace, and offers through no merit of our own to receive us to Himself, just as we are, by His grace, if we will trust in Jesus Christ.

Gracious God, we thank You for not reflecting back to us our unkind words and ugly thoughts. Thank You, instead, for reflecting back to us Your pure love. Lord, give me strength for today to forgive others since You have so generously forgiven me…

IN GOD'S STRENGTH, WE REFLECT BACK HIS LOVE.

MARCH 9

Living With Purpose

"For what will it profit a man if he gains the whole world and loses his own soul?"

— Matthew 16:26

Tragically, the false view that human beings are just the products of time and chance, and that ultimately purpose is just a mirage, dominates most of our schools today. It is not surprising when people spend the first quarter of their lives in school learning that sort of nonsense, so they have very little defined purposes for their lives.

This is supported by some psychologists, such as the late B. F. Skinner, who would say that we are "beyond freedom and dignity." To them there is no purpose; we are what we eat and are determined by those things surrounding us.

There are other psychologists who disagree and send contrary signals. They tell us that we have purposes for all we do, whatever it may be. They say to find those purposes we need to get in touch with our subconscious.

The Bible has no such contradictory signals. It makes abundantly clear the fact that God has given the entire world a purpose. Events are moving toward a definite conclusion when God will drop the curtain on history and everything will reach its appointed goal.

He has done this with the cosmos, and He has done it for every individual within it. Each of us has been given a divinely ordained purpose, and we are to fulfill that purpose in our lives. If we fail to fulfill the purpose God has given to us, our life will ultimately be a tragic failure, even if it's a success in the eyes of the world.

Lord of life, give me strength for today to finish the work You have given me to do. Thank You for the promise that You will fulfill Your purposes for me. Let me live close to You so I see them clearly…

BY GOD'S STRENGTH, OUR PURPOSE
IN LIFE WILL BE FULFILLED.

MARCH 10

Avoiding the Junk Heap

"I press toward the goal to the prize of the high calling of God in Christ Jesus."

— Philippians 3:14

The junk heap has been designed for those things that fail to fulfill their purpose. In our house, one time we had a fancy electric can opener—a wondrous thing to behold. The chrome shone brightly as a delightful adjunct to our kitchen. It was even color-coordinated with the color of the walls. It made a marvelous whirring sound when it was turned on. There was only one slight fault: It did not open cans. Guess where it is today. That's right. In the junk heap.

Outside the city of Jerusalem was a place called the Valley of Hinnom. We know it better as Gehenna, which is translated in the English version of the Bible as "hell." Into the Valley of Ge-Hinnom was cast all the refuse, all the things that had failed to serve their purposes any longer. That is what garbage is. That is where people go who do not fulfill the purposes God has ordained for them.

Paul makes it very clear that he had a purpose: "This one thing I do." This integration of all the faculties of life into one single purpose is one of the greatest secrets of success. It has been noted in anyone who has ever accomplished anything significant for good (or evil for that matter), whether it be Florence Nightingale, David Livingstone, Martin Luther or John Calvin—any person who has accomplished a great deal for humankind has had this consuming singleness of purpose.

Let us live for God's purpose and avoid the junk heap.

Oh Lord, let me not waste my life in futile pursuits, but with singleness of mind, give me strength for today to press on toward the goal. Thank You for Your high calling in Christ Jesus...

BY GOD'S STRENGTH,
WE WILL REACH THE GOAL.

MARCH 11

On Remembering and Forgetting

"When they saw the boldness of Peter and John and perceived that they were illiterate and uneducated men, they marveled. And they recognized that they had been with Jesus."

— Acts 4:13

Many people are rendered failures because they remember what they ought to forget and forget what they ought to remember. This is a tragic thing. We ought to forget those things that debilitate and keep us from reaching our greatest potential. The first among those is that we ought to forget our failures. I believe that the remembrance of our failures is Satan's chain that he uses to bind us to the ground like some chained bird. We may desire at times to spread our wings and fly up into the sky and that chain jerks us back down to the ground.

"I've tried it before, and I failed." "I tried to one time, and it did not work." "I stood up to speak and forgot my lines." "I can still remember them laughing." "I didn't do well in school. I failed the course." "I failed in business." "I failed in life." "I can't do it." "I can't." "I can't."

The apostles had their own failings. Three times Peter had denied that he knew Jesus. John and his brother James sought to be so honored that they would sit on both sides of the Lord up in heaven. The Gospels record the failings of the apostles repeatedly. But after His resurrection and the out-pouring of the Holy Spirit, now the apostles were bold changed men, so they forgot their failures and remembered God's blessing. Be careful what you choose to remember and what you choose to forget.

Dear Lord Jesus, give me strength for today to remember Your blessings, the victories You have given me, however small or great, and to remember what is good. Help me to forget my failures and hurts. I lay these at the foot of the cross. Help me to leave them there…

BY GOD'S STRENGTH, WE CAN
LEAVE OUR FAILURES BEHIND.

MARCH 12

Designed for a Purpose

"I will give You thanks, O Lord my God, with all my heart, and I will glorify Your name forever."

— Psalm 86:12

Life has purpose. The handle of an ax has only one purpose. The weighty end of the head has no other purpose than to bring the whole momentum created by the handle and the weight created by the head to bear on that small, sharp, knifelike edge. When that hits the wood, the purpose is fulfilled. So it is with a bow and arrow. The head of the arrow, the shaft, the feathers, the bow, the string, the arm and the eye are all designed for just one purpose: the front end of the arrow to hit the target.

Everything that accomplishes anything great has an integration toward a single purpose, whether it be a football team or a 747. Can you imagine a football team which is not integrated toward a single play?

Our lives are so unlike that. There are many who build huge engines but have little stubby wings and so they will not fly. Others have wings that are a block and half long but have no power to get off the ground. There is not that integration where every part moves toward the same goal.

Everything a triathlon athlete does is designed to complete that one single event. His eating, his sleeping, his exercise, what work he does to make money just to continue toward that goal, his thinking, and his study, are designed toward that one end.

Godly goals are the best type. It's good to be goal-oriented, especially if that goal is for God's glory and our good and that of others.

Lord, give me strength for today to fulfill the purpose for which You have made me. Thank You for Your promise to give Your wisdom to those who need it. Help us to live on purpose and let that purpose be to glorify Your Son, our Savior, Jesus Christ...

BY GOD'S STRENGTH,
ALL MY WORK IS PRAISE.

MARCH 13

Don't Rest on Your Laurels

"So you also, when you have done everything commanded you, say, 'We are unprofitable servants. We have done our duty.'"

— Luke 17:10

We need to forget our successes sometimes. Some of us are wonderful laurel-sitters. We have been sitting on our laurels for years. We reach a certain level of accomplishment and are satisfied. That should not be.

I recall reading that one of Napoleon's generals came to him and described a magnificent victory he had won in one of the campaigns. He described how they had brought the artillery up to just the right point and smashed the enemy. Having concluded a detailed narrative, he waited for Napoleon to commend him. There was a brief silence, and then Napoleon said to him, "Yes, and what did you do the next day?"

I think we need to hear those words because God is no doubt going to be asking us, "What did you do the next day?" What are you doing now for God? Are you resting on your laurels? We need to forget our successes. We need to have a holy discontent.

Sometimes we may be quite content and unconcerned about the advancement of the kingdom of God, but very discontented about the state we are in. We do not like the car we drive, the house we live in, the clothes we wear. We are envious of others—what they have, what jobs they hold, and what cars they drive. But we have it all backwards. There is a need for a holy discontent in the progress we have made in the kingdom of God.

Lord, give me strength for today to realize I do not need to be great in Your kingdom. I only wish to be Your servant. Neither do I wish to miss opportunities to serve and to grow and do great things for You…

BY GOD'S STRENGTH, WE PRESS ON
IN THE WORK OF THE KINGDOM.

MARCH 14

Eye on the Prize

"...reaching forward to those things which are ahead..."
— Philippians 3:13

In Philippians 3, Paul uses athletic imagery to describe his race for Christ. "Reaching forward" is a figure of a runner whose hand is stretched out way in front of his body. He is telling us that we need that eager aspiration, that enthusiasm that comes with God within us, causing us to reach out after greater things. Our soul needs to be ten or twenty paces in front of our body.

We need that eagerness of heart. Too often we go through our jobs, we go through our devotions, we go through our worship, we go through our service for Christ with a perfunctory attitude. There is no eagerness that drives us. We need to have that eagerness of spirit.

Paul adds, *"I press toward the goal to the prize"* (v. 14). In addition to eagerness of spirit, there needs to be great exertion expended to reach the mark. The words "press toward the goal" here mean to pursue, to virtually persecute, and to go after something in an intense way.

We who are saved, know that eternal life is not the result of our pursuing, of our running a race, but it is a free gift because of Christ's death on our behalf. We have then set before us a vision of the prize of the high calling of Christ where we can live our lives for His glory until that day when the King shall call us up on high and crown us with an imperishable crown. Keep your eye on the prize as you run the race.

Lord, give me strength for today to run the race. I am often weak and stumbling along. Give me the grace to keep my eyes on heavenly things. Thank You that You will lead me safely home one day...

BY GOD'S STRENGTH,
WE WILL FINISH THE RACE.

MARCH 15

Everything for Christ?

"But what things were gain to me, I have counted these things to be loss for the sake of Christ."

— Philippians 3:7

During the decade of the 1950s, a bright and brilliant star flashed across the cinematic and recording sky. It was a star that belonged to a young man with a magnificent voice. The name of that young man was Mario Lanza. But suddenly, unexpectedly, inexplicably, he died—a man who some said had, perhaps, the greatest voice ever.

His records sold more copies than any record ever had until that time. His lifetime goal was to portray the life of Enrico Caruso on the screen, a man he most admired. That dream came to pass in the mid-fifties.

My wife, knowing that I enjoyed his singing, bought several of the few motion pictures for me that he had made. One of them, *The Toast of New Orleans*, was a story about a rough-cut and unkempt young fisherman, at a bayou in Louisiana. When his talent for singing was discovered one day, the man gave him money for a suit and a haircut.

That astonished the young man. He said, "A haircut? ...for singing?"

Then the impresario said something I will never forget. He said, "From now on, everything is for singing."

When I heard those words, I thought: What a beautiful description of what it means to become a Christian. To become a Christian, very simply, is this: From now on, everything is for Christ. Every thought, every motive, every desire, every action, everything we do is to be done for Christ. Thus, our autobiography could well be called "Christ, My Life."

Jesus Christ, You are my life. Give me strength for today to be single-minded, to keep in mind that I am not my own. I belong to You. Let all I do and say and think today be pleasing to You...

BY GOD'S STRENGTH,
WE CAN LIVE FOR CHRIST.

MARCH 16

Christ – the Purpose of Life

"...I count everything as loss for the excellence of the knowledge of Christ Jesus my Lord..."

— Philippians 3:8

Tragically, many people are essentially wandering around in life, aimlessly. For all practical purposes, they are marking time. They are like the proverbial man in jail with marks on the wall, representing how many days, weeks, months, or years he has fulfilled. Many are living as if they are just waiting to die.

But when Christ changed my life, I can now say He is the purpose of my life. Is everything you do done for Christ? From now on, everything is for Christ. I believe I can honestly say that is the ordinary purpose of everything in my life, whether it be to get up or to go to sleep, to exercise or to rest, to eat or to fast, to study or to work, to do anything at all. The great over-arching transcendent purpose of everything I do is for Christ. For with Paul I can say, "For me to live is Christ." He is the purpose of my existence.

He is so, for if any man is in Christ, he is a new creation with a new purpose, new desires, and new wants to please Christ. I suppose almost every young person going through school goes on that quest in which he tries to answer the questions: "Who am I?" "Why am I here?" Where did I come from, and where am I going?" "What is my purpose for life?" Living for Christ answers all those critical questions.

El Shaddai, You are all sufficient. Thank You that there are answers to the basic questions of life. Thank You for giving meaning and purpose to life. Thank You for revealing the answers...

BY GOD'S STRENGTH, WE LIVE LIVES FULL OF MEANING.

MARCH 17

Happy Sinner Patrick Day

"But the Lord stood with me and strengthened me, so that through me the preaching might be fully known, and that all the Gentiles might hear. And I was delivered out of the mouth of the lion."

— 2 Timothy 4:17

March 17 is actually "Sinner Patrick Day." But though he was a young and rebellious youth, he was to be finally overtaken by the "Hound of Heaven." This young man from England was captured by pirates. At age 16, living as he did on the beach of the western coast of England, just south of Scotland, he and two of his friends had spent the day in the breakers in the ocean. Suddenly, they looked over here and they saw a whole group of "freebooters"—Irish pirates.

Fast forward years later, after a horrible time as a slave of the Irish, Sinner Patrick became Saint Patrick as he drew close to Jesus Christ. Eventually, he got his chance to escape slavery and escape from Ireland.

But he returned to the place of his humiliating slavery as a missionary of the Gospel after theological training. What an effective ministry he had.

His accomplishment was absolutely gigantic. No one had ever gone to convert a nation outside the rule of Rome, but Patrick did. Every day of his life he was in mortal danger. He was in the midst of some of the fiercest, cruelest people the world has ever seen—the Druids. But he trusted in Christ for his protection as he prayed regularly for the protection of Christ, "Christ before me, Christ behind me…." By the power of the Gospel, he changed that entire nation.

Lord of the nations, thank You for the example of Your servant, St. Patrick, in proclaiming Your Gospel to people who so desperately need You…

LORD, GIVE ME STRENGTH FOR TODAY
TO SPREAD YOUR KINGDOM.

MARCH 18

Is Christ the "Parent" of Your Life?

"That which is born of the flesh is flesh,
and that which is born of the Spirit is spirit."
— John 3:6

The Scripture makes it plain that as we are born by nature, we are merely flesh—flesh that is corrupting, decaying, and dying. That which is flesh is flesh, and it goes the way of all flesh. We need to have a new birth from above. Jesus said we must be born again in a new and glorious and never-dying life.

I remember one time being interviewed by a reporter who said to me, "Are you...Are you one of those...those 'born-again' Christians?" I got the very distinct impression that he was under the impression that "born-again Christians" constituted some new denomination that must only recently have come into existence.

I said to him, "Having studied the doctrines of all of the great denominations of Christendom, I am very definitely under the opinion that there is no other kind of Christian than a born-again Christian. According to the creeds and doctrines of every Christian church, it is absolutely essential that one must be born again."

To put it bluntly, and let me state it categorically: Unless, you are a born-again Christian, you are no kind of Christian at all, for there is no other kind. Furthermore, you will never see, said Christ, the inside of Paradise. But if Christ has become the parent of a new and imperishable life, that is a life that is spiritual in nature.

Dear Lord, thank You for giving me a new birth, for bringing me into Your family and making me Your child. Thank You that I am no longer a stranger nor a guest, but a child in Your home...

BY GOD'S STRENGTH,
WE ARE GOD'S ADOPTED CHILD.

MARCH 19

On Imitating Christ

"For to this you were called, because Christ suffered for us, leaving us an example, that you should follow His steps."

— 1 Peter 2:21

Christ has left for us an "example." The Greek term *hupogrammos* is an interesting one that means, literally, an "underwriting." This is a reference to that which was done in the Greek schools at the time when the teacher would very carefully write out the letters of the Greek alphabet for the primary students. Then the students would write over them in their own feeble attempts to reproduce and imitate the example the teacher had left.

Many years ago, I visited one of the Hebrew classes at our Knox Theological Seminary. The students were doing what I clearly remembered doing some 50 years ago, and that is, carefully trying to copy those Hebrew letters.

Christ has also given us an alphabet of life. He has given us an example—an underwriting by His life for us to follow. He is the great exemplar. He is the perfect person to imitate. Would you like to know what life is supposed to be like? Look at Jesus Christ; He embodies it all Himself—the perfect example of goodness and truth and love and kindness and firmness and righteousness and justice. Of course, no one can live up to His example. But after we receive His salvation, His Spirit gives us the grace to live in a way that pleases Him.

He is the pattern of our life as well as the purpose and parent of our lives. Therefore, He is our life.

Lord Jesus, give me strength for today to follow in Your footsteps. Help me to follow Your example: Your patience with Your disciples, Your compassion to all, Your kindness even to the outcasts, Your concern for Your Father's house…

BY GOD'S STRENGTH, WE CAN WALK IN JESUS' FOOTSTEPS.

MARCH 20

Christ – the Power of Life

"To them God would make known what is the glorious riches of this mystery among the nations. It is Christ in you, the hope of glory."

— Colossians 1:27

Christ is the power of my life. The Bible says that Christ will come to dwell in our hearts—that we can be strengthened with His might in the inner man and be able to accomplish many wonderful things through His strength.

We had a number of folks come over to our house one time for some fellowship. Later in the evening, one of the young men said, "I have a question."

I said, "Yes. Don't make it too hard or I will have to go and ask my wife. What is it?"

He said, "How do you do it?"

And I asked, "Do what?"

He replied, "How do you do all that you have to do over there? Do you have unlimited energy?"

I just started laughing. I can't think of anyone who naturally has any less energy than I do, or any less strength than I do, but I have discovered a wonderful secret—the secret Paul had discovered, when he said, *"I can do all things because of Christ who strengthens me"* (Philippians 4:13).

Have you discovered that secret? I know from my own experience that Christ is the power of my life, because I know that I have done innumerable things that I was absolutely certain I could not do before. He has enabled me to do them. Christ is the power. We can be strengthened with might in the inner man to do things we never dreamt we could do because Christ lives in us.

Almighty God, You are the all-powerful one. Give me strength for today to see my weakness and physical limitations, and my spiritual shortcomings. Thank You for being the strength of my life…

BY GOD'S STRENGTH,
WE ARE STRONG.

MARCH 21

Christ—the Passion of Life

"So Jacob served seven years for Rachel, and they seemed only a few days to him because of the love he had for her."

— Genesis 29:20

We are all familiar with Mel Gibson's film, *The Passion of the Christ*. But turn the words around, now that we are saved, Christ should be the passion of our lives.

Someone said that one man with a passion is worth a hundred men with an interest. There are a lot of people here who have an interest in religion, but, alas, I am afraid very few who have a passion for Christ. I have had the joy of knowing a few, and they stand out in my mind. They, indeed, are stars that flash through the heavens.

As the Scripture says, *"Those who are wise shall shine like the brightness of the firmament, and those who turn many to righteousness like the stars forever and ever"* (Daniel 12:3 NKJV). They will not suddenly be eclipsed or fade away. They will shine forever.

Is Christ the passion of your life? Jesus came with a heart full of passion. He said, *"As the Father has sent Me, I also send you"* (John 20:21 NKJV). So, too, should our hearts beat with a love for Christ.

In Genesis, we read that because Jacob so loved Rachel, the days flew by as he worked for seven years to become her husband. He was a man with a passionate goal, motivated by love.

Who or what are you passionately in love with? What do you long for and love to do?

My Savior and Lord, give me a new passion, a deeper love for You. If ever my love for You grows cold or old, bring me back to the cross and show me anew Your love for me. Thank You for loving us first…

BY GOD'S STRENGTH AND LOVE,
WE LOVE ALSO.

Avoiding Cheap Substitutes

"For to me, to continue living is Christ, and to die is gain."
— Philippians 1:21

This statement from Paul should be engraved like an intaglio upon the heart of every Christian. However, there are many cheap substitutes that clamor for our attention that we must eschew. To live is…

... NOT PLEASURE

"For me to live is pleasure," cry a whole host of voices today. For surely the Bible says that sin has its pleasure for a season—then come the consequences.

... NOT MONEY

There are others who would replace Christ with "money." "For me to live is money." They spend most of their waking hours, energy, and thoughts, trying to gain money. But to what ultimate end?

... NOT FAME

Others would say: "For me to live is fame." They give their whole lives to its accomplishment. Perhaps they rise to the top of the ladder, but where are they then? They find themselves saying, "Is this all there is?" How many realize that the ladder they have sold their soul to climb is leaning on the wrong building?

... BUT CHRIST

To live for Him is the secret of life. He goes on to say, "...and to die is gain." Consider the other substitutes: For me to live is pleasure/wealth/fame/etc., and to die is an unutterable tragedy; it is the loss of all I spent my whole life working for. How sad it is that so many do not find until they are at the very brink of eternity that they have spent their lives foolishly.

Lord of wisdom and power, give me strength for today to not accept cheap substitutes. Allow me to experience the true riches found in You. Help me to be eternally grateful for Your sacrifice for me. When I come to my own death, let it be my eternal gain…

BY GOD'S STRENGTH,
WE LIVE AND DIE.

MARCH 23

Perfect Love Casts Out Fear

"There is no fear in love, but perfect love casts out fear…"
— 1 John 4:18

How many people are prevented from ever succeeding because they allow past failures to short-circuit their faith in the Lord? They forget what God can do with us when we let Him.

Questions put to me sometimes are very amusing. One young man recently said to me, "Oh Dr. Kennedy, I so admire your intellect. You graduated from graduate school *summa cum laude*." That's not the way it was always. Before I was a Christian, I went to college for two and a half years before I quit. In the last course I took, I received an F—F for failure.

"Oh, you speak so easily. You are so articulate." I remember when I stood up and could not get out three sentences in a row. I sat down in great humiliation.

"Oh, you are such a good teacher." I can still feel the pressure on my back when the first time I taught a class. Someone had to physically push me into the room to teach my first students. I was paralyzed with fear.

But I learned something. I learned that God can use me when I concentrate on the power He gives me. His perfect love casts out our fear. Instead of focusing on your fears and your past failures, realize that God can use even those failures for His glory. He can make you a new person and remove those doubts and fears.

God of love, cast out my fears today, and give me strength for today to go forth in Your power and do the things You have set before me. Let Your love so fill my heart, mind, and soul that there is no room for fear…

BY GOD'S STRENGTH AND IN HIS LOVE,
OUR FEARS ARE CONQUERED.

MARCH 24

A Jolt From Jude

"Let him who boasts, boast in the Lord."
— 1 Corinthians 1:31

I think if you asked the average person where you would find the letter of Judas in the Bible they would be somewhat taken aback, and yet that is what we find in the second to last book of the Bible. We know it as the Epistle of Jude. His full name was actually Judas.

As many of you probably know, this man was the half-brother of our Christ. You recall that the Pharisees in Nazareth said, *"Is He not the carpenter's son… And are not His brothers James and Joseph and Simon and Judas? And His sisters, are they not all with us?"* (Matthew 13:55-56a). So we know that Jesus had four half-brothers, and at least two sisters who, in good first century Palestinian form, were not named.

As an unbeliever, Jude (along with his brothers) mocked Christ (John 7:3-5). So did James his brother, who was converted after the resurrection. James became the leader of the early church in Jerusalem. "Old camel knees," he was known as from much praying.

While little is known about Jude, other than this epistle, which we shall consider over the next few days, we should notice how he identifies himself. He writes, "Jude, the servant of Jesus Christ, and brother of James." You notice he doesn't say the brother of Jesus Christ, but the servant of Jesus Christ and the brother of James. Today, we have too many people trying to boast about who they are or who they know. We can learn a lesson in humility just from this one statement of Jude.

Father, with a humble heart I come before You. I praise You for the great examples in Scripture and ask that I may acquire some true humility. Lord, give us strength for today to walk humbly before You…

BY GOD'S STRENGTH,
WE CAN BE TRULY HUMBLE.

MARCH 25

Preservation in Faith

"I am confident of this very thing, that He who began a good work in you will perfect it until the day of Jesus Christ."

— Philippians 1:6

Jude is one of the shortest books in the New Testament, but it has much to say. For example, even in the opening, after identifying himself as the author, Jude speaks of those to whom he is addressing his letter: *"To those who are sanctified and called by God the Father and preserved in Jesus Christ..."*

We see that when we are Christians we have been called by God, by His Holy Spirit unto Him. This is that effectual calling, which by the Spirit, combining with the Word, quickens a person from the deadness of sin and brings them into a condition of saving faith and repentance. They also have been preserved.

Here is the perseverance of the saints—we are preserved by God. We are kept, as Peter says, by God. It is good to know that we are saved by Christ, we are saved by His grace, but we are also kept by that same grace.

The very same grace that saves us, keeps us, and holds us. At this point in my Christian life, after decades of following the Lord, it is more astonishing to me that He has kept me over all of these years than that I was converted in the first place. And when I think of all of the ways that I have failed Him, and have come so far short of what He would have had me to be, I am astonished that He preserves me in the faith. What the Lord has started, He promises to finish.

Faithful Father, thank You for keeping us in the faith. Thank You for upholding us by Your mighty hand and thank You that You will complete the work You started in us...

BY GOD'S STRENGTH,
WE ARE KEPT FOR ETERNITY.

MARCH 26

Liberty Is Not Freedom to Sin

"Beloved, while I diligently tried to write to you of the salvation we have in common, I found it necessary to write and appeal to you to contend for the faith which was once delivered to the saints."

— Jude 3

Jude tells us why he wrote his epistle in verse 3. Initially, he had planned to frame a general epistle perhaps something along the line of Romans, which would contain an overview of all Christian doctrine.

But as he was giving all diligence to do this, something had suddenly come up that made it necessary for him to exhort them and to write them about a particular problem, which needed their earnest attention. So we see that the rest of this Epistle of Jude is not what he set out to write in the beginning. But God had other things in mind—he was to remind them and us of a particular error, which was springing up into the church.

The gist of this error is that certain false teachers have crept into the church, *"who pervert the grace of our God into immorality and deny the only Lord God and our Lord Jesus Christ"* (verse 4).

Their coming had not been noticed; the ungodliness was not observed, but now they are in the church and now they are turning the grace of God into liberty to sin. Therefore, he contends earnestly for the faith, which was once delivered unto the saints. God has called us to liberty. But it is wrong to turn that liberty into a license to do whatever our sinful heart desires to do.

Lord, give me strength for today to never take Your grace for granted. Free us from false teachers who preach that sin is permissible and without consequences. Help us to take sin seriously…

BY GOD'S STRENGTH,
WE CAN RECEIVE GOD'S GRACE.

MARCH 27

Contending for the Faith in Love

"But, speaking the truth in love, we may grow up in all things into Him, who is the head, Christ Himself."

— Ephesians 4:15

God has called us to walk in the truth and not in error. But the minute you begin to discern truth from error, immediately there are those who spring up to denounce you, while they declare the only Bible verse they seem to know: "Do not judge or you will be judged."

The Epistle of Jude says that we are to contend for the faith that was given to the saints. We are told that we are to contend earnestly for the faith, and yet somehow or other we are to do it without being contentious.

To contend in love is the secret, and it is always a difficult one. We tend either to lose sight of love and compassion and just hack people to little pieces with our theological axes. Or we become so loving and so compassionate that we let Christian doctrine just sort of melt into a marshmallow type of thing it can be shaped however anyone wants it. But we are to contend, though non-contentiously, for the faith once for all delivered unto the saints.

There is a faith once and for all delivered to the saints. Faith here means not the subjective activity of our exercise of faith, but it means the objective body of doctrine which has been given to us, the Gospel of Jesus Christ that has been given to us.

God of truth, help us to see clearly by Your Spirit. Give us the right balance between truth and mercy, so that we may speak the truth in love…

BY GOD'S STRENGTH, WE CAN BE CONTENDERS FOR THE FAITH.

MARCH 28

Go and Sin No More

"From that time Jesus began to preach, saying, 'Repent! For the kingdom of heaven is at hand.'"

— Matthew 4:17

There are some unbelievers today who are in the church and are doing great damage to the church. Their type was around in the first century.

Jude warns about *"these ungodly dreamers,"* who *"defile the flesh"* and *"reject authority"* (verse 8). Some of them today say the church has a ministry to alcoholics and to criminals, so why can't it have a ministry to homosexuals and this sort? Wonderful, it certainly ought to have, by all means. But the ministry it has to alcoholics and criminals is one of repentance by which a gracious God will forgive you and receive you and cleanse you from your sins.

It's not that we are going to form a club of continued professing alcoholics and criminals who will come to church on Sunday and worship, and they will go the rest of the week to rob banks. How utterly absurd.

Jude adds that they are blind in their sin: *"But they destroy themselves in those things that, like unreasoning animals, they know by instinct"* (verse 10).

These are those who are sensual and not filled with the Spirit of God. My friends, the spirit of lasciviousness and license, and of lawlessness, is the very spirit that was rebuked when God says to us, "Go and sin no more"—whatever our particular sin is. Jesus may meet us in our sinful state, but if you have a true encounter with Him, He does not leave you there. Jesus said, *"Every tree that does not bear good fruit is cut down and thrown into the fire. Therefore, by their fruit you will know them"* (Matthew 7:19-20).

Holy Savior, give me strength for today to repent of any sin in my life. Let Your light shine in my soul, so that I can see my sin and run to You for cleansing and forgiveness…

BY GOD'S STRENGTH, WE
LIVE IN DAILY REPENTANCE.

MARCH 29

Fear Not

"But Jesus came and touched them and said, 'Rise, and do not be afraid.'"

— Matthew 17:7

Do you realize that all of life is a school? Through all the difficult circumstances in life, the Master is trying to teach us a few key lessons over and over, mainly to trust Him.

This is why over and over again the Bible says, *"Fear not." "Be anxious for nothing." "Be not afraid."* Why? Because Jesus said, "It is I." But in the Greek, it means "I am." It was the great *tetragrammaton,* the four letter name of God, Jehovah, in the Old Testament. When Jesus said that same word to the soldiers in the Garden of Gethsemane, they fell on their backs. "I AM." The great "I AM," is here. *"Fear not." "Do not be not afraid."*

Are you afraid? Honestly? Is there something you fear? Is there something you are concerned about? Is there something you are anxious about? God doesn't want us to be afraid. He doesn't want us to be fearful. In fact, fear and faith cannot exist in the same person about the same thing at the same time, any more than water and air can exist in the same glass at the same time. One displaces the other.

So, if you are fearful, it is because you are not trusting Jesus Christ for whatever it is you are fearful about. So, trust Him. Again we come back to the basic class, the basic lesson in all of the classes in the school of life: "Fear not, it is I."

My God, help me to know that nothing comes into my life except through Your loving hand. When I am afraid, I will trust in You. Life can be terrifying, but You are mighty and You have me in the palm of Your hand…

BY GOD'S STRENGTH,
WE CAN OVERCOME OUR FEARS.

MARCH 30

Are Your Dreams Consonant With the Bible?

"Therefore, when I have completed this and have given this blessing to them, I shall come by way of you to Spain..."
— Romans 15:28

Throughout history, those who have accomplished great things or made a great impact have always had great dreams.

- Alexander the Great had a great dream. He had a dream of overcoming the centuries' old animosity between the western cultures of Greece and Macedonia and the eastern culture of the Persian Empire through military conquest. However, his dream was not built upon the purposes of God, and it crumbled at his death.
- Napoleon's dream was to make one great European nation out of France and Germany and Italy. But his dream was shattered at Waterloo. It was not based upon the Word of God.
- Karl Marx had a dream of a classless society—a dream that does not conform with the nature of man nor the teachings of God's Word, and it is in retreat.
- The Apostle Paul had a dream based upon the truth of God. He saw men and women out of every nation, tongue, and tribe loving and worshiping the living God and coming to know the forgiveness and peace of Christ. He put feet under that dream and it is still being carried out.

Do you have any dreams? Or did they end with your childhood? How big are your dreams, my friend? Are they consonant with the teachings of the Scriptures? If so, you must then trust in Christ for their fulfillment.

Lord, You are a God of great and mighty things. Grant us great dreams for the sake of Your kingdom and the strength to live them out...

BY GOD'S STRENGTH,
WE CAN DREAM BIG DREAMS.

MARCH 31

Biblically Based Dreaming

"The slothful man says, 'There is a lion without! I will be slain in the streets!'"

— Proverbs 22:13

One problem in life is that too many people stop dreaming when they become an adult. Children have many marvelous dreams, but too many times we abandon those dreams by the time we become adults.

I think of a young boy who was but seven years old when Sputnik circled the earth. He became enamored with space. This was in Costa Rica, and he was very poor. But eventually, through hard work, he became the first Hispanic astronaut. He had a dream and would not let it go.

We must work at our dreams. Many people think this is some sort of magic wand. They erroneously imagine that it is some sort of a genie in a bottle. Not so.

One of the reasons some people do not dream large dreams is because they are too lazy to even think about putting feet under them. The very thought of it makes them tired.

Sometimes we can invent supposedly "Christian" excuses for what is really just laziness. "I can't go into politics because it's all a dirty business." "I can't work on a movie because Hollywood is just corrupt." "I can't tell my neighbor about Jesus because he doesn't want to hear it—besides, it would be unchristian for me to be so pushy." An excuse is an excuse is an excuse, no matter how we tend to mask it. May God grant us the discernment to see the difference between legitimate obstacles and just plain excuses.

God, help us to see clearly the dream You have planted in our heart as opposed to that which is there from selfish ambition and give us the wisdom to know the difference...

BY GOD'S STRENGTH, GODLY DREAMS CAN BECOME REALITY.

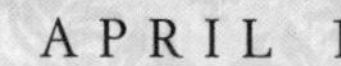

APRIL 1

RICHARD DAWKINS
CHRIS HITCHENS
JAY GOULD ROB SHERMAN
AND THE LIKE

What About Atheists? (1)

"The fool has said in his heart, 'There is no God.' They are corrupt, they do abominable deeds, there is none who does good."

— Psalm 14:1

There are many atheists today. They write bestselling books. They go on national talk shows. They seem to be all over the place. Are they beyond God's touch?

Well, over my lifetime, the best known atheist was Madalyn Murray O'Hair. Interestingly, she was the first guest on the Phil Donohue Show. He was a pioneer talk host, who liked to promote unbelief.

One of the defining moments in her life, when her atheism became solidified, was when she ran outside during a thunderstorm and defied God—if there was one—to strike her dead right then and there. He chose not to. "You see, you see." she exclaimed, "I've proved irrefutably that God does not exist." Note that she was pregnant at the time, and inside her was William J. Murray.

William J. Murray was actually a future servant of the Lord. After being exposed to a virulent form of atheism all his life, Murray came to a realization: "There has to be a God because there certainly is a devil. I have met him, talked to him, and touched him. He is the personification of evil." Soon after this insight, Murray found the Christ his mother hated so much by reading the Gospel of Luke. Today he is a powerful evangelist and also an advocate of allowing God back into the public schools. This is the very man, who as a boy, had been at the center of *Murray vs. Curlett* (1963), one of the key Supreme Court anti-school prayer decisions. God can reach anyone.

EVEN THE WORST CAN BE REACHED WITH THE GOSPEL THE WOMAN IN THE ROE/WADE ABORTION DECISION BECAME AN OUTSPOKEN BELIEVER

Lord, give me strength for today to let others know about You, even those who have bought the lie of atheism. Thank You that no one is beyond Your reach, Jesus …

IN HIS STRENGTH, WE SEE GOD'S HANDIWORK ALL AROUND US.

APRIL 2

Be Careful How You Hear

"For to everyone who has will more be given, and he will have an abundance. But from him who has nothing, even what he has will be taken away."

— Matthew 25:29

There are certain sayings Jesus repeated over and over, such as *"the last will be first, and the first last..."* (Matthew 20:16). *"…a servant is not greater than his master"... (John 13:16). "For many are called, but few are chosen"* (Matthew 22:14).

Matthew 25:29 is one of these. It is a text that is often overlooked. It is a text which is filled with meaning and pregnant with significance for our lives. On five separate occasions, Christ repeated this text in varied forms. It deals three times with the initial state of our Christian life, telling us to beware of what we hear.

We are warned early in the ministry of Christ that we are to be careful what we hear. Today it seems that people have very little care for what they hear. As long as the preacher has some eloquence and appeal or some sort of zeal, they will listen to anything. Nonetheless, false doctrine, however appealing it may appear, is always poisonous. Perhaps there has never been a time when people needed to listen more carefully to the Word of Jesus in that regard. *"Take heed what you hear"* (Mark 4:24). Few people would seem to suppose that hearing anything could be dangerous to their spiritual life. And Jesus also said, *"take heed therefore how you hear"* (Luke 8:18).

Are we not often careless hearers? May God give us the grace to listen carefully to Christ through the pages of Scripture with open ears and open hearts.

God of truth, help us to know Your voice amidst all the voices that scream out for our attention. Give us the strength to hear You correctly and to live by Your Word…

BY GOD'S STRENGTH, WE CAN DISCERN TRUTH FROM FALSEHOOD.

APRIL 3

The Just for the Unjust

"For Christ also has once suffered for sins, the just for the unjust, so that He might bring us to God..."

— 1 Peter 3:18

Before my conversion, I hadn't realized what spiritual danger I was in. But how well I remember that day when I first discovered the truth about myself, when the Holy Spirit opened my eyes to see myself as I really was. I was arraigned before the bar of God's judgment. Justice accused me, and the scales tipped precipitously against me.

The Judge looked me sternly in the face and said, "I pronounce that you shall die. Do you have anything to say for yourself before the sentence of eternal death is pronounced upon you?" For the first time in all my self-righteous life, I was speechless. The Judge brought down His gavel, and the sentence was pronounced.

Eternal death descended upon me, and I stood on the scaffold of God's judgment. I felt hopeless as I felt the black cap of eternal death placed upon my head and about to be pulled down over my eyes. Suddenly, I heard a cry, a voice that said, "Stay. Let not that man descend into the pit."

I looked and there came at a great run one whose face was flecked with blood, whose hands were pierced, who said, "Surely he deserves to die but the spear pierced My side instead. Surely he deserves to descend into the pit, but there in the blackness of midday at Calvary, I descended into the pit for him. All that he deserves I have properly taken. Now let him go free." I praise God for His gift of eternal life in Christ Jesus my Lord.

Lord Jesus, thank You that You are our advocate before the Father, pleading our cause. Thank You for rescuing us from eternal peril at the cost of Your own shed blood...

IN HIS STRENGTH,
WE STAND FORGIVEN.

APRIL 4

Don't Glory in Your Shame

"...their glory is in their shame, their minds are set on earthly things."
— Philippians 3:19

One of the sad things about our time is the fact that shame seems to have become almost extinct. When did you ever hear anyone say, "You should be ashamed"? We have so many people today that *glory* in their shame, that boast in their shame, that proclaim their shame publicly, and it is tragic that today people glory in the very things that they should be ashamed of.

And *"their minds are set on earthly things."* That, I think, is sort of the bottom line of it all because their hearts and minds are not in heaven but simply upon this earth, and if we do not have that upward calling in mind we are going to mind earthly things. Paul says our citizenship is in heaven. The Greek word we translate as citizenship is the word from which we get politics or policy. We should remember that we are citizens of heaven.

This was particularly apropos to the Philippians because Philippi, though in Macedonia, was a Roman colony. It was attached to the Roman Empire, since they had been granted by Caesar Roman citizenship, which was to be devoutly desired. They were citizens of Rome. They were citizens of Rome, even as we are citizens of heaven and most particularly of the new Jerusalem, the heavenly city. That is where our true citizenship is.

We may be involved, rightly so, and concerned about the politics and citizenship of this world, but we need to remember ultimately we are citizens of heaven; thus, we naturally are repulsed at people glorying in their shame.

Heavenly Father, You are pure and holy, and we live among a twisted and perverse generation. Help us to be more grieved when we see people flagrantly breaking Your commandments and are proud of it. Give us the strength to choose the hard right over the easy wrong...

BY GOD'S STRENGTH, WE CAN LIVE
IN THIS WORLD AS CITIZENS OF HEAVEN.

He is Risen

"But now is Christ risen from the dead and become the first fruits of those who have fallen asleep."

— 1Corinthians 15:30

The resurrection of Jesus from the dead is the greatest historical fact of antiquity. Author and speaker Josh McDowell has studied, written on, and debated about this for decades now. He writes: "After more than 700 hours of studying this subject, and thoroughly investigating its foundation, I have come to the conclusion that the resurrection of Jesus Christ is one of the "most wicked, vicious, heartless hoaxes ever foisted upon the minds of men, or it is the most fantastic fact of history."

He points out that the theories to try and explain away the resurrection make less historical sense than the resurrection itself.

When asked if the disciples stole the body of Christ, as some unbelievers assert, he says: "...here was a small band of men—most of them fishermen—just common people. They came out, fought off the Roman guard, some of the most disciplined soldiers in history, broke the Roman seal that anyone feared breaking because of the consequences of it, and then stole the body and spread abroad that Jesus had been raised from the dead."

But what if He hadn't really died, but swooned in the tomb? "Four professional executioners signed His death warrant; that was according to Roman customs. And then to try to believe that that damp tomb, instead of killing Him, healed Him, and I guess then He jumped up, hobbled over, pushed the stone out of the way, tied the guard unit up with His linen cloth and appeared to His disciples as the Lord of Life." No, the only thing to explain the facts are that He is risen. He is risen indeed!

Lord of life, we praise You that You have conquered the grave. We praise You that You changed all history, Jesus, when You walked out of that tomb. Thank You for building Your kingdom on the solid foundation of Your historical resurrection...

BY HIS STRENGTH, WE KNOW THAT WE WILL LIVE, EVEN AFTER WE DIE.

APRIL 6

On Being an Extraterrestrial Alien

"But our citizenship is in heaven, from where also we await for our Savior, the Lord Jesus Christ..."

— Philippians 3:20

I don't know if I really ought to let you know this, but I think it's time I told you. I am actually an extraterrestrial alien visiting this planet. That's true. Now before you think we are talking about the body snatchers, Christ, who is an extraterrestrial, has come to live in my heart and creating a new and heavenly nature within me. So my citizenship is in heaven, and I am an alien here on this earth. A resident for a while. We need to always remember that.

You know it is interesting in all of the sci-fi pictures that I have ever seen where there were aliens on this earth, they always seem to remember that they were from somewhere else and that they were really aliens and they had an agenda, usually malignant, for themselves while they were here.

Now we are not really illegal aliens because Christ owns this planet. He made this planet, this is His world. But we have an agenda. It is not malignant. It is most beneficial to bring about the salvation of mankind. We now look for Jesus Christ our Savior who will come from heaven and who will change our corrupted bodies. As soon as we mature, we begin to die, until finally we are a cold corpse lying in a casket.

While in this body of flesh, let us do good to others on this earth, recognizing that our ultimate citizenship is in heaven. Not bad work for an alien.

Lord of heaven and earth, give me strength today to live in this world, with my eyes fixed on heaven. Help us to remember that this is not our true home. So help us to not get too attached to this world...

IN GOD'S STRENGTH, WE LIVE
AS PILGRIMS AND ALIENS HERE.

Christ our Passover

"The next day John [the Baptist] saw Jesus coming toward him and said, 'Look, the Lamb of God, who takes away the sin of the world.'"

— John 1:29

In the obdurate hardness of his heart, Pharaoh had defied the Almighty God. So God had sent onto the land of Egypt plague after plague with ever-increasing severity. The tenth was the most severe. It is this one that gave rise to the Feast of Passover.

At God's instruction, the Hebrews were to take a bunch of hyssop, and dip it in the blood from an unblemished lamb, and strike the lintel and the door posts of their houses. They were not to go out the door of the house until the morning, because at midnight the LORD would send His angel to destroy the firstborn throughout all Egypt. But when He saw the blood upon the door post, and the lintels, He would pass over those homes.

As they waited, eventually they heard a shriek and then another…moaning and crying went up all over Egypt, as the angel of death passed over. They waited until they would hear some sound close to their own houses, but seeing the blood upon the door post and lintel, the Angel of God passed by.

The Passover celebration continued down through the centuries until Christ our Savior came. All of the lambs of God slain before, all the lambs of the Israelites were but types of that reality which should come. When John the Baptist saw Jesus, He said He was the Lamb of God. Our Passover Lamb has been slain for us. When God sees our sin, He passes over it, if we are in Christ.

Dear Lord, thank You for Your brilliant yet simple plan to show the world that only by being covered by the blood of the unblemished lamb are we to be spared from death. Thank You, Jesus, Lamb of God, for dying on the cross to pay the penalty for our sins…

BY GOD'S STRENGTH, WE SEE THAT CHRIST OUR PASSOVER LAMB HAS BEEN SLAIN.

APRIL 8

He is Risen Indeed

"...to whom He presented Himself alive after His passion by many infallible proofs, appearing to them for forty days..."

— Acts 1:3

When Jesus walked out of His own tomb 2,000 years ago, He changed all of history. His appearances to His disciples are crucial. He appeared to one, then to another, then to two, then to three and then to eight and ten and eleven and 500 people at a time, over a period of about six weeks (1 Corinthians 15:4-9). They saw Him, they heard Him, they handled Him. He fixed breakfast for them. He ate fish with them (John 21:7-15; Luke 24:42-43).

Connected to the appearances was the transformation of the apostles. One day they were cringing in an upper room for fear of the temple authorities, and soon after they were boldly upbraiding the Sanhedrin and proclaiming the resurrection of Christ.

Consider also their martyrdom. They were crucified, crucified upside down, sawed in half, stoned to death, and killed in many other ways, all except John, who was exiled to the island of Patmos by Nero. Why would they give their lives for what they knew to be false?

One could argue that they were deceived in believing Jesus rose from the dead. However, the notion that they knew He wasn't really raised from the dead, but they made it up anyway? Why? So they could face horrific deaths? That does not make sense. People do what is in their own best interest. The apostles spread the Word everywhere because they knew Jesus rose from the dead from firsthand experience. He is risen indeed!

Lord Jesus, give me strength for today to boldly transform my world around me by letting others know You are risen from the dead. Thank You for showing the world for all time that Your truth is based on the unshakable foundation of Your historical resurrection...

BY HIS STRENGTH, WE CAN TELL OTHERS THAT DEATH HAS BEEN DESTROYED.

APRIL 9

If Christ Has Not Risen

"If Christ has not risen, then our preaching is vain,and your faith is also vain."

— 1 Corinthians 15:14

Some people begin with the assumption that miracles don't happen; therefore, Christ could not have been raised from the dead. But this does not explain any of the facts. It is also circular logic. It's merely a presupposition that disallows the possibility of the resurrection.

But the truth is that Christ rose from the dead. The greatest problem mankind has ever faced, generation after generation, century after century, millennia after millennia, has been solved by Jesus. Death has been with us since the fall of man, and always people have asked, "If a man dies, will he rise again?" Jesus Christ has given us irrefutable evidence that the answer is "Yes!"

The greatest efforts of the most brilliant, unbelieving skeptical minds of the last 2,000 years to disprove the resurrection have all come to naught. There is not one of them that could stay afloat in a debate for 15 minutes when the evidence is given a fair examination.

Notice even the transformation of the Sabbath from the Jewish Saturday to the Christian Sunday. The resurrection took place amidst Jews who were committed and zealous Sabbatarians. How is it that suddenly the Christian church changed from the seventh day Sabbath to the first day? Because the resurrection of Jesus Christ from the dead happened on the first day of the week.

When Jesus walked out of the tomb, He changed human history for all time. He put His seal on everything He said. We can believe in Him because He is truly alive forevermore.

Dear Lord, thank You that what we believe has been sealed for all time. Thank You that You have solved once and for all our greatest need and by successfully taking on death, You have solved life's biggest problem...

BY GOD'S STRENGTH, WE CAN PROCLAIM THAT DEATH IS DEAD.

Amen

Ultimate Success, Ultimate Failure

"For to everyone who has will more be given, and he will have an abundance. But from him who has nothing, even what he has will be taken away."

— Matthew 25:29

In the Greek text the words of Jesus have a certain forcefulness about them that often is lost in the translation. I read the words of Jesus after one of His judgment parables in Matthew, *"Then He will say to those at the left hand, 'Depart from Me, you cursed, into the eternal fire, prepared for the devil and his angels'"* (Matthew 25:41). I thought to myself, "What must it be like for a human being to actually hear those words intoned by the Judge of all of the earth upon himself?" It seemed to me that every single person on this earth ought to cast himself upon his knees and pray, "O God, may these ears never hear those words come from Your mouth."

The great 19th century British preacher Charles Spurgeon said that there are two great principles of grace enunciated in the Bible. The first one is this: God gives grace to the empty...to the needy...to the poor...to the humble. Second: to those whom God has granted His grace, He is in the habit of granting more. This is the great truth of our text above, Matthew 25:29.

If you are in Christ, in one sense you are already a success. If you are not in Christ, no matter how well accomplished you may be, you are ultimately a failure. What does it profit you if you gain the whole world, but lose your soul? Serve the Lord with all your heart, and He will bless you with more opportunity and joy to serve Him.

Father God, Giver of all great gifts, thank You for Your grace in our lives and the abundance of Your blessings. Help us to be mindful of our responsibilities to share with others...

BY GOD'S STRENGTH, WE CAN SERVE HIM WITH JOY.

APRIL 11

Use It or Lose It

"For to everyone who has will more be given, and he will have an abundance. But from him who has nothing, even what he has will be taken away."

— Matthew 25:29

As we continue to look at this verse, we note that many people often lament the fact that it seems that the rich get richer, and the poor get poorer. Money makes money; nothing succeeds like success. However, this is a principle Christ built into the universe and enunciated in his earthly ministry.

The essence of that principle is: Use it or lose it. Money does not make money, unless it is put to use. In the parable of the talents, there was the third servant who hid his talent in the ground. His money was buried and produced nothing. If he had used it, it would have produced more.

The principle certainly applies in the physical realm of the body. Build your muscles; don't let them atrophy. This is also true in the case of our work. Is it not a fact that the person who is able to do something finds that he is given it to do? We will then unquestionably find that opportunities will grow with the exercise of our gifts.

It is also true in the moral area of conscience. Our characters will develop in due proportion to those aspects we give our time to exercise and develop. Would that more of that time were spent studying the Word of God.

If you are not being used by God as much as you wish, make yourself available to Him.

Divine Master, give us strength today to serve You well. We desire to be good stewards of Your gifts to us, and we know that You reward service with more service...

BY GOD'S STRENGTH, WE SERVE HIM BY SERVING OTHERS.

APRIL 12

Divine Growth

"And other seed fell on good ground, and it yielded grain that sprang up and increased by thirty, sixty, or a hundred times as much."

— Mark 4:8

Divine grace always grows. The good seed of God will inevitably grow. There is no doubt about it. Place a live bulb in the ground; and a stalk and buds will appear, and the lilies will eventually sway in the breeze. Put a post and a sapling into the ground and what happens? Immediately the post begins to decay and the sapling begins to grow. Come back twenty years later and, should the post still be there, you will find it completely decayed, but the little sapling will be a huge tree.

So it is with our lives. If it is true that divine grace always grows, then it is vitally true that this teaching of Jesus would instruct us to make certain that we have the true spiritual principle within.

I would ask you, are you a post or a tree? Go back twenty years. There are many people who grew up in the church, attended regularly, but there was never any divine principle of life within them. Are they growing in love and zeal and service to God, or do they actually find that there is less zeal, less desire for prayer, less interest in the Word of God, less interest in the worship of God, less interest in the service of God? If so, then you are a post and not a tree. Over the years you have decayed. You have not grown, and you need to seriously consider whether or not you have the true principle of life within you.

Lord of the harvest, may Your strength, Your power, Your Holy Spirit bring forth the fruit in our lives that You desire. Weed out and prune us that we may yield an eternal harvest a hundredfold…

BY GOD'S STRENGTH, WE
CAN GROW AND BEAR FRUIT.

Don't Confuse Activity With Growth

"I tell you that to everyone who has, more will be given, but as for the one who has nothing, even what they have will be taken away."

— Luke 19:26 NIV

There are a lot of people who are like a little boy riding on his rocking horse. There is a great deal of motion and action, but very little progress. A lot of people in the church are like that. They may go through a lot of motion, be involved in all sorts of things, but they do not really make progress in their spiritual life. True use of the means of grace: i.e., the Word and the Sacraments, will inevitably cause us to grow because grace always grows. It is always progressing. Those who grow will be given more (Luke 19:26). That is the absolute law of God.

One farmer in a country church used to say at testimony time: "Well, I haven't made much progress, but I am established." One day he was bringing his wagon full of logs into town; the road was wet and the wheels sank into the mud. One of his fellow church members, who did not really agree with his view of the Christian life, happened to be passing by. He said, "Well, Farmer Jones, I see that though you are not making much progress, you are established." What some people call "established in the faith" may be little more than established in the mud.

If you truly have the grace of God, the principle of life within you, there is growth. That means you will be growing in faith and love, peace, joy, and all the other fruit of the Spirit will show themselves in your life.

Jesus, the true Gardener, let Your grace produce fruit in my life. Give me the strength today to partake regularly in the means of grace…

BY GOD'S STRENGTH, THE FRUIT OF THE SPIRIT WILL ABOUND IN US.

APRIL 14

A Lesson From the Titanic

"But he who does not believe is condemned already, because he has not believed in the name of the only begotten Son of God."

— John 3:18

A minister once said, "I have the most marvelous news for lost sinners, if only I could find one." He added, "The problem with most people in America is not getting them saved. They think they are saved already. The problem is getting them lost."

Unless we understand the bad news, we can't begin to appreciate the good news. Jesus says the world is condemned already. But so many people suppose that if they just live a reasonably decent life, it will be all right with them in the end and they will finally make it.

It was 12:45 A.M. on April 15, 1912, when the first lifeboat was lowered from the stricken *Titanic,* one hour after the ship struck the iceberg. The passengers were told that they must leave the ship. Many of them didn't believe it. Even if the ship was taking on water, they were quite confident they were in no danger. Surely this ship couldn't sink, after all, a White Star Line employee at the time of *Titanic*'s launch on May 31, 1911 had said, "Not even God himself could sink this ship."

So they went inside into the warmth of the interior chambers and refused the offer of a lifeboat. Most of them died. They couldn't accept the good news that there was a place in the lifeboat for them, because they wouldn't accept the bad news that they were in danger of perishing.

We cannot be saved until we first recognize that we are lost and need to be saved.

Dear Lord, how permanent this life seems to be. But in reality, how fleeting it is. Help us to live for eternity and not just for the very short time of our earthly sojourn. Give us strength for today to share the Gospel with those who are lost, even if they don't know it…

BY GOD'S STRENGTH, WE REALIZE WE ARE LOST AND IN NEED OF BEING SAVED.

APRIL 15

Governmental Theft

"You shall not covet your neighbor's house; you shall not covet your neighbor's wife, or his manservant, or his maidservant, or his ox, or his donkey, or anything that is your neighbor's."

— Exodus 20:17

In modern America, we are like mice wandering in a maze—we don't know where we are going. We don't know which way to head, or even which way is which way, because we have turned away from the Word of God and from the instructions that our Founding Fathers believed in and looked to and upon which this great country was built.

One of those areas in which we have lost our way is the realm of economics. While the Soviet Union imploded because of forced socialism, many in our own country have been clamoring for less violent versions of socialism.

Though we have seen the greatest experiment in socialism in the history of the world in the Union of Soviet Socialist Republics come to a disastrous end, crash in flames and burn, bring utter disaster and bankruptcy and perhaps famine to that nation, still socialism is alive, though not well, in America. I think one of the great lessons we need to learn from the events of recent years is that socialism doesn't work. It doesn't work in the Soviet Union. It doesn't work in Poland. It doesn't work in East Germany. It doesn't work in Cuba. It doesn't work in China. It doesn't work in America. What is it going to take to wake us up to that fact?

Socialism is built on covetousness, but the Bible says, *"You shall not covet."* The Bible also says, *"You shall not steal"*—not even if you are the federal government.

Lord, give me strength for today to see through the politicians' wily plans to buy votes from the unsuspecting. Lord, forgive us for stealing from our neighbor through exorbitant taxation. Help us to work for our daily bread and to share with others…

BY GOD'S STRENGTH, WE ARE CONTENT, NOT COVETOUS.

APRIL 16

How Deep Are Your Roots?

"But when the sun came up, the plants were scorched, and they withered because they had no root."

— Mark 4:6

A man who owned a vineyard noticed that one of the plants was not doing well. It was sickly for two years, and it had never produced grapes of any significance. He wondered why all of those around it were quite filled with fruit, and so he decided to dig down around it and see if there was some problem in the soil. He dug down about six inches and ran into boards underneath the plant covering an old abandoned well. When he took away the boards he noticed that the roots of the plant had gone down between the cracks and were dangling in the empty well, trying desperately to get nourishment. The plant could not grow. What a picture that is of many Christians. They do not grow and they do not produce fruit because their roots are not into the Word of God.

I would ask you this: Are the roots of your faith reaching down into the Word of God? If they are not, you will not be growing. If the true principle of grace is in your life, it will be giving you a hunger for the Word of God.

If you are growing in faith, you will be growing in repentance, too. Are you growing in that area in your Christian life? Our whole life is a continuation of repentance. Failure to repent is one of the sure ways to stop spiritual growth. Is there some sin in your life that is keeping you from growing? Ask God to show you.

Lord, help me to be mindful of the depravity in my own soul. Help me to live in daily repentance, always taking time to confess my sins before You. Thank You for Your blood that washes away my sins and cleanses me from all unrighteousness...

BY GOD'S STRENGTH, WE CAN SEE OUR SINS, CONFESS THEM, TURN FROM THEM, AND BE FORGIVEN DAILY.

Avoid Idolatry Like the Plague

"Thus says the LORD, 'In this you shall know that I am the LORD: Indeed, I will strike the waters of the Nile with the rod that is in my hand, and they shall be turned to blood.'"

— Exodus 7:17

In the Book of Exodus, we see the great confrontation between Moses and Pharaoh. This is the Old Testament counterpart to that confrontation between Christ and Pilate, the representative of the pagan Roman Empire, with Pharaoh being the representative of the pagan empire of Egypt.

Here is a classic confrontation between good and evil, Christ and Satan. It is the high point in the Old Testament. It is that point to which the Jews looked for centuries afterward remembering the great acts of God.

Now these ten plagues are not simply punishments upon Pharaoh and the people of Egypt, but they are a concerted effort on the part of Jehovah to destroy the idolatry of the Egyptian people and to bring to naught their many gods. And so, in the plagues, we have a systematic, cumulative crescendo of attacks on the gods of Egypt before the watching Egyptians.

Take, for example, the first plague, the attack that God made was upon the River Nile, which was a great god to the Egyptians because it was the source of all their livelihoods. Egypt of course is a huge desert with the Nile River running down it, giving about a 50 mile wide swath of greenery and life. Without the Nile, that nation would dry up and blow away. And so first of all, God attacked that, the great god of the Nile.

God alone is to be worshiped and not any false idols.

God above all gods, give us the strength of heart to worship only You. We ask that You cast down any idol in our lives and that our worship might be true and right…

BY GOD'S STRENGTH, WE CAN AVOID IDOLATRY AND DESTROY ANY IDOLS IN OUR LIVES.

APRIL 18

Confronting the Egyptian Frog and Earth Gods

"But if you refuse to let them go, then I will plague all your borders with frogs....All the dust of the land became gnats throughout all the land of Egypt."

— Exodus 8:2, 17

In the 10 plagues of Exodus, we have a confrontation between the one true God and the false gods of the Egyptian people.

Plague number two was an attack by frogs. The frogs were one of the many gods of Egypt. It was the goddess Hekt, which is a form of the Egyptian word Hathor, who was the goddess of love and mirth and joy. It is from this goddess Hathor that the Greeks got the name of their goddess Aphrodite, the goddess of love and mirth and joy.

But when the frogs started hopping over everything—in their houses, into their ovens and into their food, even into their beds—they didn't have much mirth and joy. And then when they all died and the nation stank, they were not too thrilled, I believe, with the goddess Hekt or Hathor.

Plague number three was probably fleas. Now one of the gods of the Egyptians was the god of earth, Seb, and they worshiped the earth. We can picture those fleas hopping up all over the place. The Egyptians' reverence for their earth god Seb would no doubt have cooled when they saw their land covered with trillions of fleas. These two hard lessons underscore the fact that we should worship the one true God alone.

Lord of lords, free us from all false worship and spirituality of our day. Make us aware of subtle forms of idolatry that are attached to seemingly good causes. May we worship You, the Triune God, and You alone...

BY GOD'S STRENGTH, WE CAN OVERCOME FALSE RELIGION.

The True God Confronts the False Gods of Egypt

"...if you will not let My people go, indeed I will send swarms of flies on you...all the livestock of Egypt died, but not one of the livestock of the children of Israel died...and it became a boil breaking forth with blisters upon man and beast..."

— Exodus 8:21, 9:6, 10

In the ten plagues, the Lord God did not just judge the Egyptians for their 430 year enslavement of the Hebrews, He also judged their false gods, as we have seen.

The fourth plague involved the flies. The Hebrew word means swarms. Scholars say they probably were not flies, but were were the beetles common to that area, called the *scarabaeus* from which we get the word scarab, which is a black beetle. I am sure after they had a couple hundred thousand of those in every home in Egypt they were not too thrilled with the god of Scarabaeus.

The fifth plague was a disease of cattle. The god Apis was the sacred bull. You've seen many Egyptian figures of a man with the head of a bull that they worshiped.

And sixth, there was the god Typhon. This was when the dust caused the breaking forth of boils and blisters. Typhon was a magical genie that was worshiped in ancient Egypt. Here was a god who was connected with the magicians, who were the priests of the Egyptian religion. We find here that the magicians could not stand before Moses because of the boils, for the boil was upon the magicians and upon all of Egypt. So their power was broken.

God alone is to be worshiped.

Lord of all, today we see people turning to false gods and playing with spiritual forces they know nothing about. Free us from Beelzebub, "The Lord of the flies." Thank You for calling us out of darkness and into Your marvelous light...

BY GOD'S STRENGTH ALONE,
CAN WE STAND AGAINST EVIL.

APRIL 20

The Last Four Plagues

"For I will at this time send all My plagues upon you and your servants and your people, so that you may know that there is none like Me in all the earth."

— Exodus 9:14

As noted, when Moses confronted Pharaoh, God judged the false gods of the Egyptians, one by one in each of the plagues.

The seventh plague was hail that came down from the sky. One of the gods of the Egyptians was the god Shu, who was the god of the atmosphere. Now it is hard to go out to worship the god of the atmosphere when you are being pounded with large hail stones.

And then there were the locusts that swarmed all over the land, and this was a rebuke of the god Serapis, who supposedly was the protector against locusts. Their prayers to him were of no avail as the whole country was black with locusts.

And then there was the darkness that came upon the land for three days, which was an assault upon the chief god of the Egyptians, the god Rah. Rah was the sun god, the principal deity of ancient Egypt, and here this deity was blotted out.

And finally, in the last plague upon Pharaoh himself who was supposedly descended from the sun god Rah, his first born was killed. This was God's attack upon Satan and Egypt. Egypt here is a picture of the world—an unbelieving, godless, pagan world. And Pharaoh is a picture of Satan, who is the god of this world. Moses was a representative of the living God who took on all of the gods of Egypt.

In the ten plagues, God shows the world for all time that He alone deserves our worship.

Sovereign One, give us the strength to worship You alone. When we see plagues coming back on a worldwide scale, we tremble. Keep us close to You and keep us safe from demonic power…

BY GOD'S STRENGTH, WE ARE SEALED AND KEPT SAFE IN AN EVIL WORLD.

APRIL 21

Plagues and God's Judgment

"The rest of mankind, who were not killed by these plagues, did not repent of the works of their hands."

— Revelation 9:20

The greatest confrontation that is to be found in all of the Old Testament and perhaps in all of literature, save that confrontation of Christ himself with Pilate, is Moses' confrontation of Pharaoh. Here we see the true God dealing with unbelief and bringing these ten grievous plagues upon the nation of Egypt and destroying it.

These were not the end of plagues in the Bible. We find throughout the whole Old Testament that there were plagues that came upon not only the pagan nations around Israel, but came upon the people of Israel repeatedly because of their sins. And down through the last 2,000 years there have been plagues that have come upon the people of this earth, most notable of which was the bubonic plague in the 14th century, which killed one-third of all of the people of Europe.

And now we are asked could God send a plague today? Well, we do know that some of the sexually transmitted diseases, including AIDS, are ravaging some populations in our world. In effect, we sent a letter to God, and we said, "God, we have thrown off Your law. We have rebelled against your Commandments. We are in revolt against your dominion, and we will now go our own way and do our own thing."

But people are now suffering the physical, emotional, and spiritual consequences of defying God's law. STDs are a type of plague upon all sexual promiscuity, whether heterosexual or homosexual. God will bring it to an end.

Dear God, thank You so much that You spare Your obedient children from all sorts of diseases when we follow You. Of course, the ultimate healing is when You take us home and free us from this body of death. Help us to show compassion to those suffering for whatever reason…

LORD, GIVE ME STRENGTH FOR TODAY TO AVOID SEXUAL SIN.

APRIL 22

Lord, Increase Our Love for You

"Yet I hold this against you: You have forsaken the love you had at first."
— Revelation 2:4

Do you love the Lord more than you did ten years ago? I can think of a little girl of about six who was kneeling beside her bed saying her prayers. Her mother was sitting on the bed, helping her by suggesting things for her to pray about. Finally, her mother said, "Darling, why don't you pray that God might enable you to love Jesus more."

The little girl looked up in astonishment and said, "But mommy, I am just crazy about Him now." I wonder how many could really say that today. Paul said, *"If anyone does not love the Lord Jesus Christ, let him be cursed!"* (1 Corinthians 16:22).

In one of the great art museums, a poor man, not well dressed, was standing in front of a picture of Christ on the cross. He was standing there with his hat in his hand, looking at the picture for a long time. Finally, totally oblivious of those who were in the museum about him, he said, "Bless Him. Bless Him. I love Him. I love Him." The quiet mumbling stopped and all turned their eyes upon him.

Another man walked up to him, took him by the arm, and said, "I love Him, too."

A third said, "And so do I."

A fourth, "And I, also." A little group of people, totally unknown to one another, was drawn together by the love they had for Christ.

It is God's grace in our hearts that causes us to love the Savior.

Oh, Lord Jesus, forgive me for ever taking Your cross for granted. Please, increase my love for You. As the hymnist said, "let me never, never outlive my love for Thee"...

IN GOD'S STRENGTH, OUR LOVE
FOR JESUS GROWS DAILY.

APRIL 23

Zeal for God

"…for the zeal of Your house has consumed me…"

— Psalm 69:6

There was a man who was watching sailboats out on a large lake. The breeze was brisk and the sails were filled, and he noticed one boat did not seem to be moving. He asked a friend, "That boat does not seem to be moving. Why not? The sails are full." And his friend replied, "It is anchored."

A lot of Christians may come to church and put up their sails; they may even read the Bible. Yet they are anchored into some sin, some carnal habit, something they refuse to give up. Thus, they make no progress in their spiritual life.

Christ would have us to grow in our zeal for Him. If the divine principle is within us, if we truly have that which comes from God, it will produce within us a zeal, a flame, and a fire. A flame consumes everything about it. It will continue to grow, transforming everything it touches into its own nature of fire, but a painted flame, a painted fire, will never grow.

As Jim Elliot said, "He makes his ministers a flame of fire." Let's ask ourselves: Are we ignitable? Are we weak? Yes, weak in ourselves, but strong in God. May our prayer be that cry of young David Brainerd, the missionary to the American Indians, who said, "O God, would that I were a flaming fire in Thy service." Wouldn't it be a fantastic thing if ten thousand sparks would spread out from our churches and set afire our communities for Jesus Christ?

Father, forgive us that we can be wildly enthusiastic about those things that interest us here on earth, while remaining diffident to You. Give us strength for today, Lord, to love You above all…

LORD, GIVE ME STRENGTH FOR TODAY
TO BE MORE ZEALOUS FOR YOU!

Be the Bishop of Your Thoughts

"Finally, brothers, whatever things are true, whatever things are honest, whatever things are just, whatever things are pure, whatever things are lovely, whatever things are of good report, if there is any virtue, and if there is any praise, think on these things."

— Philippians 4:8

We can make a sincere effort to try to counter our thoughts and to bring them into subjection to Christ and obedience to Him, and we will discover that they will affect the life that we lead. I would urge you to look these over from day to day (what Paul lists here) and ask yourself are these the things that you are thinking about?

Now ordinarily we don't stop and consciously ask ourselves what thoughts are going through our minds, but I think that we need to do that more often. We need to be as it were a supervisor of our own thoughts—a bishop, which is an overseer, of the thoughts of our minds to see what kind of thoughts we are dwelling on.

When we see that we are beginning to go down one of those well-worn channels again, that we say, "Stop, you are not going down that channel anymore." We want to replace the ungodly thoughts with godly ones.

Unholy thoughts lead to unholy living. Holy thoughts do lead to holy living. Some people have said that a person is what he thinks about all day. That may not be totally true, but the old saying is true: garbage in, garbage out. Be the bishop of your thoughts.

Father, give us strength for today to control what we think about. Forgive us for allowing our minds to dwell on evil things. Lord, renew our mind and so renew our lives…

BY GOD'S STRENGTH, WE TAKE EVERY THOUGHT CAPTIVE FOR CHRIST.

APRIL 25

Paul: Do What I Say *and* What I Do

"Do those things which you have both learned and received, and heard and seen in me, and the God of peace will be with you"
— Philippians 4:9

Many people say in effect, "Do as I say, not as I do." But Paul says in effect, "Do what I do, as well as what I say." Paul tells the Philippian Christians to put into practice that which they saw him do: *"Do those things which you have both learned and received, and heard and seen in me, and the God of peace will be with you"* (4:9).

He says something similar to the Corinthian Christians: *"Follow me as I follow Christ"* (1 Corinthians 11:1). Paul is not giving merely theoretical advice, he is saying follow me. Now that is a bold statement. How many of us could say that to others?

"What I want you to do, new convert, is watch me closely and do what I do in my life." That's how we ought to live. This is a tremendous statement from Paul. They had learned from him in his oral instruction when he had preached to them and taught them when he was at Philippi. They had received this epistle from his hands which they had read. They had heard from others of how he was enduring the punishment in the Roman imprisonment, and they had seen with their own eyes how he had acted while he was in Philippi when he had been persecuted and imprisoned and beaten in stocks while he was among them. Follow me, be emulators of me, as I emulate Christ. And he adds, *"the God of peace will be with you."*

Lord, give me strength for today to so live my life that if others were to imitate me, that would be a good thing. Help me to be a good example that I would want people to follow me as I follow You...

BY GOD'S STRENGTH, WE ARE GOOD EXAMPLES FOR OTHERS TO FOLLOW.

APRIL 26

Guard Your Heart

"Keep your heart with all diligence, for out of it are the issues of life."
— Proverbs 4:23

There is a large corporation whose motto is "Think." Well we all think all of the time. God is more specific. In Philippians 8, after giving a list of good and wholesome things, He says think on *these* things. Don't just think. Hitler was a man who thought, as was Stalin and Mao and Nero and Judas, but the important thing is not merely to think, but *what* we are to think about.

Paul says in Philippians 4:9, if we control these thoughts, if we bring every thought into obedience to Christ, then the God of peace will be with us. So the peace of God within us, the God of peace around us, and that is the kind of life that everyone of us certainly would covet. I would urge you to look at the two verses—verse 6 (don't worry, instead pray) and verse 8 (think on these positive things)—which precede these two promises of the peace of God and endeavor to put them into application in your own life. God's peace will be your reward.

God's Word truly gets to the heart of the matter—out of which there proceed the issues of life. We pray we should learn to bring every thought into subjection to Christ and obedience to Him. We should pray the Lord would create new channels where positive, loving, pure, honest thoughts may run, which will result in God's peace filling our hearts and lives and surrounding us in our homes and wherever we go.

Dear Lord, in our age of incredible moral pollution, help us to keep our lives pure. Lord, I ask that You would guard my heart and give me strength for today to feed my soul with good things, while keeping away from that which is harmful...

BY GOD'S STRENGTH, WE BRING EVERY THOUGHT INTO SUBJECTION TO CHRIST AND OBEDIENCE TO HIM.

Moses and the Promised Land

"The Lord spoke to Moses and Aaron, 'Because you did not believe in Me, to sanctify Me in the eyes of the children of Israel, therefore you will not bring this assembly into the land which I have given them.'"

— Numbers 20:12

Moses did not get to lead the Israelites to the Promised Land, yet his whole life's work was moving in that direction.

Some will say, "Well, it is because Moses smote the rock." We see in Exodus 17:6 that God said to him, *"you shall strike the rock, and there water shall come out of it,"* and he did. But later on, in Numbers 20, there is another smiting of another rock, and that time God told him to go and *speak* to the rock, and the water would come forth. Instead, on that occasion, Moses struck the rock and angered God, who then punished him by not letting Him go to the Promised Land.

Sometimes we have to obey without fully understanding, but we know we can trust God because He has proven Himself fully trustworthy. Jesus is the Rock of Ages, but Moses had no way of knowing that God was in a sense demonstrating Christ's role and work. Jesus was struck once on the cross, and living water flowed forth. After that, we only need to speak to Jesus Christ, and He gives us the living water. Obedience in small things matters. May we always drink of this water that becomes for us a spring of eternal life.

Moses lived by the law and was judged by the law. Thank God for His mercy and grace in Jesus Christ. Remember, G-R-A-C-E means "God's Riches At Christ's Expense." F-A-I-T-H MEANS "FORSAKING ALL, I TRUST HIM"

God, thank You for Your grace poured out in Jesus Christ. Help us to show our love for You by striving to obey You in all things. Thank You, Jesus, for being struck on Your own body, taking on Yourself the penalty of our wrong-doings…

BY GOD'S STRENGTH, WE EXPERIENCE HIS UNMERITED FAVOR IN CHRIST.

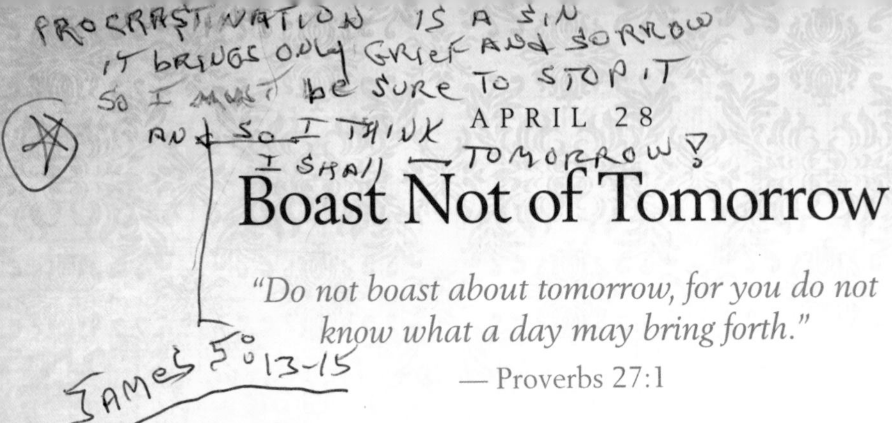

APRIL 28

Boast Not of Tomorrow

"Do not boast about tomorrow, for you do not know what a day may bring forth."

— Proverbs 27:1

Though we usually joke about it, psychologists tell us that procrastination can be a very harmful addiction with disastrous consequences. Many people addicted to procrastinating just can't seem to stop, no matter what.

During the American Revolution, General Washington had conceived his bold plan to cross the Delaware in the midst of winter and to surprise the Hessian army at Trenton on Christmas night 1776, but a British sympathizer saw what he was doing and sent a messenger across the river with a note to Colonel Rahl, the Hessian commander. When the courier arrived at the camp, he found the Colonel in his tent playing cards with his officers. He gave him the letter, and Rahl, without opening it, put it in his pocket, and said, "Later, but first, let's finish the game."

He finished the game just in time to stand up, surprised at the American attack. It cost Rahl his honor, his command, and his life—all because of procrastination. It can, indeed, have disastrous consequences.

In the business realm, procrastination can have disastrous consequences. Many a person, who, though he is outstandingly talented, educated, and equipped, does not progress nearly as well as some of lesser abilities and talents simply because he procrastinates and the others don't.

When it comes to the spiritual world, procrastination is eternally disastrous. Many important things are left undone because of procrastination. Most vital of all is to not postpone accepting Christ. Let us live today for Christ. Tomorrow may never come.

Lord, give me strength for today to do that which I should do today. Forgive me for so often putting off today's task until "tomorrow," which often never comes. Help me to truly live for You today…

BY GOD'S STRENGTH, WE LIVE FOR HIM *TODAY*.

"When Time Permits"

"After several days, when Felix arrived…he sent for Paul and heard him speak concerning faith in Christ…Felix was afraid and answered, 'For now, leave! When time permits, I will send for you.'"

— Acts 24:24-25

How true it is that has been said, "Of all the sad words of tongue or pen, the saddest are these: it might have been." We all know that the road to hell is lined with good intentions. But why? Because of procrastination. Procrastination is what keeps good intentions from materializing into good works.

If procrastination is harmful in the spiritual exercises of this life, it is most deadly and fatal when it comes to our eternal salvation. We see a spiritual procrastinator in the example of Felix, a Roman leader.

Now Felix was a despicable character, far lower than the average Roman governor. He was indeed, the Roman historian Tacitus tells us, "a man of lust and cruelty;" who "exercised the office of a king with the spirit of a slave."

In Acts 24, this man, who did not hesitate to get involved in the most immoral kinds of activities, was now listening to Paul preach. As he talked about these things, Felix began to tremble. Because his sins were crying out against him and his conscience was calling for relief, he should have repented, but he was a procrastinator. So he said, *"For now, leave! When time permits, I will send for you"* (Acts 24:25). He would take care of it *mañana*. To our knowledge he never did. How tragic. He provides a great example of what *not* to do.

Heavenly Father, forgive us for our spiritual procrastination. Give us strength for today to share the Gospel with those You have put in our path. Help us to not be like Felix or anyone else who would postpone such important news…

BY GOD'S STRENGTH, WE WILL
HEED HIS VOICE TODAY.

APRIL 30

Dealing With Worry

"Who of you by worrying can add one cubit to his height?"
— Luke 12:25

The French word for "wooden shoe" is *sabot*. From this word comes "sabotage," and it seemed that Dutchmen had a way of sabotaging French plants by casting their wooden shoes into the machinery. Worry is sabotage to our lives. Worry is a great destroyer of the body as well as the mind.

Worry is also harmful to the spiritual life. Jesus said that the cares of this world choke out the good seed and keep it from being fruitful. Cares of this world cause some people never to enter the kingdom of God. I remember talking one time to a person that I dearly loved, talking to him about the kingdom of God and about the salvation which Christ offered. And I remember how he cut me off short by telling me that he had so many problems and so many cares and so many worries in the world that he did not have time to think about that.

Many people think about worry as a weakness. The Bible tells us that it is a wickedness; that it is because of unbelief. Because, you see, where worry starts, faith ends. You cannot have faith and worry about the same thing at the same time. As water in a glass replaces the air, so worry replaces faith. Worry is practical atheism. But we should cast our cares on the Lord and trust Him. Over and over we see He helps, and most of our worries never materialize.

Dear Lord, forgive us for our unbelief. Forgive us for taking on ourselves burdens, which overwhelm us, instead of turning those problems over to You. Thank You that You are more than capable to handle all these problems…

BY GOD'S STRENGTH, OUR PROBLEMS ARE HANDED OVER TO THE GREAT PROBLEM-SOLVER.

MAY 1

Heavenly Calling

"Go therefore and make disciples of all nations..."

— Matthew 28:19

We are called to something altogether different than the things of this world. We are called to advance the kingdom of Jesus Christ. We are called to be those who never lose sight of the fact that we have been made for eternity and that human beings are either saved or lost. They are on their way to eternal paradise or eternal perdition and it is up to us to bring to them that message.

I think of a lay minister of our church who had a clear focus in his mind of the high calling of God in Christ Jesus and was more continually faithful to that calling than perhaps anyone I have ever known. Before he died of Lou Gehrig's disease, he was going out three times a week on Evangelism Explosion, even though someone had to carry him up the stairs in order to go into a home.

He was a man who went to the prisons five or six times a week, spent hours there sharing the Gospel. Because of his deteriorating health, the prison officials would no longer let this lay minister in without help for fear he might get hurt. So he always found a volunteer to accompany him. One day, co-author Jerry Newcombe was that volunteer and thus had his first experience visiting a prison.

This lay minister never lost sight of his heavenly calling. We each have a heavenly calling in Jesus. If you struggle to know your calling, ask the Lord for wisdom and seek out godly counsel for direction.

Lord, give me strength for today to find my calling and to fulfill it with joy. Please use me in Your vineyard...

BY GOD'S STRENGTH, WE CAN
BE FAITHFUL TO THE END.

MAY 2

Enemies of the Cross

"For many are walking in such a way that they are the enemies of the cross of Christ. I have told you of them often and tell you again, even weeping."

— Philippians 3:18

I remember my old pastor telling me one time when he visited me at seminary, "James, remember that the enemies of Christ will always attack the Cross, the blood of Christ and this will be the object of their attack and their ridicule," and I have found that to be so.

Paul notes in 1 Corinthians 1:22: *"For the Jews require a sign, and the Greeks seek after wisdom."* And so it is; there are those who seek miracles and unless they can find the miracle they can't seem to believe. The Greeks sought after wisdom and philosophy, like the humanists of our time.

Paul adds, *"But we preach Christ crucified, a stumbling block to the Jews and foolishness to the Greeks"* (verse 23). Then He notes that the foolishness of God is wiser than the wisdom of the world.

Meanwhile, it is the blood of the Savior that is most despised and hated by an ungodly and unregenerate world. But as Paul says in Philippians 3:18 of the enemies of the cross, their end is destruction. That is one thing you need to remember about all of the wise men of this world—all of those who in their utter sophistication attack Christianity and Christians and the Bible and Christ and His cross—their end is destruction. What lies before them is naught but Hell. They are going away into everlasting perdition and pain.

I don't hate the cross; I am eternally grateful for it. I trust you are too.

Lord, give me strength to always glory in the cross, as the attacks on You, Your Gospel, Your name, and Your cross continue to increase. Give us the strength to gladly bear reproach and shame for Your name's sake…

BY HIS STRENGTH, WE CAN LIFT HIGH THE CROSS.

MAY 3

Those Whose God Is Their Belly

"Whose end is destruction, whose God is their belly..."

— Philippians 3:19 KJV

Paul talks about enemies of Christianity *"whose god is their belly."* As commentators would agree, I think here he is referring not merely to food. Though many of them no doubt are gluttons, this would be a metaphor for an inordinate love of all earthly, worldly and material things.

Jesus said, *"Give us this day our daily bread."* Thus, it is fine to ask God to meet our material needs. But the person whose god is his belly loves the material things of this earth beyond normal appetites.

In his first epistle, Peter refers to such people and rebukes those who would abuse the Gospel as a means for filthy gain: *"Shepherd the flock of God that is among you, take care of them, not by constraint, but willingly, not for dishonest gain, but eagerly"* (1 Peter 5:2).

And so Peter is warning us of the same thing that Paul is warning us of—we are not to minister for money's sake, and we need always to be watchful for those who wear the clerical garb and yet do it for money's sake. I am always concerned when I see would-be ministers that are too concerned about the things of this world.

Paul tells us that the workman is worthy of his hire. But people should not go into the ministry for money's sake. The Gospel is good news. It is not for sale. The only price paid for the Gospel is the price of the blood of Jesus.

Lord, give us the strength to seek You and not to seek after pleasures. We thank You for what You give us. Help us to be ever mindful to seek Your kingdom and Your righteousness...

BY HIS STRENGTH, WE CAN
SEEK GOD'S KINGDOM FIRST.

MAY 4

Money and the Ministry

"Feed the flock of God which is among you, taking the oversight thereof, not by constraint, but willingly; not for filthy lucre, but of a ready mind..."

— 1 Peter 5:2 KJV

How often do we hear accusations against ministers or ministries, "Oh, they're just in it for the money"? The Bible tells us that those who work should be paid, including ministers. But no one should pursue the "ministry" for greed's sake. Yet tragically some do.

I receive a great many invitations to speak, and I turn down well over 99 percent of them. Very frequently I am asked ,"How much do you charge to speak? What honorarium do you require?" And there are ministers who have set honorariums, sometimes running into thousands of dollars. I have always replied that that is their problem (as to how much to pay me) and I leave it with them.

We are not to minister for money. We are not to feed the flock of God *"for filthy lucre,"* and I would say to those going into the ministry that I think this is a very vital thing and we need to trust in God for our provision and not trust in men.

I am not in the ministry for money, nor should anyone be. I have been absolutely convinced that God was going to provide for all of my needs and, therefore, that was just not something that was an issue. I can say that God has certainly provided abundantly for all of my needs over the years.

Lord, give us strength for today that we never do a good deed for money or recognition or any gain, but let us always serve You out of love. Thank You, Jehovah-Jireh, for Your provision...

BY HIS STRENGTH, WE CAN BE FREED FROM GREED.

Distinguishing Justification and Sanctification

"And I will take away the stony heart out of your flesh, and I will give you a heart of flesh."

— Ezekiel 36:26

The term "salvation" in Scripture is a broad term that includes within its compass all of the acts and processes of God whereby we are saved. Initially, these include justification and regeneration. We are quickened by God, brought to life, which is regeneration, and we are granted faith and repentance on the basis of which we are then justified. These are both acts of God and they are instantaneous.

Then, however, there is the process of sanctification, which is a long process that is never completed in this life. Our sanctification takes place slowly. It has its ups and downs. There may be great spurts. There may be times of great backsliding, but this process continues on as God continues to sanctify us.

When we are in Christ and growing in Him, we are being sanctified by God, the Spirit. God is working in our hearts to cleanse us and to separate us from sin. The interesting thing about sanctification is that the more you have of it, the less you are aware of it. It is like a man who is both filthy dirty and totally blind having two operations performed on him at once. He is slowly and progressively being cleansed and slowly and progressively being given his eyesight, so with his increased acuity of vision, he is able to see more and more sin or dirt as it were on himself than he was able to see before.

Justification is a one-time act, but Scripturally speaking, sanctification is more of a process.

Lord, You who sanctifies me, give me strength for today to grow in holiness. As I do, forgive me for my sin, which I see more clearly. Let this process ever go forward in my life, until You bring me safely home and then glorify me…

BY GOD'S STRENGTH AND HOLY SPIRIT,
WE ARE SET APART FOR GOD.

MAY 6

Are You a Saint?

"To all who are in Rome, beloved of God, called to be saints..."
— Romans 1:7

I am always amazed when I go up to someone and I say, "How are you today, Saint Sue?" or Saint Mike. Many times people will say, "Well, I'm not a saint." Well, you better be. There is not going to be anybody but saints who are going to go to heaven.

Now, of course, many people have sort of a Roman Catholic concept of that—a saint is somebody who has won sort of the prize of the year for being exemplary. The first thing you need to do to become a saint according to the Roman church is be dead a long time, and then they will look the thing over very carefully and decide if you are a saint.

But it is a very interesting thing to me that Paul and the other apostles wrote their epistles to saints. And, of course, the saints receiving these letters were very much alive. A saint is someone who has been sanctified and is being sanctified, which means essentially that person is set aside unto God. So to be called a saint is at once an honor, it is also an exhortation. It is an honor that we are called those that are sanctified, set aside unto God. It is an exhortation that we should live as saints and that we have a high calling to live as those who are separated from sin and cleansed and godly.

Holy Father, give us strength for today to live holy lives. Thank You that we are already Your saints. Help us to grow in holiness and always live a life worthy of belonging to You...

BY GOD'S STRENGTH AND POWER,
WE ARE SAINTS.

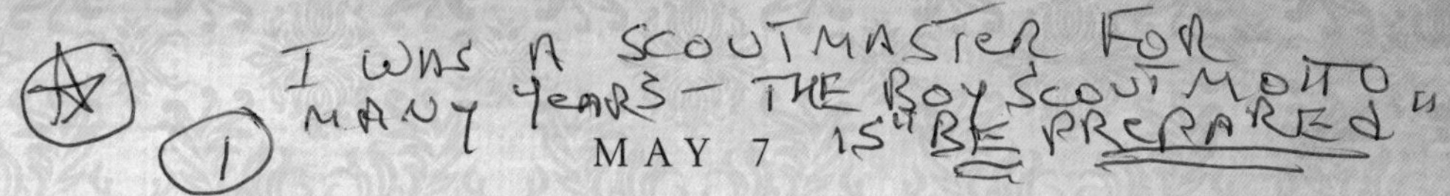

MAY 7

Defending the Word of God

"Always be ready to give an answer to every man who asks you for a reason for the hope that is in you..."

1 Peter 3:15

Today we live in a day when it is necessary to contend for the faith. Peter said that we should always be able to provide a defense for the faith. We are called upon to proclaim the Word.

I remember I used to hear in seminary all the time men who would give sermons on how there was no need to defend the Word of God. It is like my having a trained, powerfully strong dog on a chain, and I have to go out and defend my dog? Of course, there is a certain element of truth in there, but we are called upon to defend the teachings of the Gospel.

God has been pleased to commit the Gospel into the hands of men, who can twist it or distort it, deny it, or whatever, and so we are called upon to defend it. We are to contend for this faith lest it should be perverted, as it has been so many times in the past. Thank God for the Reformers and men who were able to see the need of purifying the Word and bringing us back to the true meaning of it.

Years ago I saw a painting which I have never forgotten. It was a painting of a large anvil. Around the anvil on the floor lay scattered scores of shattered, smashed hammers and, underneath, the words of the text: "The word of the Lord endureth forever." The attacks on the Bible break, but God's Word stands strong.

Father God, we thank You for Your Word, and we ask that You give us strength for today that we might be true defenders of the pure doctrine You have revealed and not let it be perverted and twisted...

BY GOD'S STRENGTH, WE CAN
EMBRACE TRUE DOCTRINE.

MAY 8

Freedom to Obey

"For freedom Christ freed us. Stand fast therefore and do not be entangled again with the yoke of bondage."

— Galatians 5:1

We must avoid two heresies: either turning the Gospel of liberty into licentiousness or into legalism.

The Gospel gives us freedom. But some encourage us to pervert that freedom into a freedom to sin freely. That is license, not liberty. Jude describes it this way: *"For there are some men who secretly crept in, who were marked long ago for this condemnation. They are ungodly men, who pervert the grace of our God into immorality and deny the only Lord God and our Lord Jesus Christ"* (verse 4).

Paul warns against such abuse of liberty: *"What then? Shall we sin because we are not under the law but under grace? God forbid!"* (Romans 6:15).

But the other extreme is trading liberty for legalism. In Galatians, we have one overall thrust of this book, which is God's antidote against legalism. You will recall in Galatians we are to stand fast in the liberty Christ has given us. Galatians opposes legalism.

Legalism essentially says that by obeying some set of laws or rules, one may in some way make oneself acceptable to the Almighty. Martin Luther said, "The most damnable and pernicious idea which has ever plagued the minds of men is the idea that poor, sinful, fallen, depraved man could ever make himself good enough to live in the presence of an all-holy and sin-hating God."

May God give us the grace to walk in the liberty Christ has made available to us. It is freedom to obey His commands out of love.

Lord, give me strength for today that I might glory in the freedom You have given us without misusing it. Thank You for setting us free from all bondage and strivings to make ourselves acceptable to You…

BY GOD'S STRENGTH, WE CAN WALK IN FREEDOM.

MAY 9

The Problem of Legalism

"For by the works of the law no flesh shall be justified."
— Galatians 2:16

Some professing Christians think they can keep God's law and thereby get to heaven. I have often asked such people to name the Ten Commandments, and usually they can name only three at the most.

A legalist is a person who says that we are not saved by grace alone through faith alone, but rather, we are saved by faith plus obedience to the law. This is the doctrine of some of the more traditional churches, the doctrine of most all of your cults, and it is the doctrine of vast numbers of other people who may belong to one or another organization.

But it would add to the grace of God and the finished work of Christ some effort, some works, some doings of ourselves. The Apostle Paul makes it very plain, however, that as soon as we place ourselves under the law as a means, either in whole or in part, to get us into heaven that immediately we become debtors to do the whole law. Salvation is either of grace or it is of law. And it is not a combination of both.

If we choose to put ourselves under law, then if we offend in any point we would, therefore, become guilty and would be culpable and could be punished.

God's law points us to the need for Christ. While we can't fulfill it perfectly, after we get saved, it provides some of the standards we strive to live by to show our love for Christ.

Lord Jesus, help me to see clearly that You have saved me purely by Your grace. Now that You have saved me, give me strength for today to walk in obedience to Your commandments, unto good works. Let me in gratitude keep Your law…

BY GOD'S STRENGH, WE
CAN LIVE IN OBEDIENCE.

MAY 10

The Problem of Antinomianism

"For we are His workmanship, created in Christ Jesus for good works, which God prepared beforehand, so that we should walk in them."

— Ephesians 2:10

Nomos is a Greek word for law. *"Anti-nomianism"* would describe the position of those who are against the law. They do not realize that we are saved by grace alone, through faith alone, in order that we may serve God, and that we can only serve God by obeying His commandments.

There is nothing that anyone of us can do that is pleasing to God except to obey His commandments, even as Jesus humbled Himself and showed his humility by becoming obedient, and He always pleased His father by keeping His commandments.

So also, since we have been saved by the grace of God, we are saved unto good works. Ephesians 2:8-9 says that we are saved by grace through faith. The next verse is the text above. This does not mean we are saved by faith plus good works. No. We are saved by faith alone, but that faith is never alone. If it is genuine, it results in good works.

Paul says in Titus that it is not by works of righteousness which we have done, but according to His mercy that He saved us.

Antinomianism is the spirit of the age. Some have perverted the Gospel to mean that we can live like we want and not have to worry about a holy God because He has already forgiven us. This is cheap grace. Salvation actually is by good works—the good works of Jesus Christ who died on the cross on our behalf.

My Savior and Lord, thank You for Your work on my behalf. Thank You for living in perfect obedience and for always pleasing Your Father. Lord, give me strength for today to do with joy the works You have laid before...

BY GOD'S STRENGTH, WE CAN
LIVE LIVES PLEASING TO HIM.

Beware of Those Who Pervert the Gospel

"...not by works of righteousness which we have done, but according to His mercy He saved us...and these things I want you constantly to affirm, so that those who have believed in God might be careful to maintain good works."

— Titus 3:5, 8

Paul tells us that we are saved not by our works. But once we are saved, we are empowered by the Holy Spirit that in order that we might endeavor to keep God's law to show our love and gratitude to Him. That is the biblical doctrine.

But there are some perverters of the faith who are turning the grace of God into lasciviousness. This antinomianism (anti-law) error sprang up early in the church.

We have this idea today, too; it is rampant everywhere. I could probably produce 100 books that have been written in the last five years that are popular even in evangelical circles which teach antinomianism; i.e., that now that we are Christians we don't have to obey the law.

We have professing Christians engaged in all sorts of sexual perversions, and they act as if it's okay because we are under grace.

But they are following the very example of Sodom and Gomorrah, having the absolute audacity to form themselves into churches of the Lord Jesus Christ, practicing the same perversions that brought Sodom and Gomorrah beneath the fierce wrath of God.

True Christianity always results in true transformation of the human heart. Many people may *profess* salvation, but not everyone who does so *possesses* salvation.

Dear God, I know grace is not cheap. It cost You dearly, and I want to praise and thank You for my salvation. Lord, give me strength for today to live in obedience to Your commandments...

BY GOD'S STRENGTH, WE CAN STRIVE TO LIVE ACCORDING TO HIS LAWS.

MAY 12

Mother's Day

"…remembering the genuine faith that first lived in your grandmother Lois and your mother Eunice and that I am persuaded lives in you also."

— 2 Timothy 1:5

On Mother's Day, we need to remember that there is no gift that we could give them that compares to the gift that they have given us—the gift of life.

In fact, the hand that rocks the cradle rules the world, for without the moral law of God taught them by their godly mothers, men find it extremely difficult to govern rightly. This has been echoed by innumerable great men of history. Abraham Lincoln said, "All that I am and all that I hope to be, I owe to my angel mother."

Sometime ago a lady in this church told me she had been at a large social occasion, a dinner I believe it was, and before they sat down the people were milling around the room getting acquainted. One man walked up to her, introduced himself, and said to her, "And what do you do?"

She replied, "Oh, I'm a wife and a mother."

He gave a small smile and turned to a woman standing nearby and said, "And what do you do?" She said she was deeply hurt.

"And what do you do?" What should she say? Well, I told her what I am going to tell you moms and housewives when you are asked that question, and you frequently are. "And what do you do?"

"Oh, I . . . well sir, I rule the world." And then walk away.

Mothers play a pivotal role in God's design for our world.

I thank You, Lord, for my mother today. Help me to honor and love her (or her memory) and be a good child of hers all the days of my life…

BY HIS STRENGTH, WE CAN PASS ON THE FAITH TO THE NEXT GENERATION.

God's Guarantee of Success

"This Book of the Law must not depart from your mouth. Meditate on it day and night so that you may act carefully according to all that is written in it. For then you will make your way successful, and you will be wise."

— Joshua 1:8

"It's guaranteed," the sign says. "Double your money back," the label declares. Many a product has been sold with such a promise only to have the purchaser discover later that it contained a slight flaw. The person who made the guarantee, as you often see on TV, is counting on the fact that you won't bother to pack it up and ship it back; or if you try to get your money back, find that the salesman has skipped town and left you with a very faulty product.

Today, I would like to talk about a guarantee that can never fail; a wonderful guarantee that is backed by the bank of heaven. In the promise of the above text, we have the guarantee of success.

Theologians have a Greek phrase, *hapax logomenon*—the only occurrence of the word. Sometimes in the Bible there is only one instance of something. That is the case in Joshua 1:8 with the word success. God, who can never lie and who will never go out of business, has set forth a divine guarantee of success.

Let us consider what the conditions to this guarantee are. The conditions are predicated upon meditating on and obeying God's book. In Joshua's time there existed only the first five books (the Pentateuch) given through Moses by God. Today, we have the completed volume, the Book of God, and what a wonderful book it is. Meditate on His Word, and you will succeed in life.

Almighty God, Your Word is precious to us. It is our inheritance. Lord, give us strength for today to live by it and pass it on to others. Thank You for the wisdom it gives us…

BY GOD'S STRENGTH, WE CAN BE KEEPERS OF THE WORD.

MAY 14

God and Predestination

"For by grace you have been saved through faith, and this is not of yourselves. It is the gift of God, not of works, so that no one should boast."

— Ephesians 2:8-9

The Bible teaches that God is the sovereign Lord and controls all things. And in His sovereignty, He allows men to do what they wish.

Now when He allows a person to sin, it is the person who is acting according to his own evil nature that does it. Now this is where people say, "Well, is not predestination simply allowing people to act according to their own will and to receive Christ?" But it won't work that way because the whole world is a fallen race. We are all totally depraved. We are dead in trespasses and sin. We are blind to the Gospel; we cannot understand the things of the Spirit of God. Therefore, if we are left to our own natural inclinations we will one and all decide to continue in our sin to the very end.

For anyone to be saved, God has to come down into this stream, this mass of humanity, which is pressing ever downward in more and more ungodliness and sin, and He has to come and pluck people out of it, bring them unto Himself, and turn them around. He then steers them upstream and gives them empowering to go the other way. That is why when we get to heaven all of the praise goes to God. He did it all. There is none that seeks after God, no not one. That is why we should be most humble about salvation. It is accomplished by the Savior.

Beautiful Savior, thank You for choosing me to be Yours forever. I thank You for Your work in my life and the grace that You have so freely given...

BY GOD'S STRENGTH AND POWER,
WE CAN KNOW HIM.

MAY 15

Something To Really Look Forward To

"But as it is written, 'Eye has not seen, nor ear heard, nor has it entered into the heart of man the things which God has prepared for those who love Him.'"

— 1 Corinthians 2:9

For the Christian, death is not an enemy. It will lead us to the great blessing as we come to meet Him face to face and experience that joy of which this world has never conceived. Of course, we should do nothing to hasten our death. That is in God's hands.

There have been many reports of people who have "died" and found themselves in heaven. Then they come back. I have known some personally who told me their stories. All such reports must first and foremost be tested by the Word of God.

If for you to live is Christ, then for you to die is unspeakable gain. You will be rejoined to all in Christ whom you have loved, and restored to all you have lost. You will walk through the meadows of flowers that never fade; alongside of rivers whose waters forever sparkle; near fountains whose spray is crystal diamonds; through bowers whose leaves are never seared; through gardens whose fragrance never surfeits. You will then know what it means to be among the immortals. Your body will be filled with an energy that never flags, with a power that you have never known. Your mind will enlarge and dilate with electric thoughts, noble ideals, and vast expansions.

Above all, you will see Jesus face to face and spend time with Him. He is the one who opened up heaven to us in the first place by His death on the cross.

Heavenly Father, thank You that You have made us for eternity. Thank You for preparing a place for us and for the total restoration that awaits our souls, bodies, minds, and spirits…

BY GOD'S STRENGTH,
WE CAN ENTER HEAVEN.

MAY 16

What is Life?

"What is your life? It is just a vapor that appears for a little while and then vanishes away."

— James 4:14

I am convinced that the vast majority of people on this earth live and die without ever having the slightest idea of what life is all about. Now that is a sweeping judgment. I make it, however, in compassion and love. It is tragic beyond words. I have given my whole life in an effort to try to solve that problem. Many live as if it will all end after their life "vanishes away."

May I call to witness a few people who should, because of their education and their genius, understand what life is all about. One of the most applauded authors of the twentieth century, no doubt, was Somerset Maugham. He said this: "When I look back on my life, it seems to me strangely lacking in reality. It may be that my heart, having found rest nowhere, had some deep ancestral craving for God and immortality, which my reason [his fallen reason] would have no truck with."

Or consider the British author—another skeptic—Thomas Hobbes, who gave us that concept of government as "leviathan." He said this: "The life of man is solitary, poor, nasty, brutish, and short." Not a very high view of life.

For such unbelievers, there was no future, there was no hope, there was no meaning for life. What a contrast we have with a Christian view of life where we are eternal beings created to glorify God and enjoy Him forever. Too bad so many will miss out on that which human beings were created to enjoy.

Lord of life, thank You for giving me life abundantly. You came to give us this rich and full and purposeful life, and You gave Your own Son to make it all possible…

BY GOD'S STRENGTH, WE LIVE FULL AND PURPOSEFUL LIVES.

MAY 17

A Contrasting View of Life

"He who did not spare His own Son, but delivered Him up for us all, how shall He not with Him also freely give us all things?

— Romans 8:32

There is a big difference between a Christian view of life and a pagan one. For example, the prince of atheists, the Frenchman Voltaire, once said: "I think we human beings are indeed contemptible creatures. I exhort you to enjoy as much as you can life, which isn't much."

Of course Shakespeare's Macbeth said:

Life's but a walking shadow
A poor player
That struts and frets
His hour upon the stage
And then is heard no more.
It is a tale told by an idiot,
Full of sound and fury, signifying nothing.

But the Christian view says that God has made us in His image. He has made us a little lower than the angels. The Scriptures say that God cares for us so much that Christ left the glories of heaven and became man in order to suffer a horrible but atoning death on our behalf. We are a part of His bride, which He has bought with His own precious blood. We are looking forward to the beginning of eternity with Him by attending the marriage feast of the lamb. Thus, life to the Christian is of infinite worth and value.

Lord, give me strength for today to live life to the full for Your glory and others' good. Thank You for letting us bear Your image and making us "just a little lower than the angels." We are so grateful for all the gifts You give us so freely…

BY GOD'S STRENGTH, WE CAN
SEE HIS LOVING HEART.

MAY 18

To Be or Not To Be

"Surely goodness and mercy shall follow me all the days of my life, and I will dwell in the house of the LORD forever."

— Psalm 23:6

We can't always say that what Shakespeare's characters say is what he believed. Nevertheless, I believe Shakespeare was a Christian, and his testimony on that is clear.

Consider the character Shakespeare paints of Hamlet, the melancholy Dane. Consider his view of life as contrasted with that of the devout Christian.

In this famous scene, Hamlet has an unsheathed dagger in his hands. He is wondering whether he should kill himself or not:

> To be, or not to be: that is the question…
> To die, to sleep;
> To sleep: perchance to dream: ay, there's the rub;
> For in that sleep of death what dreams may come,
> When we have shuffled off this mortal coil,
> Must give us pause…

The philosophy of life and death reflected in this passage is vastly higher than the awful secular philosophy of life portrayed by much of the media today, who believe that by simply committing suicide, by flinging the gift of life back into the face of the Giver, by deserting our post, by showing our cowardice, that we are going to solve all of our problems. Hamlet chooses against suicide because the Almighty has set His canon (law) against self-slaughter.

What a vast difference there is to those who come to know Jesus. Through all the difficulties of life, the Savior can sustain us until He brings us safely home.

Lord of life and death, we acknowledge that You decide when we are born and when we die. Thank You that our time is in Your hands. When life becomes too burdensome for us, then help us to cast our burdens on You…

BY GOD'S STRENGTH, WE CAN ENDURE LIFE UNTIL WE'RE SAFELY HOME.

MAY 19

All Things New

"Rejoice in the Lord always. Again I will say, rejoice!"
— Philippians 4:4

I remember the words of the classic song, "Old Man River": "I gets weary an' sick of tryin', I'm tired of livin' An'skeered of dyin'." Tragically, that is the picture of so many people.

But Paul the Apostle is a great model to us on how to live and how to die. He had become the possessor of a new life through Jesus Christ, who makes all things new. He tells us: *"Therefore, if any man is in Christ, he is a new creature. Old things have passed away. Look, all things have become new"* (2 Corinthians 5:17). Even though he sat in a Roman prison waiting to face a possible death sentence, he still rejoiced, and again he said, *"I will rejoice."*

He said for me to live is Christ. There is the secret of the fullness of life: Me, live, Christ.

Someone said it is like an arc lamp. When the two components of the self and Christ are put together, they glow with a brilliant incandescence. But if you replace Christ with anything else—with fame, or fortune, or wealth or success or whatever—then you have the smoldering dim smoky lamp that is produced by anything other than Christ.

When the love of Christ takes over the life of a soul, it produces the power of a life which can have a magnetic attraction even for the most scandalous and can change even the hardest of hearts.

Whatever happens in life, we can choose to complain or we can choose to rejoice, through it all. Paul chose to rejoice, and, therefore, they couldn't keep him down.

Dear Father, give me strength for today to rejoice even when I don't feel like it. Help me to remember that in You all things work out for the best for those who love You and are called according to Your purpose…

BY GOD'S STRENGTH, WE CAN
REJOICE IN ALL CIRCUMSTANCES.

MAY 20

Pride vs. Trust in the Lord

"God resists the proud, but gives grace to the humble."

— James 4:6

I saw a book in a bookstore many years ago with an intriguing title. I didn't buy it, and now I regret it. The book was entitled *Not Made for Defeat*. You and I were not made for defeat. We were made for triumph. That, of course, is a picture of a Roman general or emperor coming back from war, his soldiers behind him, flags flying from his chariot. Behind them, in chains, was the army of those who had been defeated and now were being brought as slaves to Rome. But there is a danger in victory—pride. When David faced Goliath, he did not boast. Instead, he put his confidence in the Lord.

It always amazes me how many Americans, even professing Christians, will frequently teach their children: "Be proud." God gives grace to the humble, but He will tear down the proud of heart.

Pride (in the sense of arrogance, not self-dignity) says that pride is the worst of sins and leads to destruction. C. S. Lewis puts it, "It was through Pride that the devil became the devil." Trusting in self is like resting on a broken reed that will break completely and pierce your hand.

If we trust in ourselves, if we succeed, we will be proud, and when we run into something too big, we will then be saddened, defeated, and dejected. But if we trust in Christ, we will succeed, and the glory will go to Him and not unto ourselves. That is the Christian way.

Oh God, our help in ages past, I praise and thank You for being my constant helper. Thank You for what You have helped me accomplish and thank You for the victories won. Help me always to give You the glory…

BY GOD'S STRENGTH, WE ARE KEPT FROM THE DEADLY SIN OF PRIDE.

MAY 21

The Peace That Passes Understanding

"And the peace of God, which surpasses all understanding, will protect your hearts and minds through Christ Jesus."

— Philippians 4:7

James Cash Penney, better known as J.C. Penney, built that tremendous chain of retail stores. Penney was a Christian, but he, like many Christians, had not yet fully learned the lesson of walking by faith. Though his business survived the economic crash of 1929, he had become involved in some personal commitments that were causing him great trouble and stress. In fact, the stress was so severe that it caused the dormant virus of chicken pox, which he had had as a child, to spring to life again in the form of that very, very painful disease of shingles.

He was so crushed and overwhelmed by the constant pain and agony of this disease that he came to the very end of himself and had to be hospitalized. That night in the hospital he was sure he would not survive, so he wrote farewell letters to his wife and son.

He finally went to sleep. The next morning he awoke to singing. It was coming from the hospital chapel just a few doors from his room. He managed to get up, put on his bathrobe, and shuffle into the chapel where he heard a group singing a hymn. As he listened to the words, he was transformed. This was the turning point for him. He said later, "I am seventy-one years old, and the most dramatic and glorious minutes of my life were those I spent in that chapel that morning: 'God Will Take Care of You.'"

Oh Lord, our hearts cry out to You for Your grace and Your protection from ourselves. Indeed, lead us not into temptation but deliver us from the evil one. Thank You that You alone are able to keep us from falling and to present us before Your glory...

BY GOD'S STRENGTH, WE MAY LIVE OUR LIVES SO THAT ONE DAY WE WILL HEAR HIM SAY, "WELL DONE."

MAY 22

Christ vs. Anti-Christ

"…and every spirit that does not confess that Jesus Christ has come in the flesh is not from God. This is the spirit of the antichrist, which you have heard is coming and is already in the world."

— 1 John 4:3-4

Much ink has been spilled over the issue of the Anti-Christ. Just who is he or will he be—or as some want to say, Who was he?

Jesus said in Matthew 24 that many false prophets would arise and lead many astray. We see that one of the aspects of the *anti-christos* is to be a deceiver as well as an opposer of Christ, and he also will have false prophets as well.

Furthermore, said Jesus, some of these deceivers will be able to do supernatural things: *"For false christs and false prophets will rise and show signs and wonders to deceive, if possible, even the elect"* (Mark 13:22).

We see the activity of Satan directed against Christ, for example, at the temptation. The devil claims to be able to dispose of the kingdoms of this world at his whim. This claim is not denied by Christ.

Furthermore, we have the parable of the tares and the wheat and while we slept, said Jesus, an enemy came and sowed the tares. That enemy would be the antichrist or the devil.

Meanwhile, some people have read too much into the number 666. But in every city in the world, there are probably hundreds of streets at which somebody lives at 666 First Street, 666 Second Street, Third Street and Fourth Street and on and on and on.

John tells us that the spirit of the antichrist is found in those who deny that Jesus has come in the flesh. The spirit of antichrist is to ultimately reject Jesus.

Dear Jesus, we see how many people reject Your holy name and Your divinity. We see how people fight against Your name and claim all sorts of roads to heaven. Thank You for being Who You claim to be…

IN GOD'S STRENGTH, WE CAN STAND AGAINST THE SPIRIT OF ANTICHRIST.

MAY 23

Can You Have God Without Christ?

"Whoever denies the Father and the Son is the antichrist."

— 1 John 2:22

As noted before, we hear much said about the beast and the Anti-Christ. But interestingly, John tells us that those who deny the incarnation of Jesus makes one an "antichrist." Now, therefore, there are a great many individuals and movements and even churches that would fit quite plainly and incontrovertibly into that category. John adds, *"No one who denies the Son has the Father"* (verse 23).

Now I think it is commonplace among nominal Christians to think that there are those who deny the Son, but nevertheless have the Father. But when someone challenges me about this, I respond: "Just tilt your chin up and talk to God because your argument isn't with me. I wouldn't have the gall to say it, but God did, right here, "No one who denies the Son has the Father." This opponent of Jesus is advertently knocking out the ladder between heaven and earth, between God and man.

Obviously this verse in John referred in ancient days to numerous heretics at that time, such as the Gnostics: they said that Christ came upon Jesus at His baptism and left before His passion, and they separated between Jesus and the Christ and made Christ something other than the person of Jesus.

Of course, all who are agnostic and who are atheists would quite obviously be antichrist in both the senses of opposing Christianity: opposing both the revelation of God and the redemption that Jesus Christ has brought.

Lord Jesus, You are the divine Son of God. We know that no one can come to the Father except by You. Help us to never water down this truth, even in an age of rampant political correctness…

IN GOD'S STRENGTH, WE PROCLAIM THAT JESUS IS LORD.

MAY 24

What About Christians Who Fall Away for Good?

"They went out from us, but they were not of us, for if they had been of us, they would no doubt have remained with us. But they went out, revealing that none of them were of us."

— 1 John 2:19

How are we to understand it when someone seems to become a Christian, they seem to actively grow, and then eventually they fall away? They leave, and they never come back. The first thing we think of is that these people are somewhere out there someplace. But they were right in the church.

They went out from us, but they were not of us. They were among them, a part of the church, but they really were not of it in its essence. *"For if they had been of us, they would no doubt have remained with us."*

Many people ask about those that leave the church and apostatize and deny Christ. Have they fallen from grace and ceased to be Christians, or were they never really Christians at all? Two theological systems have been built in response to that question. The Calvinistic system, which says they never were Christians at all and that is why they left. And the Arminian system, which says they once were Christians and now they have ceased to be Christians.

I think John settled once and for all that controversy in this very verse. Their apostatizing is a part of the continual purification of the church.

Father God, it is with deepest sorrow that we think of the people we know who have left the church. We ask You to bring them back to Yourself. You who received the prodigal son with open arms, quicken and make alive those who are spiritually dead...

BY GOD'S STRENGTH AND POWER ALONE, CAN THE DEAD BE MADE ALIVE.

MAY 25

Be Filled With the Spirit

"Do not be drunk with wine, for that is reckless living. But be filled with the Spirit."

— Ephesians 5:18

The church of Jesus Christ began in earnest on Pentecost, when the Holy Spirit was poured out on the believers in Jerusalem with great fanfare as recorded in Acts 2. This was 50 days after Christ's resurrection.

A lady said to me one time, "I wish you would preach a sermon on the Holy Spirit. What is it?" It? Suppose when you get up tomorrow morning, your husband says to you, "Well, good morning, Thing. How are you today, Thing?"

It is obviously a gross insult to depersonalize someone. And to depersonalize the Holy Spirit of God is an insult. So let us consider just who the Holy Spirit is. Now if you were to ask any of the cultists, they would all tell you the same thing: The Holy Spirit is a "thing"; The Holy Spirit is a "force." It is like gravity, or magnetism, or nuclear energy, or electricity. It is not a person.

But the Bible teaches that the Holy Spirit is a person. Along with the Father and the Son, the Holy Spirit is one God, in three persons. The Scripture says, *"He who searches the hearts knows what the mind of the Spirit is, because He intercedes for the saints according to the will of God"* (Romans 8:27).

Does the Spirit have emotion? The Bible tells us in Ephesians 4:30 that we are not to grieve the Holy Spirit. We are to be filled with the Holy Spirit. This is not a one-time experience but an ongoing one.

Come, Oh Holy Spirit, and convict us again of our sins. Call us to the Father. Glorify Jesus before our eyes. Melt me. Use me. Fill me.

BY GOD'S STRENGTH, THE HOLY SPIRIT CAN REIGN IN MY LIFE.

God Does Not Grade on the Curve

"Therefore be perfect, even as your Father who is in heaven is perfect."
— Matthew 5:48

I lived for years in the church without understanding the basic message of Christ myself. That message is good news! Good news that Jesus Christ came and suffered and died that we might have eternal life freely as a gift.

It is not earned or deserved, dear friend. It is absolutely free. In order for us to earn it we would have to pass the test and the passing grade is 100 percent. Since Jesus tells us we're supposed to be perfect, we realize that all of us have fallen short. The whole class has failed and God doesn't grade on a curve.

If you realize that you have sinned and if you are not sure that you have eternal life, then I would urge you today to consider what Christ has done. He suffered on the cross for us. He suffered infinitely in our stead. And when He had finished His atoning work He declared "*Tetelestai*"—it is done, it is paid, it is finished. The wrath of God was paid in full.

We may receive the gift of eternal life by repenting of our sins, which is a sincere determination of our heart and mind to turn from that which is displeasing to God and trust in Jesus Christ his Son. Trusting in Christ doesn't simply mean an intellectual assent, but saving faith is resting one's entire hope of eternal life in what Christ did for sinners on the cross.

Lord Jesus, I turn from my sins and come to You for forgiveness and cleansing. Thank You for taking away my sins and making me clean and holy before You. Help me to never tolerate any sin in my life, but to always bring them to You…

BY GOD'S STRENGTH AND HIS WORK, WE ARE SAVED BY FAITH.

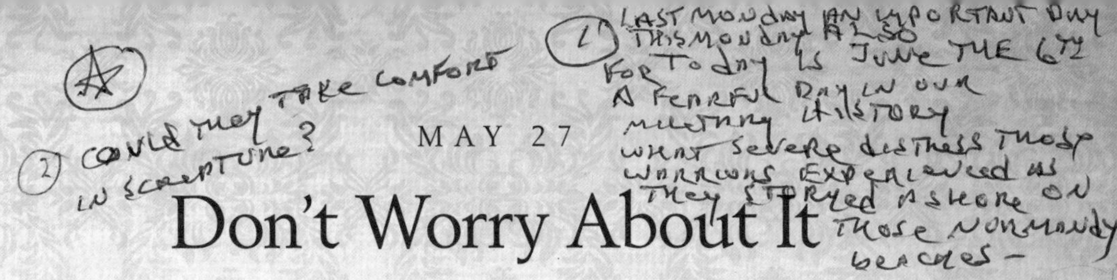

MAY 27

Don't Worry About It

"Do not fear, for I am with you; do not be dismayed, for I am your God."

— Isaiah 41:10

What a useless thing it is to worry. It does not accomplish anything. This does not mean that we are not to give some forethought and planning; but it is talking about going over and over and over again those things which we cannot, at the time, do anything about. Worry never accomplishes anything. It does not improve business; it does not bring our children home safely; and it does not improve our health.

I wonder how many today have been blinded by the corroding effects of worry and care. They have been blinded to the joys and happiness of life. All serenity and peace have been removed from them.

Worry and anxiety both come from the same root: one from Latin, the other from Anglo-Saxon. The root means "to choke or to strangle." And that is what worry does. It chokes us; it strangles us so that we do not think or see straight. The antonyms for "worry" are "serenity," "peace," "joy," "boldness," and "confidence." And when worry is there, all of those things are gone. One physician said that there are innumerable people who die and their deaths are listed for various reasons, but in fact, they were killed by worry.

I wish today that the Spirit of God might rub away some of those worry lines, might relax some aching limbs, that you might hear the Word of God saying to you to rejoice forevermore—that you might be delivered from the dread scourge of worry. Instead of being anxious, cast your cares on the Lord.

Oh Lord, give me strength for today to cast all my cares on You. Forgive me for worrying about things, instead of turning them over to You. Thank You for Your promise to strengthen and uphold me. Thank You that through You I need not fear anything…

BY GOD'S STRENGTH AND CARE, ALL FEARS ARE GONE.

MAY 28

The Spade of the Archaeologist

"For we have not followed cleverly devised myths when we made known to you the power and coming of our Lord Jesus Christ, but we were eyewitnesses of His majesty."

— 2 Peter 1:16

The school of higher criticism began in the late eighteenth century. It seemed the higher critics considered themselves called to demolish all traditional views concerning the Bible. For example, they said that it was quite obvious that Moses could not possibly have written the Pentateuch because writing had not even been invented in his day.

It is interesting that not long after the time that higher criticism began, the science of archaeology began as well. But the spade of the archaeologist has been the utter frustration of the higher critic for it was discovered not long after, that writing certainly existed in the time of Moses—actually long before Moses.

Isn't it astonishing to see how many times God's Word, though doubted by skeptics, is confirmed by the spade of the archaeologist? I have preached whole messages, providing example after example in which the critics assumed the Bible was wrong, but the Scriptures were proved right after all.

The Bible is not some kind of fable. The Bible is not some kind of fairy tale. It is not something that happened up on a cloud in never, never land somewhere, but as people have dug into the sand and into the rock and unearthed thousands, tens of thousands of inscriptions and tablets and symbols of every kind, they have discovered over and over again that what the Bible has been saying all along is indeed the actual facts of history and of God.

We can believe it, rest our souls upon it, and share it with a lost and needy world.

God of truth, Your Word is truth. Thank You for the dependability of the Scriptures, not just as historical facts, but as the means we learn of the bedrock of our salvation and eternal destiny...

BY GOD'S STRENGTH AND POWER,
HIS WORD STANDS FOREVER.

MAY 29

The Fiery Furnace, Lion's Den, and Walls of Babylon

"And whoever does not fall down and worship shall the same hour be cast into the midst of a burning fiery furnace."

— Daniel 3:6

When skeptics read about three certain Jews, Shadrach, Meshach and Abednego, being cast into a fiery furnace, they scoffed. Same thing when they read about Daniel being thrown into a den of lions.

But archaeologists working in the ruins of Babylon discovered an ancient library on clay tablets. Included on these tablets were the punishments for violations of various regulations.

For the offense of impiety to any god, one was to be cast alive into a fiery furnace, and huge furnaces have also been discovered. For an untoward act relative to a king, like failure to worship his image, one was to be cast alive into the den of lions. Cages with iron bars have also been found in the ruins and the diggings of Babylon.

Furthermore, when Babylon was at the height of its glory, Ezekiel prophesied that the great walls of Babylon would be utterly destroyed. These walls were 60 miles long and as thick as 150 feet and 300 feet high, where a number of chariots could race on the top of those walls.

Archaeologists were digging down in the ground and they ran into the base, the foundation of the walls because they were utterly destroyed, just as God said they would be. If you ever see a picture of Babylon, it looks like it has been cut off by a scythe. Once again, the critics are wrong; the Bible is right.

Almighty God, as we consider what happened to Your people in ancient Babylon, we can't help but think of Your people today in various parts of the world facing persecution for the name of Jesus. Grant them strength, grace, and perseverance until the end...

BY GOD'S STRENGTH, WE CAN FACE DEATH.

MAY 30

A Time to Remember

"These stones will be a memorial for the children of Israel continually."
— Joshua 4:7

Memorial Day: It is a good thing to remember. There are more than a dozen different words in the Bible that are translated "remember." When Joshua led the people of Israel into the Promised Land, he had them build a memorial of stones to remember what God had done for them.

We must remember what God has done for us as a nation. Did you know that America is unique because this is the first nation in the history of this planet to have freedom of religion? Religious tyranny prevailed all over the globe. Gradually some nations rose to religious tolerance, like England, but only in America was full religious freedom granted for the very first time.

This continent, hidden between two great oceans, was reserved by God for that religious freedom, for that expression of the true Gospel of Jesus Christ—where His Word would be read, where He would be worshiped, where He would be trusted, and His Gospel would be proclaimed both here and throughout the whole world.

Today I would like for us to remember not only those men and women who laid down their lives in the wars, but that One who fought the longest to give us what we enjoy most and who often is the most forgotten. In fact, there is a strange lament we find in Scripture that says, *"My people have forgotten Me for days without number"* (Jeremiah 2:32). Ultimately, God is the source of our freedom, and we should remember that.

Thank You, God, that we still have freedom. Help us to remember that it was given us at great price, first by the blood of Jesus, then by men and women who laid down their lives for our country. Please turn our country around before it's too late, lest their sacrifice be in vain…

BY GOD'S STRENGTH, WE RECOGNIZE
THE HIGH COST OF FREEDOM.

MAY 31

Philosophy vs. Wisdom

"Beware lest anyone captivate you through philosophy and vain deceit, in the tradition of men and the elementary principles of the world, and not after Christ."

— Colossians 2:8

The word philosophy comes from the Greek and literally means "the love of wisdom." The Hebrews received God's revelation, which was greater than human philosophy. The ancient Greeks had no such advantage, and though wise in their way, they were like blind men searching for light in a darkened room, whereas the Hebrews were in a room which was brilliantly illuminated. For them all that was possible was to approach unto the light and try to penetrate into it more deeply and understand it more thoroughly. This was called by the Hebrews not philosophy, but wisdom, and there is a great difference between that "vain philosophy" as it is called in the New Testament and the wisdom of God.

When the Bible speaks about wisdom, it is talking about an understanding of the revelation of God. It is talking about a heart that seeks to know and to understand, and that seeking to know and understand is aimed particularly at an understanding and knowledge of God. Over and against this are set all of those who either have no desire to learn. The person who does not desire to learn is repeatedly set forth in the Scriptures as a fool—as a man or woman of folly whose end is destruction.

It is tragic that many people today reject God's wisdom because they falsely assume it has somehow been discredited by philosophy. Such "philosophers" are described by Paul: *"Claiming to be wise, they became fools"* (Romans 1:22).

God of wisdom and might, thank You for revealing Yourself to us mortal beings. Help us to become wise by studying Your Word and knowing You. Thank You that with You, there is wisdom and understanding…

BY GOD'S STRENGTH AND KNOWLEDGE,
WE CAN BECOME WISE.

JUNE 1

On Hypnosis

"Do not be conformed to this world, but be transformed by the renewing of your mind, that you may prove what is the good and acceptable and perfect will of God."

— Romans 12:2

Don't let the world hypnotize you into inaction for the Lord. Why don't we all do something of significance with our lives? I recall seeing a magician at a stage performance ask for a volunteer. A man came forward and was asked to sit down on a stool. The magician began to hypnotize him. Finally the man apparently fell into a deep hypnotic sleep. But before he was brought out of that sleep, the magician told him and the entire audience that could hear, "When you wake up, you will not be able to move your right arm. You will not be able to even lift your right arm. Now, you wake up at the count of three—one, two, three."

This was a man about 40 years old, quite physically capable. When he woke up, the magician said to him, "Now, sir, would you raise your left arm?" and he did. He then said, "Now, will you raise your right arm?" the man said, "I can't." He didn't know what had happened to him. No matter how hard he tried, he could not raise his right arm.

I am absolutely confident that there are many of us who can't do many things simply because we don't believe that we can. May God help us to not be hypnotized by the world, so that we are conformed more and more into its image. I'm reminded of how the J. B. Phillips version paraphrases Romans 12:2: *"Don't let the world squeeze you into its mold."*

Dear Father, give me strength for today that I might conform myself to You and to no longer be hypnotized by this world's negative and evil influences. Help us, Lord, to be conformed to Your image and not that of this sinful world...

BY GOD'S STRENGTH, WE MARCH TO HIS BEAT AND NOT THAT OF THE WORLD.

JUNE 2

The Benefits of Wisdom

"…for wisdom is better than rubies, and all the things that may be desired are not to be compared to it."

— Proverbs 8:11

God's wisdom is personified in Proverbs 8, calling out to the people to follow her ways. We see in this passage various excellencies of wisdom—how it is able to touch the locks and open the latches of all of the doors of wisdom and knowledge and inventions. All things open in the face of wisdom. By wisdom kings reign and princes rule, and judges judge the earth. Wisdom says, *"I love those who love me, and those that seek me early will find me"* (Proverbs 8:16).

How true it is with even the knowledge of this world that those who love knowledge find that they are loved by it. And yet often they merely heap up to themselves empty facts, which have little eternal significance. But if we truly love wisdom, we will find that we will be loved by it and blessed by it. Not only riches, but *"riches and honor are with me"* (Proverbs 8:18). Honor comes from the wisdom of God and His word. It is durable riches which shall last.

Verse 21 says *"… I may cause those who love me to inherit wealth, and I will fill their treasuries."* Now this is an amazing promise—those who seek God's word will be blessed with substance and their treasuries will be filled. This is the promise of wisdom. Above all, seek not the gifts of life but the Giver of life.

Almighty God, wisdom and strength are with You. Make me wise, God, so that I can discern right from wrong. Give me strength for today that I can see the right path and take it and impart wisdom to others…

BY GOD'S STRENGTH AND WISDOM,
WE TOO MAY BE WISE.

JUNE 3

The Bible's Amazing Unity

"God is not a man, that He should lie, nor a son of man, that He should repent. Has He spoken, and will He not do it? Or has He spoken, and will He not make it good?"

— Numbers 23:19

First there is an idea, which the author develops into an outline he can take to a publisher. When one is found, they usually work jointly to complete the manuscript, taking it through various stages of editing until the final version is ready to be printed.

However, with the Scripture there was no outline, no topic assigned, no editorial committee on this earth, no plan for production, no completion or publication dates. Indeed, some 40 different writers—over a period of 60 generations and some 1,500 years, writing in three different languages (Hebrew, Aramaic, and Greek), on a number of different continents, in numerous countries (including Palestine, Rome, Greece, Turkey, Patmos, Babylon, and Persia)—produced this incredible book. Writers who came from totally divergent backgrounds—kings and peasants, shepherds and fishermen, philosophers, and what have you—all conspired to produce a book that has the most incredible unity.

The book begins in a garden in Paradise and ends in a garden in Paradise. It begins with Paradise lost and ends with Paradise regained. There has never been another book so produced with such incredible unity as this wondrous book.

God of the Bible, make us truly "people of the Book." Thank You that we live in a time where we have complete copies, in multiple versions and languages, with innumerable aids to help us understand Your Word better. Help us to be diligent in our studies of the Bible that we may apply it to our lives…

BY GOD'S STRENGTH, WE KNOW HIS WORD AND LIVE BY IT.

JUNE 4

Like No Other Book of Antiquity

"I, Tertius, who wrote down this letter, greet you in the Lord."

— Romans 1:22, NIV

Consider, if you will, the wonder of the certainty that we may have concerning the Bible. Since no original autograph of any ancient writer is extant today, we always have to rely upon copies of copies.

In many cases concerning historical writings, we cannot be absolutely certain if we have what was originally written by the author. The level of certainty primarily depends upon two factors: First, the number of manuscripts that are extant, and secondly, the time span since they were written. Obviously, if you have but one manuscript, you have no idea if it is what the author actually wrote. If you have two and there is a divergence, you can flip a coin and decide whether he went in or whether he went out. If you have three, four or five, you are beginning to move toward a little more assurance concerning the manuscript. But even this number is hardly enough to give you any great assurance.

Plato, one of the greatest philosophers of all time, has left us seven manuscripts. There are only five of any of Aristotle's works that are extant. Thucydides, Herodotus and Suetonius, all historians, have each given us eight.

In the case of the New Testament, there are more than 5,000 extant Greek manuscripts. There are more than 10,000 additional manuscripts in other ancient languages. So we have well over 15,000 manuscripts of the New Testament. There is nothing that vaguely approaches this in any other writing of any sort whatever of antiquity. It is, indeed, unique.

Lord, we thank You that we can trust Your Word. Thank You for all the preserved manuscripts. Thank You that in spite of all the attempts to destroy the Bible, it is still the Book of books…

BY GOD'S STRENGTH, HE SPEAKS
TO US THROUGH HIS WORD.

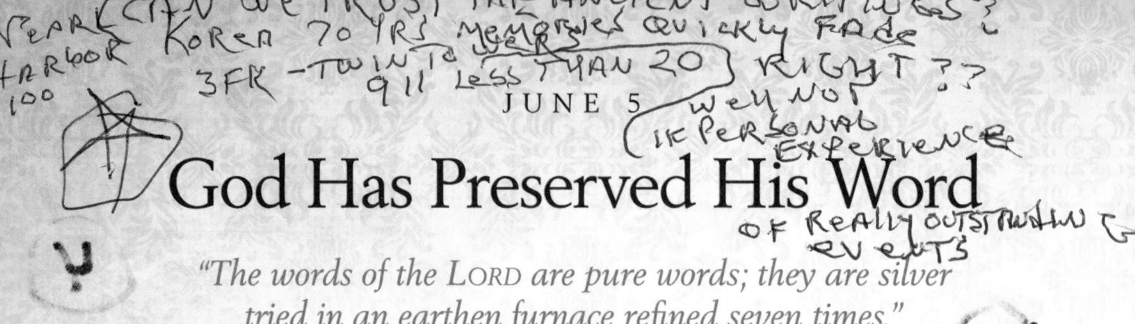

JUNE 5

God Has Preserved His Word

"The words of the LORD *are pure words; they are silver tried in an earthen furnace refined seven times."*

— Psalm 12:6

Not only are there more manuscripts of the New Testament in existence than any other ancient writing, but the time lapse between the original writing and the oldest existing copy is shorter. Obviously, if that time span increases, there is more time for corruption to creep into the manuscripts.

For example, the time that elapsed between the time that Plato wrote and the earliest extant manuscript of his writings is 1,200 years. In the case of Aristotle, it is 1,400; Thucydides, 1,300; Herodotus, 1,300, and Aristophanes, 1,200.

Compare that with the earliest extant manuscripts of the New Testament. The earliest fragment of the New Testament that has been preserved is called the "John Rylands fragment," written 35 years after the completion of the New Testament in about 95 A.D. These are names of manuscripts of the New Testament or portions thereof in a relatively short time (by ancient standards) after the completion of the New Testament: the Bodmer Papyrus II written 55 years after the completion of the New Testament; Tatian's Diatessaron, 75 years; Codex Vaticanus, 230 years; Codex Sinaiticus, 255 years.

Compare these dates with the 1,200, 1,300, and 1,400 years which elapsed in the case of the other writings of antiquity. Do we actually have today what was inspired back then? The New Testament stands upon firmer historical and scientific grounds than any other writing of any kind ever written in antiquity.

Dear God, we thank You that Your Word has been preserved for us and that it was written down by eyewitnesses and the early Christians. Thank You that when all other writings disappear, Your Word will stand…

BY GOD'S STRENGTH, HIS WORD REMAINS FOREVER.

The Imperishable Word

"As Jehudi read three or four columns, the king cut it with a scribe's knife and cast it into the fire that was on the hearth, until all the scroll was consumed in the fire that was on the hearth."

— Jeremiah 36:23

In the days of Jeremiah the prophet, Jehoiakim, an evil king, did not like hearing the Word of God. So he burned it. No other writings in history have been so intensely and consistently vilified over such a period of time as have the Scriptures. Even during the Old Testament period, the evil Jewish king Manasseh attempted to destroy all of the writings of the Scriptures. Yet, twenty years later, his grandson, Josiah, found a copy of the Scriptures hidden in the temple, and with that discovery began a great spiritual revival.

In 303 A.D., the Roman emperor Diocletian instituted another of the long line of terrible persecutions against the Christians and ordered all copies of the Scriptures to be burned. Ten years later, the Emperor Constantine issued the Edict of Toleration. Twenty-five years after Diocletian's order to destroy the Scriptures, Constantine officially ordered the historian Eusebius to produce numerous copies of the Bible for the Roman Empire.

Voltaire, who died in 1778, said that within 100 years of his death Christianity would have become extinct. One hundred years after Voltaire died, an original copy of the writings of Voltaire sold for $0.11 while that same year a manuscript of the Bible sold for $500,000. The Word of God will stand forever.

Almighty God, it could only be by Your power that the Bible has escaped destruction. It is still under attack. Thank You for Your watching over Your Word as You watch over Your people...

BY GOD'S STRENGTH,
HIS WORD STANDS.

Avoiding the Will to Fail

"I must do the works of Him who sent Me while it is day. Night is coming when no one can work."

— John 9:4

Have you ever noticed how sometimes, just on the eve of victory, someone will sabotage his own success by doing something foolish, even if it took him a while to get to that point? He subconsciously gave in to what some psychologists call "the will to failure."

In her 1936 classic book, *Wake Up & Live!*, Dorothea Brande devotes a chapter to the "Will to Fail." She talks about people who are "unconsciously…trying to fail." She says that the people who essentially waste their lives, either explicitly or subtly, are given over to the Will to Fail. For example, she writes, "Easiest of all to recognize as lovers of failure are the heavy drinkers."

She lists other examples of this "will to fail." "There are the takers of eternal post-graduate courses, turning up on the campus year after year like so many Flying Dutchman." Pursuits that basically cause us to waste our lives manifest the Will to Fail, and so she concludes: "…[If] we are not doing what we are best equipped to do, or doing well what we have undertaken as our personal contribution to the world's work, at least by way of an earnestly followed avocation, there will be a core of unhappiness in our lives which will be more and more difficult to ignore as the years pass."

God has given us the privilege to walk in the good works that He has prepared for us to do. Just ask Him to show what those are and then do them.

Heavenly Father, give us the strength today to do the work You have called us to do. Guide us and help us to obey You in all things…

BY GOD'S STRENGTH, WE ARE NOT CAPTIVES OF THE WILL TO FAIL.

JUNE 8

Science, a Gift From Christians

"...when He appointed the foundations of the earth, then I was by Him, as one brought up with Him..."

— Proverbs 8:29-30

In Proverbs 8:22-31, there is a creation poem. Creation is described here as something that is not accidental. The Creator is not a blind force, but rather an intelligent being. The Word has been eternally generated by the Father. His first creation was wisdom. And this of course is the wisdom by which all other things have been created.

Now this contrasts marvelously with all of the heathen conceptions. In those schemes, caprice is supreme and accident and fortuitousness are involved, and blind forces work through a compulsion of necessity. But God, through His wisdom, has established laws and the whole world is an ordered process. Without the Christian concept of an ordered universe with God-given laws continually operating in the same way, science would never have come into existence.

Modern science was born in the 1500s and 1600s when a Christian worldview was dominant. And yet this same science, having turned its back upon God has adopted the materialistic and atheistic view of evolution. One of the things that is seldom discussed in evolution is the fact of the impossibility of physical laws ever arising by blind chance. You would not have laws operating always the same way throughout all of the universe continually the same, but you would have everything working by accident and continually changing. On the very premises of evolution, science would never have come into existence.

Our Heavenly Creator, all praise is due to You. We glorify You—the One who flung the stars into existence, who merely spoke and created all things. Help us to lift up our eyes and behold Your glory...

LORD, GIVE ME STRENGTH FOR TODAY TO ADVANCE TRUE KNOWLEDGE IN THE WORLD.

Transformed By the Word of God

"But put on the Lord Jesus Christ, and make no provision for the flesh to fulfill its lusts."
— Romans 13:14

In the 19th Century a famous skeptic in England challenged a noted minister to a debate. The minister said he would gladly involve himself in this debate under one condition: that the skeptic would bring with him two people who could testify that the teachings of this skeptic had bettered their lives. The minister said he would bring 100 people who would testify that what he had taught had bettered and transformed their lives. The skeptic withdrew from the debate because he said he could not meet the condition.

Mel Trotter, an inveterate drunkard in Chicago, squandered money on alcohol rather than meeting the needs of his family. He came home one day to find his family famished from lack of food and his little son dead of malnutrition and neglect. What did he do? Though his heart was broken, he was so constrained and in bondage to alcohol he took the baby shoes off his little son and sold them for another drink. Having gotten that drink, he was so overwhelmed with remorse that he determined to throw himself into Lake Michigan and end it all. On the way to the lake, he heard, coming from a mission in one of the worst parts of Chicago, the glorious story of love of Jesus Christ for sinners. Mel Trotter became a new creature in Christ, resulting in the establishment of 56 missions around the United States for derelicts such as he had been. The Word of God changes lives.

Dear God, thank You that You can do the miraculous. Thank You that one of the greatest miracles of all is the transformation of the human heart. Change our hearts of stone into hearts of flesh. Thank You, Jesus, for changing us from the inside out…

BY HIS STRENGTH, WE ARE TROPHIES OF GOD'S GRACE.

JUNE 10

True Success

"To him who overcomes and keeps My works to the end, I will give authority over the nations…"

— Revelation 2:26

What the Bible means by success has less to do with the end than with the aspirations—has less to do with reaching our goal than it has to do with setting the goal. That is, it is much more important to aspire toward a noble goal than it is to achieve a lower goal.

The Bible talks about this in terms of faithfulness—to be faithful unto God's goal for our lives. Was the Apostle Paul a success? He died without leaving any material estate. He died with a headsman's axe separating his head from the body. Was Jesus a success? He was nailed to a cross and had naught but that which He had on His body. Yet everyone knows that they were great successes because their lives were aimed at the glorious object of the glory of God.

Many people today may aim at wealth and fame. Whether they achieve these or not and whether the whole world applauds them as a success, if their goals have not been consonant with the goals that God has given us in His Word, they are not a success at all. We are to seek first His kingdom and righteousness (Matthew 6:33). *"Be faithful unto death, and I will give you the crown of life."* (Revelation 2:10). The Apostle Paul said at the end of his life: *"I have kept the faith"* (2 Timothy 4:7). That is true success.

Dear Father, we live in a world that is obsessed with worldly success. Help us to not fall for this deception. Help us see that true success in this world involves overcoming this world through Your grace. Lord, give me strength for today to keep the faith…

BY GOD'S GRACE AND IN HIS STRENGTH,
WE CAN BE FAITHFUL UNTO DEATH.

JUNE 11

The Lost Art of Meditating on the Word

"I will meditate on Your precepts and keep my eyes on Your ways."
— Psalm 119:15

We need to begin and end the day reading the Word of God, memorizing the Word of God, hiding it in our hearts, and then meditating upon it through the day and night: in the morning, to fortify us for the battles of the day; at night, to close the day in the presence of our God who shall make even heavy seasons light through His Word. As we meditate upon the Word of God, He is sculpting us through that Word into His own image and making us what He would have us to be.

It is tragic that there are many people who determine to live according to only part of God's Word without seeing the big picture of God's will. They are like the aliens who were brought into Samaria after the people of Israel had been deported into Babylon. The Scriptures say that they feared the Lord Jehovah and served their own gods.

Many people will try to be a little bit righteous but then they want to reward themselves with a little bit of sin. With one foot in the church and the other foot in the world, they suppose they will find the best of both worlds. The truth is that they discover the best of neither, and they miss out on the blessings of good success, which God promises to those who will determine to do all that is written in His Word through obedience to the divine precepts.

Lord, forgive us for our intellectual laziness. Forgive us that we have all sorts of time for recreation and diversions, but no time for Your Word. Give us strength for today to let Your holy Word saturate our minds and hearts…

BY GOD'S STRENGTH, HE IS OUR "BEST THOUGHT BY DAY OR BY NIGHT."

JUNE 12

Hiding God's Word In Our Heart

"I have more understanding than all my teachers, for Your testimonies are my meditation."

— Psalm 119:99

It has been well said that prosperity is the natural consequence of acting on good advice. Many people have received advice from counselors concerning their financial lives—investments in stocks, bonds or businesses. They have acted on that advice only to discover that the advice given was poor and they destroyed their lives and ruined themselves in the process.

But the advice that is contained in the Word of God is invariably good advice. He who consults Omniscience will be helped by Omnipotence. That is a great truth we should remember. If we will meditate upon His Word day and night and determine to live our lives according to it, then God says that He will make our way prosperous and then we shall have good success.

Marion E. Wade, through meditating on the Scriptures, discovered that success in life would come through reading, meditating, and living according to them. He determined to do precisely that and became the founder and chairman of Servicemaster, Inc., one of the great corporations of this nation.

One popular Bible teacher, as a young man in school, wasn't doing well with his grades. Someone asked him if he would like to become wiser than all of his teachers. How? By meditating upon the Word of God and hiding it in his heart. And so he learned great passages of Scripture. He went on to teach popular seminars. By hiding the Word of God in our heart and meditating upon it, God will shape us into the person that He would have us to be.

Lord, thank You that You know all things and can do all things, yet You have taken the time to reveal Yourself in the pages of holy writ. Help us, Lord, to do our part in learning what You have shown us there. Forgive us for biblical illiteracy…

BY HIS STRENGTH, WE STUDY TO SHOW OURSELVES APPROVED.

Angels and Their Roles

"Then I looked, and I heard around the throne and the living creatures and the elders the voices of many angels, numbering ten thousand times ten thousand, and thousands of thousands..."

— Revelation 5:11

A comforting truth in the Scripture is that there are innumerable angels—these supernatural servants and messengers of God. There are myriads of myriads of kiliads of killiads, vast hundreds of millions of billions of angels, and there is no doubt that the angels of God outnumber the enemies of God. Not that they need to. If one of them can handle 185 thousand fully armed soldiers in one night (2 Kings 19:35), they don't need to outnumber them, but they do outnumber them.

One of the things about angels is that they are present a lot more than we realize. I'm sure they are all about us all of the time. They are sent to minister unto the heirs of salvation Hebrews tells us, and they are watching over us. They have a great interest in and they are commanded to watch over the people of God. Now what a wonderful thought that is. Nonetheless, we are not to worship them, but only God alone.

There are different times when human beings encounter angels, and they mistakenly bow down to worship them. Here is an example: *"I, John, am he who saw and heard these things. When I heard and saw them, I fell down to worship at the feet of the angel who showed me these things. But he said to me, 'See that you not do that. For I am your fellow servant, and of your brothers the prophets, and of those who keep the words of this book. Worship God!'"* (Revelation 22:8-9).

Father, thank You for Your servants, the angels. Thank You that we who are saved have received something they have never experienced, Your divine redemption. We praise You that You are so holy that the angels hide their faces from You...

BY GOD'S STRENGTH,
WE RECEIVE DIVINE HELP.

JUNE 14

A Time to Weep, A Time to Act

"So the king said to me, 'Why is your face troubled though you do not seem sick? This is nothing but a troubled heart.'"

— Nehemiah 2:2

Nehemiah was the cupbearer of the Persian king, Artaxerxes. He was among the Jews left in Persia who had originally been taken into captivity by the Babylonians. When Nehemiah got word that the walls of Jerusalem and its temple were in total ruins, he was very sad.

We might go out in this day as Nehemiah did and survey the spiritual wall around America; then ask ourselves the question: Is that wall broken down or is it in good condition? It was true in Nehemiah's day that if the wall was destroyed the temple would be destroyed and the faith of the people of God would be greatly set back. So today, if America falls, the Church of Jesus Christ will be greatly set back, since about 75 percent of all the money and manpower for the world mission cause of Jesus Christ originates from North America.

What did Nehemiah do when he heard about Jerusalem's broken walls? He wept. He fasted! He prayed! We need to pray that that wall around America may be built again.

Lastly, Nehemiah went to Jerusalem to work. God grant us the faith to pray and the faith to work that the nation may survive, that the Church may continue, and the Gospel of Christ may go out into all of the earth. There comes a time when we have to pause from the ordinary course of things to take a look at the walls which make all of the rest possible.

Lord, if ever a nation needed to turn back to You, such is the case with our land. Thank You that You care about the broken walls in our country. We ask for Your grace that there be true repentance and revival throughout our nation…

BY GOD'S STRENGTH, WE
WEEP AND THEN WE ACT.

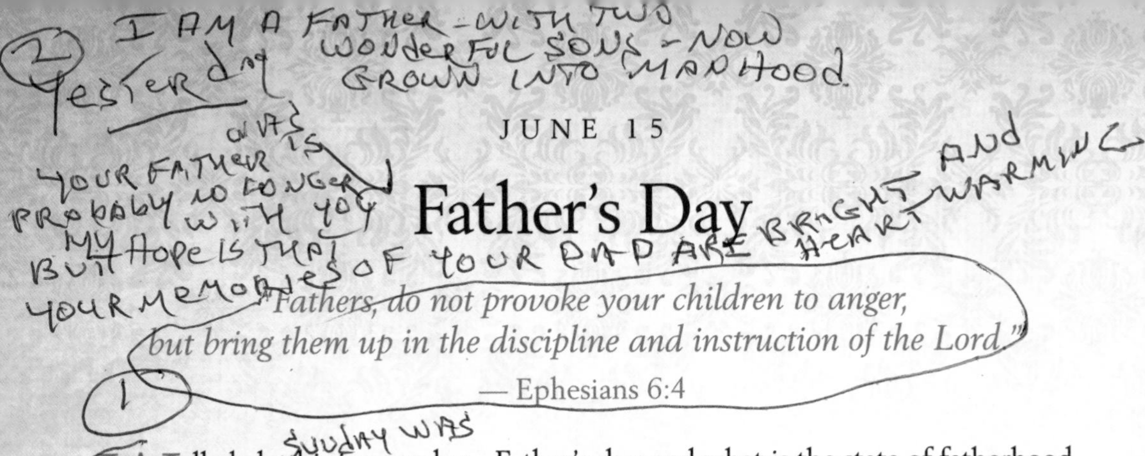

JUNE 15

Father's Day

"Fathers, do not provoke your children to anger, but bring them up in the discipline and instruction of the Lord."

— Ephesians 6:4

Well, dads, this is your day—Father's day, and what is the state of fatherhood in modern America today? One lady, a few decades ago, put it like this: "Women need a man like a fish needs a bicycle." That is what she said. That is what Gloria Steinem, one of the leading gurus of the feminist movement said.

And so, men, fathers, it seems that we are obsolete. We are unneeded. There has been a huge denigration of fatherhood and maleness in our country in our generation. It is even said that maleness is a recessive and repressive gene, and it's a big mistake. We'd be better off without any men in this world. I've got news for those ladies. There wouldn't be any civilization without men, but I guess they are working on that next.

America is suffering from a serious case of fatherlessness. An absentee or brutish father, an abusive father, a weak father, has an enormous impact upon the children. Scientists have discovered that you, gentlemen, as godly fathers, as faithful fathers, have an impact and an importance which is vastly greater than anybody imagined many years ago. Yes, it seems that fish need bicycles, doesn't it?

God has chosen earthly fathers to essentially be His representative on earth to their children. Therefore, let all Christian fathers strive to be great examples to our children.

Lord, help us to realize the importance of our relationship to our children. Help us to fulfill our vows that we made to bring up our children in the nurture and admonition of the Lord…

IN HIS STRENGTH, WE CAN REFLECT OUR HEAVENLY FATHER TO OUR CHILDREN.

God Keeps Watch Over His Own

"Then the king of Aram was fighting against Israel, and he took counsel with his servants, saying, 'At such and such a place will be my camp.'"

— 2 Kings 6:8

God uses different means to achieve His good purposes. In the days of Elisha the prophet, Ben-Hadad, the wicked king of Aram, wanted to go to war against Israel, the northern kingdom. So he sent one of his bands of marauders into Israel to take prisoners and gather substance and treasure. These marauding bands of Ben-Hadad were sent frequently into Israel. But all of sudden something had happened. Every time they would go to lay a trap for the king of Israel, he would be forewarned and he wouldn't be there.

Finally Ben-Hadad was much troubled. He thought there must be a traitor in their midst, but his captains assured him there was no traitor among them. Rather, it was that prophet Elisha who was being such a problem because he could hear the very words of the king of Aram, which were spoken in his bedchamber, in a distant land.

Now the fame of Elisha had spread since he had cured the general Naaman of Syria of his leprosy, and the word had gone all out. They knew he was the prophet of Israel, and so Ben-Hadad, foolishly, decided he was going to capture him.

Despite Israel's many shortcomings, God was keeping watch over His own. He used the man of God Elisha to prevent His people from being destroyed. God uses different means to protect His own. Only in heaven will we be able to see the myriad ways in which the Lord has protected us.

Lord God, Keeper of Israel, thank You for also keeping me. Thank You for keeping me from sin and keeping watch over my comings and goings. Most of all, thank You for keeping my soul safe for eternity…

BY GOD'S STRENGTH,
WE ARE KEPT SAFE.

JUNE 17

Chariots of Fire

"When a servant of the man of God rose early in the morning and went out, a force surrounded the city both with horses and chariots. And his servant said to him, 'Alas, my master! What will we do?'"

— 2 Kings 6:15

As noted yesterday, Ben-Hadad, the king of Aram, found out that Elisha the prophet was revealing to Israel Ben-Hadad's inner secrets for attacking Israel. Ben-Hadad decided to capture Elisha.

So he sent a large group of chariots and horses and soldiers to take Elisha. First the spies tell him that Elisha is in Dothan, and they make a march by night and then the sun rises. That morning, a young man who is a servant of Elisha goes out to look around, and he discovers in the valley all around are the horses and chariots and enemy soldiers. He is filled with terror, with trembling.

How many times in our life do we exclaim, *"Alas, my master! What will we do?"* There was no escape. They were completely surrounded. There was no army there, no soldiers, just two of them. They were totally outnumbered. They were helpless.

But Elisha said, *"Do not be afraid, for there are more with us than with them"* (2 Kings 6:16). Then he asked God to open his servant's eyes, so He did, *"and he saw that the mountain was full of horses and chariots of fire surrounding Elisha"* (2 Kings 6:17).

Dear friends, if that concept really filled our hearts and minds it would literally change our lives—most particularly in the difficult places of life. With the eyes of faith, Elisha could say, *"Do not be afraid, for there are more with us than with them."*

Sovereign Lord, we praise You that You know and see all. We ask that You give us strength for today to go about our lives with the assurance of Your sovereign watch over our lives. Forgive us for harboring secret fears and unbelief…

BY GOD'S STRENGTH,
WE ARE PROTECTED.

On Wealth and Poverty

"The generous soul will be made rich, and he who waters will be watered also himself."

— Proverbs 11:25

If I wanted to know about your real spiritual commitment, one of the means to check would be with how you handle money. It is an important indicator of our real, not just professed, priorities.

No moral system is complete unless it deals clearly and fully with the subject of wealth and the procurement and dealing with such. Since we live in a materialistic universe, it is quite evident that the individual cannot be moral unless he has food to eat, or should I put that more accurately, he cannot be moral or virtuous for very long unless he has food to eat.

Without clothing to wear it is not even possible to have civilization. In the case of the nation, it is vital that the nation rise beyond a bare subsistence level. There needs to be some people who do not have to engage in merely trying to get enough food and shelter to continue, but they may go on into education and the arts, music, and culture, and of course religion.

The Book of Proverbs has a great deal to say about the matter of wealth and our acquisition of it and its proper uses, as do more generally some of the other significant texts in the Bible.

Through Proverbs, God teaches us to be diligent workers, to plan ahead (while recognizing that the outcome is in His hands), to save as the ant does, and to be generous with everyone, especially the poor.

Lord, give me strength for today to be generous, to be genuinely concerned by other people's needs, and to help where I can. Help me to refresh others and thus be refreshed myself...

BY GOD'S STRENGTH, WE CAN LIVE GENEROUS LIVES.

JUNE 19

The Character of Elijah the Tishbite

"But what is the divine reply to Elijah? 'I have kept for Myself seven thousand men, who have not bowed the knee to Baal.'"

— Romans 11:4

Elijah the Tishbite—his name no doubt conjures up certain images. He was a man of the wilderness and the desert. John the Baptist was a prophet like unto Elijah. He was a man of solitude—a man whom God had prepared for a most difficult time. He was a man of unbending character. He was an austere man. A man whom perhaps many people would not find particularly likeable. He was what some people would call rigid in his beliefs. He was a diamond hard man for the hard days that were there.

To set this in context, in the early years of the reign of Ahab, he married Jezebel, who was the daughter of the king of Tyre and Sidon and she brought the Sidonian religion of the worship of Baal into Israel. This religion prospered and grew and Jezebel had set herself up to see Baalism replace the worship of Jehovah in Israel. She had killed a great many of the prophets of the Lord and provided hundreds of prophets of Baal. Baalism was rampant in Israel so that there were very few worshipers of the true God.

Elijah said that they have slain the prophets of the Lord and that he was the only one left, and they were seeking his life. But God encouraged him, as seen in the verse above, that there was still a faithful remnant.

May God help us to have resolute character to faithfully serve Him for our tasks at hand.

Righteous Father, we see our own country turning away from You and we too are discouraged by all the ungodliness. Thank You that there are many more than seven thousand in our land who have not bowed their knees to Baal...

BY GOD'S GRACE AND STRENGTH, WE CAN STAND FIRM AND STRAIGHT IN A CROOKED WORLD.

JUNE 20

The Radiance of the Church

"Who is this who looks forth like the dawn, fair as the moon, radiant as the sun, awesome as an army with banners?"

— Song of Solomon 6:10

A beautiful description of the church of Jesus Christ was uttered centuries before she was officially inaugurated at Pentecost. Although the Song of Solomon has much to teach about human love between a man and a woman, it is also ultimately the story of the relationship of the heavenly Bridegroom and His earthly bride—the church.

Who is she? We are the bride of Christ. Who is she who looks forth as the morning? In the midst of the blackness of night of despair and death, it is the church that brings the hope of the coming morning.

Even in the Old Testament when darkness still covered most of the earth, God's people were like the moon—that fair moon that gave borrowed light to a needy and hopeless world...a world that could see nothing beyond that hole in the ground where life had little meaning and no hope.

There was the church (as in God's congregation), even back then, that was fair as the moon. That is, of course, an idealized picture of the church. Unfortunately, there are many who would be seen merely as pockmarks on that moon; but, nevertheless, that is the picture He draws of the church.

And yet there came a glorious day when the night would fade away. On that bright and marvelous morning when Jesus Christ walked out of the tomb and the darkness of death faded away forever, the church became clear as the sun.

Lord of the church, we thank You, Jesus, for the miracle of the church. We praise You that by Your strength, she has endured through the centuries and will stand triumphant and glorious on the last day as Your beautiful and spotless bride...

BY GOD'S STRENGTH, THE BRIDE OF CHRIST PREPARES FOR THE BIG WEDDING.

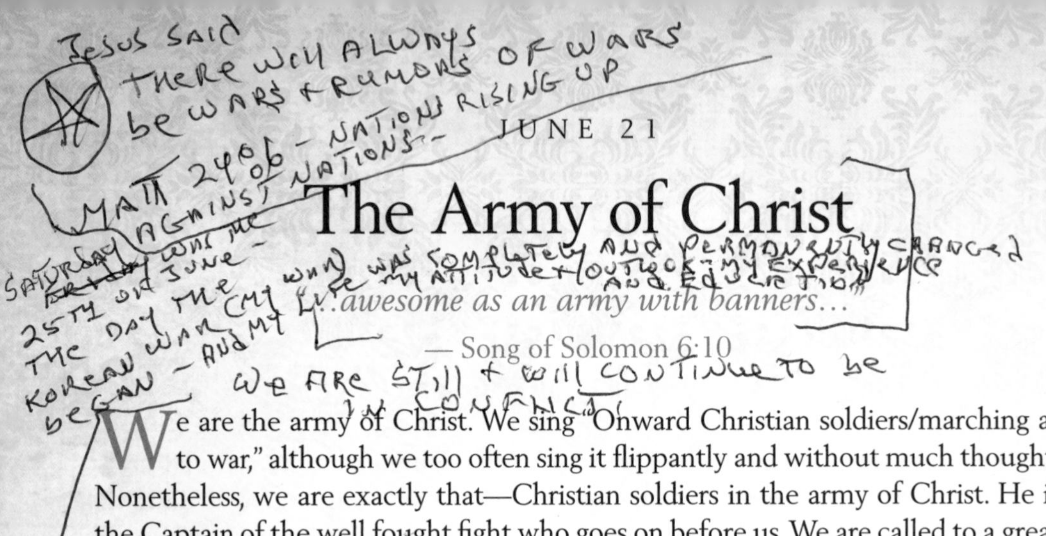

JUNE 21

The Army of Christ

"…awesome as an army with banners…"

— Song of Solomon 6:10

We are the army of Christ. We sing "Onward Christian soldiers/marching as to war," although we too often sing it flippantly and without much thought. Nonetheless, we are exactly that—Christian soldiers in the army of Christ. He is the Captain of the well fought fight who goes on before us. We are called to a great battle with the forces of darkness, with principalities and powers of the air.

We are called to go forth "awesome as an army with banners." We have a banner. It is the Gospel. The Church has many other banners. "Jesus Christ is Lord" was one of the earliest ones. "He will never leave us" is another. "He always leads us forth in triumph" is yet another. "He is King of kings and Lord of lords," is yet another. "He goes forth upon a white horse, conquering and to conquer" is yet another of the banners of Christ.

Have you noticed that with the armies of this world, sometimes, when they see the flag, the national emblem, lifted up, even soldiers who are fatigued will get new strength? So we, as the army of Christ are to go forth in that way. And we should indeed strike fear into those who are the enemies of God and the enemies of righteousness and godlessness—not because we would take up a literal sword, but because we would proclaim the Word of God to a lost world, which contains many elements that don't want to hear it.

Lord God, thank You for the transforming power of the Gospel. Thank You for transforming my heart and daily conforming me into Your own image. Thank You for making us part of Your story…

BY GOD'S STRENGTH, OUR HEARTS ARE TRANSFORMED.

JUNE 22

Fear Not

"For He has said: 'I will never leave you, nor forsake you.' So we may boldly say: 'The Lord is my helper; I will not fear. What can man do to me?'"

— Hebrews 13:5-6

How easily we are brought to fear. How often the dark clouds on the horizon seem to gather and they instill fear in our hearts. May I ask you this: Is there anything that is causing you to be afraid right now? Is there some dark cloud gathering on your life? Do you already feel the cold drizzling rain? Is there some terrible calamity that you feel is coming upon you?

Consider how God took care of Elijah, His choice servant, even when he was on the run from the wicked queen who demanded he be executed.

After the brook Cherith ran dry, God continued to care for him. And though the brook dried up, we see that God's resources had not dried up, and that God's love and care was shown in that He gave him the command as to precisely what he was to do. Even in the midst of this trial, God led him to Zarephath, which belonged to Sidon, and there a widow provided for him.

This widow was preparing to eat her last meal, but when Elijah came, God provided for her and her son, and also for Elijah. And he says, "Fear not." This is a great statement we have so often in Scripture—words that were so frequently on the lips of Jesus Christ Himself, and words which we often need to hear. God takes care of His own.

Lord Jesus Christ, Your perfect love casts out fear. Forgive us for limiting in our own minds what You can do. You are a big God and great and can do the impossible, and You care for us. Thank You that You are our helper.

BY GOD'S STRENGTH,
WE WALK IN COURAGE.

JUNE 23

Preparation for Big Tasks Through Little Ones

"The word of the LORD came to him, saying, Arise, go to Zarephath, which belongs to Sidon, and live there. I have commanded a widow there to provide for you.'"

— 1 Kings 17:7

Sometimes God prepares us with little tests to prepare us for the bigger ones to come. Elijah, one of the great Old Testament prophets, lived in Zarephath with a poor widow and her son, no doubt an unusual relationship for a man who had spent most of his life in the desert. He spent about three years there, about half that time there was no rain.

One day the widow's son grew sick and died, and the widow became very distraught. Elijah took the boy up to the loft where he stayed and laid his body out over the boy: *"Oh LORD, my God, I pray that You let this child's soul come into him again."* The Lord heard his prayer, and the boy began to breathe again. The great prophet brought the child down to his bereft mother, and there was rejoicing. She said, *"Now, because of this, I know indeed that you are a man of God, and that the word of the LORD in your mouth is truth!"*

This was all preparation for the great test that Elijah was to have in the great showdown on Mount Carmel with the hundreds of false prophets of Baal versus just him, representing Yahweh. Don't despise the little tests God puts in your path. He may well be preparing for larger tasks. Make sure you pass all the tests, or you might just have to take them over again.

Father, help me to not shun small tasks. For it is in the mastery of the basics, so often You shape our lives to take on the much larger assignments You have for us. Lord, give me the strength for today to make myself available to You for big tasks or small…

BY GOD'S STRENGTH, WE MAKE OURSELVES AVAILABLE TO HIM FOR TASKS, BIG OR SMALL.

 AMEN

JUNE 24

One of the Shortest Prayers

"But when he saw the strong wind, he was afraid, and beginning to sink, he cried out, 'Lord, save me!' Immediately Jesus reached out His hand and caught him, and said to him, 'O you of little faith, why did you doubt?'"

— Matthew 14:30-31

One of the shortest prayers in the Bible gets right to the point. It was said by Peter when he began to sink after briefly walking on water. When he looked away from Jesus and at the sea, then he sank and cried out, *"Lord, save me!"*

Is your life filled with troubles? Christ can help you. Some of you may not even know Him. If so, there will come a day when you will find yourself sinking into a different kind of sea—a sea of fire from which there is no help. Right now you are sinking in your sins. Peter prayed his shortest prayer, "Lord, save me," and instantly Christ stretched out His hand and saved him. If you have never experienced His salvation, if you will merely pray from your heart that prayer, "Lord, save me," you will find that Christ has stretched out His hands for you and will instantly save you. Whatever your sin may be, Christ can wash it all away.

If you do know Him, I hope you will learn that lesson. Whatever troubles you may face now or yet in the future, the great lesson is: Trust Christ, and He will teach you to walk on the waves of the storms of life.

Jesus Christ, our Lord and Savior, thank You that You can save us when we are drowning. Give me strength for today to keep my eyes focused on You and not the problems of life pressing in around me…

BY GOD'S STRENGTH, WE FIND SALVATION IN CHRIST.

JUNE 25

Follow the True God

"Elijah said to the prophets of Baal, 'Choose one bull for yourselves and prepare it first, for there are many of you, and call on the name of your god, but do not light a fire underneath.'"

— 1 Kings 18:25

In the days of Ahab, the wicked king of Israel, there was mass apostasy in the land. The people worshiped Baal instead of the true God. One day, Elijah called for a showdown on Mount Carmel between Baal and Jehovah. Elijah was one man versus 450 priests of Baal and 400 false prophets.

Elijah gathered the people and said, *"How long will you stay between two opinions? If the Lord is God, follow Him, but if Baal, then follow him"* (I Kings 18:21). Sadly, this compromising and equivocating spirit is still alive in the world today. How many there are who have one foot in the church and one foot in the world, and they cannot make up their mind whether to fully follow Christ or to fully seek for the things of the world.

The showdown involved two altars, both with sacrificed bullocks. One for Baal; the other for Jehovah. The priests of Baal went first. But as much as they prayed to him, called on him, and even cut themselves bloody, there was only silence from their god.

When it was Elijah's turn, he ordered them to drench the sacrifice on the altar of Jehovah. Then Elijah looked to God in prayer to show Himself. Suddenly, the fire of God fell out of the heavens and consumed the sacrifice and consumed the stones of the altar and consumed the dust and consumed the very water itself. This was a victory for belief in the true God. He alone is the one we should worship and not any false gods.

Great Jehovah, God of all gods, we praise You that You alone are worthy of worship. You alone have made us. Forgive us for straying from the path. Help us to be hot for You and not equivocating between worldliness and godliness…

BY GOD'S STRENGTH, WE FOLLOW HIM AGAINST THE TIDE OF THE WORLD.

JUNE 26

Am I the Only One?

"Still, I have preserved seven thousand men in Israel for Myself, all of whose knees have not bowed to Baal and whose mouths have not kissed him."

— 1 Kings 19:18

Elijah, the bold prophet of the Lord, thought that he was the only one left in Israel who worshiped the one true God. But God told him there were seven thousand who did not bow the knee to the false god, Baal.

In the great struggle that we have with the forces of unbelief, we need men and women of faith like Elijah. Men who have something of that unyielding spirit, that iron in their backbone that will enable them to stand up against the forces of evil and godlessness. Men and women who will see the great battle that is really before us.

But so many people in America today seem oblivious to the great spiritual struggle of our time. We need men and women of faith today who are not afraid to stand up and confront the unbelief of our day.

When Elijah confronted the forces of Baal on Mount Carmel, God answered powerfully with fire from the sky, proving that He alone was God. What consequences hang in the balance for this nation if the forces of godlessness succeed in completely overthrowing the followers of Christ? We thank God that in our day there are far more than seven thousand who have not bowed their knee to Baal. May God grant us that we may have something of the courage and something of the faith and something of the determination and steadfastness of Elijah in the critical hour in which we live today.

Lord, we marvel that You would have saved Sodom and Gomorrah for the sake of even ten righteous people there. As it is, You delivered Lot and his family. Lord, send a great revival that the millions of people who bear Your name will truly live for You…

BY GOD'S STRENGTH, WE BOW THE KNEE TO THE TRIUNE GOD ALONE.

AMEN

JUNE 27

Jezebel

"But there were none compared to Ahab, who sold himself to evil deeds in the sight of the LORD, which Jezebel his wife stirred up."

— 1 Kings 21:25

When you hear the name Jezebel, what images are conjured up in your mind? She personifies evil. Jezebel is certainly an intriguing character.

She is the Lady Macbeth of the Scripture. She was in many ways a remarkably strong woman. In fact she was the worst of all combinations. She was a very strong character and a very bad character. These are the types of people who wreak havoc on their centuries, and Jezebel most certainly did that.

She was the daughter of the king and high priest of the worship of Baal, the king of Sidon, a Phoenician city on the west coast of the Mediterranean by Tyre. Her father, Ethbaal, was the king of that city of the Phoenicians and he was also high priest of the temple of Baal. It was into this powerful home that Jezebel was born and molded. Molded as a woman who was born to rank and power, and secondly, as a woman who was taught all of the cruel and licentious and evil ways of Baal worship, which was a most venomous form of pagan superstition.

The name Jezebel means "unexalted," and she was a great defender and propagator of her religion, and here we see an example of the damage that an evil religion can bring. Unfortunately, there are many Jezebels around in our day. But one day their due punishment will come. Hopefully, some of them will repent and turn to Jesus before it is too late. Meanwhile, we pray for deliverance from her seductive spirit.

Oh God, purge the wickedness in our hearts. Remove from us the Jezebel spirit that seeks to pull us ever downward and away from You. We live in a land that glorifies Jezebel, without coming to grips her true end...

BY GOD'S STRENGTH,
WE ARE UNSEDUCEABLE.

JUNE 28

Prayer Helps Save the Constitution

...and call on Me in the day of trouble;
I will deliver you, and you will glorify Me."

— Psalm 50:15

The Constitution was written, as it says, "in the year of our Lord 1787." And during that long, very hot summer in Philadelphia, tempers flared and the progress was slow. Indeed, the fact that they ever finished the whole enterprise was a "miracle" to quote George Washington, for they almost gave up midway through.

The turning point came on June 28, when Ben Franklin rose to his feet and appealed to them to pray. He said, "In the beginning of the Contest with Great Britain, when we were sensible of danger, we had daily prayer in this room for Divine protection—Our prayers, Sir, were heard, & they were graciously answered... And have we now forgotten that powerful Friend? or do we imagine we no longer need His assistance?..."

He added, "I have lived, Sir, a long time, and the longer I live, the more convincing proofs I see of this truth—that God Governs in the affairs of men. And if a sparrow cannot fall to the ground without His notice, is it probable that an empire can rise without His aid?"

After that they attended a worship service at a local Christian church and prayed together. Much of the acrimony subsided. They were finally able to produce the Constitution. My friends, this is one example among many that testify that if it weren't for the Christian faith, there would not be an America as we know it. If you are facing a crisis in your life, can you honestly say you have prayed about it? Don't let prayer be a last resort, as almost happened with the Founding Fathers.

Thank You, Lord God, for blessing the undertaking of those godly men who gave us our nation by Your wisdom and guidance. Lord, give me strength for today to expand Your kingdom in our nation...

BY GOD'S STRENGTH, WE CAN RECOGNIZE HIS HAND IN THE RAISING UP AND TEARING DOWN OF NATIONS.

Ahab Went to the Wrong Place to Choose a Wife

"The sins of Jeroboam the son of Nebat were seen as minor for him to walk in, for he took Jezebel the daughter of Ethbaal, king of the Sidonians, as his wife and went and served Baal and worshipped him."

— 1 Kings 16:31

Ahab, king of the Israelites, chose a wicked bride, Jezebel, a Syro-Phoenician princess. She was bad and her father was bad. Her children were bad. And her husband was bad. And her grandchildren were bad. She produced calamity in whatever she did, and everything she touched was poisoned by her false belief.

She was part of a very prosperous and highly sophisticated people. The Phoenicians are the ones that gave us the alphabet. The Tyrians and Sidonians had great navies, since they had access to the Mediterranean, and they accomplished many things, like establishing Carthage, and sailing to Spain and Britain.

But they were molded according to their religion and therefore they were a very bold and cruel people. It was into this nest of the Priest King of Sidon that the weak and wicked king of Israel, Ahab looked for his mate. Now this was a gross mistake.

It may very well have looked to be politically a very attractive move. But, it was a violation of the law of God, which had forbidden the Israelites to take wives of the Canaanites or the other unbelievers. That has always been God's law; we are not to be unequally yoked together with unbelievers. A sin like this can have a negative impact on everyone, and in Ahab's case, on the nation.

Lord, forgive us for serious compromise on major issues. Forgive us for allowing ourselves to be allied with the world in the wrong way. Give us strength for today that we might glorify You in all our relationships…

BY GOD'S STRENGTH, WE CAN STAY FAITHFUL TO CHRIST, INCLUDING IN OUR KEY RELATIONSHIPS.

JUNE 30

To Sin Against God's Wisdom Is to Sin Against Oneself

"...but he who sins against me wrongs his own soul; all those who hate me love death."

— Proverbs 8:36

In Proverbs 8, God's wisdom cries aloud in the street and beckons men and women to live their lives according to His precepts. She then concludes with today's verse. I think that there is a great truth found here. It is a very far reaching truth.

For example, none of us would ever think of pitting ourselves against the law of gravity. One would not climb up the Empire State Building and jump off just to see if sometimes it doesn't work. We know that it works.

One knows that if we violate it, the law will break us every time. The moral law is not different or elastic; it is one. The law is all one given by the same Law Giver and therefore we can but break ourselves against that law. Although Jesus Christ has taken the eternal punishment—the wrath of God—for our breaking those laws, how slow we are to realize that when we sin against the law of God we invariably bring the chastening and displeasure of God upon ourselves. Have we not been foolish? Have we not been slow to realize that the law is all one and that we can no more break the moral law of God than we can break the physical laws of God? All we can do is break ourselves upon them by violating His laws. May God grant us greater wisdom to experience the joy of obedience to Him.

Lord, thank You that You are the source of all wisdom. This day we choose life and eschew death. Thank You that You are the Lord of life. Give us strength for today to follow after You and not break Your laws...

BY GOD'S STRENGTH, WE CAN EMBRACE HIS WISDOM.

Is Evolution a Fact?

"For if through the trespass of one man [Adam] many died, then how much more has the grace of God and the free gift by the grace of the one Man, Jesus Christ, abounded to many."

— Romans 5:15

Jesus is the second Adam. Through His death He undid the sin of the first Adam for all who believe. But some people today assume that the first Adam is a myth; therefore, they reject the second Adam and His gift of eternal life. They assume that human origin via evolution is a proven fact.

Well, did Darwin present overwhelming facts? It has been noted by scientists that he did not by any means ever demonstrate the origin of any species. He simply showed how there were variations in species. In his classic book, *The Origin of Species*, the fourth chapter is the key chapter of the book. It deals with natural selection.

Natural selection is a scientific fact, but as one observer noted about a generation before Darwin, it removes the oddities that occur on either side of the spectrum of the species, thus preserving the order of species.

But Darwin tried to transform natural selection into a process that creates new species, and there is not the slightest bit of evidence that such a thing has ever happened. In that one chapter, Darwin uses phrases like this 187 times: "may have been," "is supposed to," "perhaps," "it is probable," and "I have assumed." They are not scientific facts at all. Isn't it tragic that many people reject the fact of Christ to choose instead mere hypothesizing?

Lord God, may we not create any false assumptions about You or Your creation. You have said repeatedly that You are the Creator of heaven and earth, and we believe that You are who You say You are. Increase our trust in You…

BY GOD'S STRENGTH, WE CAN SEE CLEARLY THE REALITY OF BOTH ADAMS.

The Importance of Fellowship

"And they continued steadfastly in the apostles' doctrine and fellowship, and in breaking of bread, and in prayers."
— Acts 2:42

My friends, we are the witnessing community of Jesus Christ, and we today live in a world where it is possible that we shall one day pay the same price for that witness that the early Christians paid in the arena. What a oneness is created when we realize that among us are those who also are placing their lives upon the line as they boldly witness for the living Christ.

Furthermore, we are the branches, and Christ is the vine, and, thus, we know that there is the same life-giving power flowing through each one of us. We are the body and Christ is the head. We are members of the same body.

All of these are but a few of the pictures the Bible paints of this strange fellowship, this koinonia, this partnership, this oneness, this mystical union we have in Jesus Christ. Ah, my friends, there is nothing like it in the entire world. Despite our differences, there is some ineffable union of heart and mind that has been created by Jesus Christ.

One third of all Americans are involved in small groups today, which is astounding. That is tens of millions of people, and 60 percent of those are in the church. Christians can find that much of their strengthening, their discipleship, and their spiritual growth take place in these caring, sharing, praying, Bible studying groups, which are going to build up men and women to do the work of Christ better than ever before.

Dear Lord, thank You for adopting us into Your family, the largest family in the world. Thank You for the millions of brother and sisters in Christ with whom we are one. Give us strength for today, Lord, to serve You by serving Your body on earth…

BY GOD'S STRENGTH, WE CAN BE
ONE IN CHRIST WITH OTHER CHRISTIANS.

For Such a Time as This

"But he disdained to lay hands on only Mordecai, since they had told him of the people of Mordecai. So Haman sought to destroy all the Jews throughout the whole kingdom of Ahasuerus."

— Esther 3:6

At one time, the fate of the entire Jewish people rested in the hands of one young Jewish woman, Esther. This is the story of that short book in the Old Testament and how God in His sovereignty saved the Jews. But if Esther had given in to her natural inclinations, they might have perished, or God would have saved them through some other means, but she and her family would have perished.

The wicked Haman had convinced King Xerxes of the Medo-Persian Empire that all the Jews must be destroyed on a certain day. The laws of the Medes and the Persians were irreversible. Haman selected that day of massacre by the lot. The plural for the Hebrew word for lot is purim, and it is the Feast of Purim that the Jews continue to celebrate until this day, remembering when their people were saved.

Esther's cousin Mordecai told her that she must go see the king, but she told him that it was absolutely against the law—she could be executed for going to see him unbidden. But Mordecai said to her, *"For if you remain silent at this time, protection and deliverance for the Jews will be ordained from some other place, but you and your father's house shall be destroyed. And who knows if you may have attained royal position for such a time as this?"* (Esther 4:14). These are classic words. At one time or another, every Christian, down through the centuries, has no doubt asked, "Is this not true for me as well?"

Lord, You who are our protector, give me strength for today to do what is right rather than what is easy. Give me Your sure protection and thank You for the time and place in which You have set me…

IN GOD'S STRENGTH, WE CAN STAND BEFORE KINGS.

Independence Day

"For freedom Christ freed us. Stand fast therefore and do not be entangled again with the yoke of bondage."

— Galatians 5:1

In 1776, fifty-six men, representing three million people, voted to adopt one of the most revolutionary documents in history: the Declaration of Independence. If the fledgling colonies succeeded in defending themselves from the most powerful nation on earth, it was worth the risk. If they failed, these fifty-six men were signing their death warrants.

The level of the signers' commitment and their willingness to sacrifice in order to secure liberty under God's law is evident in the final words of their declaration: "And for the support of this declaration, with a firm reliance on the protection of divine providence, we mutually pledge to each other our lives, our fortunes, and our sacred honor."

They trusted in God and laid it all on the line. It will take courage, sacrifice, and, above all, trust in the Lord to turn things around in this country.

The late Dr. M. E. Bradford of the University of Dallas researched the founding fathers, including the Christian commitments of the signers of the Declaration of Independence. He concluded that of the fifty-six men who signed the nation's birth certificate, definitely fifty, maybe fifty-two, were Trinitarian Christians. Other scholars note that 29 of them had the equivalent of seminary degrees.

Paul Johnson, author of *A History of the American People*, says, "There is no question that the Declaration of Independence was, to those who signed it, a religious as well as a secular act..." Thank God for our freedom, which was bought by God and by their sacrifice.

Thank You, God, for this nation and the freedom secured for us by the signers of the Declaration of Independence. May we always depend on You and Your Providence. Help us, Lord, to do our part to work toward renewal of this great country...

BY GOD'S STRENGTH, WE CAN PLEDGE TO HIM OUR LIVES, OUR FORTUNES, AND OUR SACRED HONOR.

Study to Show Yourself Approved

"Study to show yourself approved by God, a workman who need not be ashamed, rightly dividing the word of truth."

— 2 Timothy 2:15

God has made us unique creatures in this world. We are the only beings on this planet who have been given an intellect; all others operate by blind instinct. God expects us to use our minds. If we do not, we will stand in the judgment and give an account of the reason that we have not. Now I think that very often people do not consider that mental laziness is a sin. There are some people that say that they have no desire to learn much, and as soon as they get out of school, for all practical purposes they stop learning anything of significance. They suppose that this is just like some people like carrots and some people don't, and they don't particularly care about learning. The Bible says this is wrong.

The Bible also makes it clear that if a person does not endeavor with this eagerness to learn to seek after the things of God—after that practical wisdom that comes from God, that he, too, is a fool and has missed the point of Jesus Christ. Now there are those who deny this. Jesus says wisdom is justified of her children, and I think that the best of interpreters agree that here is an allusion to the passage in Proverbs 8, where wisdom incarnate cries out in the streets for people to listen and heed. Some people believe this is a preincarnate Christ who is the incarnate logos of God. We should be lifelong students of the living Word of God.

Omniscient God, You who know all things, give me strength for today to keep learning and growing and using the mind You gave me. Thank You that You are the source of all wisdom. I ask that I might be wise in the matters of Your kingdom...

BY GOD'S STRENGTH, WE CAN ACQUIRE WISDOM.

JULY 6

Come to the Feast

"Wisdom has built her house…She has killed her beasts, she has mixed her wine, she has also furnished her table… 'Come, eat of my bread'"

— Proverbs 9:1-2, 5

In Proverbs 8 and 9, we see wisdom personified. In the latter chapter, she holds a feast and sends forth servants to invite others to come. In the Greek *Septuagint** we find exactly the same words as are found in the New Testament where Jesus talks about a feast and servants are sent out to compel others to come in. So I think that there is a biblical reason for believing this applies to Christ.

Some object to the idea that wisdom personified in Proverbs could be a preincarnate Jesus since it is personified in the female gender and Jesus, of course, is male. This cannot be, they say. Well, I do not believe that God is a sexist, and I think that is of no problem to Him. If anyone has a particular difficulty with that, let me remind you that the Hebrew word for spirit is feminine, as is the Greek word for spirit. So I don't have a problem with the notion that wisdom is personified here in the female form, and it still relates to Jesus.

God is preparing a great feast for us. We are welcome to come. But some, blinded by their pride, choose not to come to His great feast and, thus, will miss out.

God of plenty, thank You for inviting me to Your feast. I gladly accept the invitation, first to the Wedding Feast of the Lamb and then to this feast of wisdom. Lord, give me strength for today to always seek Your wisdom and guidance…

IN GOD'S STRENGTH, WE CAN FEAST ON HIS RICHES.

---

*The *Septuagint* was the translation of the Old Testament from Hebrew into Greek made by 70 (hence the name "Septuagint") scholars from Alexandria, Egypt. It was begun in the late 200's B.C. and was finished about a century and a half before Jesus was born.

JULY 7

Always Seek Wisdom, No Matter How "Mature"

"Does not wisdom cry out, and understanding lift up her voice?...
She cries out at the gates, at the entry of the city,
at the entrance of the doors..."

— Proverbs 8:1, 3

In the book of Proverbs, we find an interesting contrast between two women. One represents wisdom and life. The other represents sin and death. In Proverbs 8, we see what wisdom does, contrasted with what the strange woman in the preceding chapter does. In chapter 7 we see the strange woman in the twilight, in the evening, in the black and dark night.

There she is crouching about in the doorways, from corner to corner, lying in wait to catch the unwary. In stark contrast to this, in the broad daylight, standing at the entrance way to the city in the open places at the gates and at the door, wisdom cries to all to come. There are no whispered intimations in the ear, no secret agreements, but rather there is an open declaration, and invitation to all. So too, Jesus boldly proclaimed His Word for all to hear and said to His accusers, *"Why do you ask Me?... I spoke openly to the world. I always taught in the synagogue and in the temple, where the Jews always meet, and I said nothing in secret"* (John 18:21, 20).

The message of wisdom is for all of us, even those who think they are so mature they no longer need to heed the message. Too many times people will go through many years of Sunday School and then they grow up and they think they don't need it any longer. But God wants us to continue to seek after His wisdom.

Wise and wonderful Savior, thank You for the openness and clarity of Your Word. It is not a secret message for the select few. It is freely proclaimed to all of us...

BY GOD'S STRENGTH, WE CAN CONTINUE TO GROW IN KNOWLEDGE AND WISDOM.

JULY 8

Who Is Wise?

"Where is the wise? Where is the scribe? Where is the debater of this age? Has God not made the wisdom of this world foolish?"

— 1 Corinthians 1:20

There is a great contrast in the Bible between the wise and the foolish. Proverbs 8:5 says, "*O you simple, understand wisdom, and you fools, be of an understanding heart.*" We see that not only the wise and mature, but also the simple and the foolish, are invited to come and hear. This is in stark contrast to the Greek philosophical schools where only the wise and the best were invited to come and partake of the teachings of those schools. But here is a broad invitation for all to come.

Do you consider yourself to be foolish, to be simple? Then come and understand wisdom. I suppose the height of wisdom is to realize how vast is our folly. The greatest strength is to realize how infinite is our weakness and the greatest righteousness is to know that we have none at all, that Christ is our righteousness. Even as He, according to the New Testament, is wisdom. He is made unto us wisdom and righteousness and redemption.

Wisdom is so great that it is desirable even among precious things of this world. Is the Word of God, the wisdom of God, the wisdom that is in Jesus Christ, better to you than all of the other things which you may desire?

Jesus, joy of man's desiring, I do desire You and Your wisdom. I am a foolish mortal in great need of You. Keep me from sinning. Keep me from making mistakes and keep me on the right path…

BY GOD'S STRENGTH, WE DESIRE THE RICHES OF WISDOM.

JULY 9

Spiritual Selftalk

"Why, my soul, are you cast down? Why do you groan within me? Wait for God; I will yet thank Him, For He is my deliverance and my God."

— Psalm 42:5

When we read this verse, we might think, "The poor psalmist. He has come to the place where he is talking to himself." But the Word of God would have us understand that he is doing exactly what he ought to do.

Dr. Martyn Lloyd-Jones, one of the greatest preachers in England in the second part of the twentieth century, says this in his excellent work, *Spiritual Depression, It's Cause and Cure*: "Most of your unhappiness in life is due to the fact that you are listening to yourself rather than talking to yourself."

Remarkable? Most of your unhappiness in life comes from listening to yourself. Think about it. You wake up in the morning and right away there are streams of thought coming into your mind. You haven't invited them, you didn't ask for them, you are not consciously doing anything to produce them; they just come. They start talking to you. It is the old nature, discounting what God can do in your life.

The psalmist, says Lloyd-Jones, "stands up and says, 'Self, listen for a moment. I will speak to you.'" God's Word tells us, *"Do not fear, for I am with you"* (Genesis 26:24 and throughout Scripture), and *"I will never leave you, nor forsake you"* (Hebrews 13:5). *"Be of good cheer"* is repeated in Matthew, Mark, John, and Acts. God also reassures us, *"…all things work together for good to those who love God, to those who are called according to His purpose"* (Romans 8:28). Let us allow God to renew our minds by dwelling on His promises.

Dear Lord, give me strength for today to listen to the new person in Christ within me, instead of my old, carnal nature. Let me rejoice as I consider Your promises in Christ Jesus, which are guaranteed by Your flawless character…

BY GOD'S STRENGTH, WE ARE PEOPLE OF GOOD CHEER.

Overcoming Life's Obstacles

"For I am not ashamed of the gospel of Christ. For it is the power of God for salvation to everyone who believes..."
— Romans 1:16

Have you ever noticed how any time we try to pursue something worthwhile, we always seem to be beset by a number of obstacles? Look at Paul's goal to spread the Gospel in the first century; a goal made possible by Rome's incredible roadway system, by the unifying language of everyday Greek, by the Pax Romana, and by the many synagogues in far-flung places that often became Stop 1 in his entrance to a new town.

His efforts to spread the Gospel over most of the Roman world have continued until the Gospel has been spread into every nation on the face of the earth. If you asked Paul how he was doing, I don't think he would have told you the terrible travails he had undergone in persecution and in difficult travels. Today, we think nothing of getting on a superhighway or a jetliner and usually arriving at our destination in comfort or ease—not so in antiquity in most cases. But Paul wouldn't generally have told you the suffering he underwent in his travels. Instead, Paul chose to look at things through the eye of faith, thus, in effect, he was going from glory to glory.

Anyone who thinks that it was easy for Paul ought to read 2 Corinthians 11, which shows that he faced one problem after another. Anything worthwhile may be fraught with difficulties. But those difficulties may not be a sign that you're on the wrong track but rather on the right track after all.

Father God, You know how easy it is for us to give up when we face obstacles. Help me to see them as a sign that I'm doing something worthwhile and not an indication that I should quit...

BY GOD'S STRENGTH, WE CAN OVERCOME
THE OBSTACLES IN OUR PATH.

With God…

"But Jesus looked at them and said, 'With men this is impossible, but with God all things are possible.'"

— Matthew 19:26

One of the great saints of the last century, A. W. Tozer, said that if someone were able to extract from your mind the thoughts you have when you think of God, they could very accurately predict your spiritual future, because people rise no higher than their concept of God.

Certainly the disciples of the first century had an exalted view of God. Their God could do anything. To paraphrase them: "O Lord God, Creator of heaven and earth, nothing is too hard for You." And so, therefore, they set out on a glorious task. Here they were, eleven men (i.e., the twelve minus Judas). God told them to do a little simple thing: Go change the whole world—and they set out to do it. They have, in great measure, already succeeded. These men who were so absorbed in the characteristics and attributes of God were able to do fantastic things.

The late Bill Bright, the founder of Campus Crusade for Christ, told us to remember that as believers in Christ we are called to live supernatural lives. We are no longer ordinary people, but our lives are now joined with the One who spoke and the worlds were framed. We belong to the One whom God has given all authority over heaven and earth, and He has come to dwell in our lives with all of His resurrection power.

Bright said that living a supernatural life begins with thinking supernatural thoughts. Pray for supernatural results and watch God do great things.

All Powerful Omnipotent God, I praise You for Your might. Give me a clear picture of You and let not my finite mind distort Your image…

BY GOD'S STRENGTH, WE CAN WORSHIP HIM AS HE IS.

JULY 12

The Father of Modern Missions

"He said to them, 'Go into all the world, and preach the gospel to every creature.'"

— Mark 16:15

One of my great heroes of the past is William Carey (1761-1834) of England. I trust that every Christian knows who he was. Carey was a poor uneducated man who did nothing but fix shoes, and yet he had a dream. On the wall in front of him in his shop he had placed a map—a map of the world. He sat there fixing soles, but dreamt of fixing souls in lands where the Gospel was not known.

Carey was laughed at. He was told to shut up and sit down, but he wouldn't do it because there was a dream. And so he set out on a long trip to India. He launched something 200 years ago called "The World Missionary Movement." To take the words of Winston Churchill and apply them much more accurately, we can most certainly say that "never did so many owe so much to so few." With so little support and help, missionaries have done the greatest work in the history of the world. Today, 200 years later, the work William Carey dreamt of has been started and planted in virtually every nation on earth because he had a dream and with God's help, he fulfilled it.

Carey learned a number of languages. He wrote a dictionary in English and the Indian language of Bengali. He translated the Bible into numerous different languages. He became a scholar. He let God use him fully for the Gospel. May God help all of us to fulfill the task He has for us, one that helps spread His eternal kingdom.

God, Giver of dreams, give me dreams and visions for You. Let me fulfill the dreams You have planted in my heart. Thank You for the ones that have already been fulfilled…

BY GOD'S STRENGTH, WE CAN FULFILL THE DREAMS HE GIVES US.

AMEN

JULY 13

The Christian Adventure

"These men who have turned the world upside down have come here also..."

— Acts 17:6

Several decades ago, I read a statement in a book entitled *The Strong Name*. It was written by a professor at the University of Glasgow. His name was James Stewart. No, he never went to Hollywood—he had greater things on his mind. This is what he said:

> If we could but show the world that being committed to Christ is no tame, humdrum sheltered monotony, but the most exciting adventure the human spirit could ever know, then those who have been standing outside looking askance at Christ would come crowding in to pay allegiance, and we may well see the greatest spiritual revival since Pentecost.

I wonder what your friends think of your Christianity, of your religion? Is it some tame, humdrum sheltered monotony? Sadly, for some of us our friends could say, "That describes it pretty well." Or is it the most exciting adventure the human spirit can ever know? Well, I'll tell you, it's going to inevitably be the first and not the latter unless you believe Paul's text: *"I can do all things through Christ who strengthens me"* (Philippians 4:13 NKJV).

Peter once said to Jesus: *"See, we have left everything and followed You. What then shall we have?"* Jesus replied, *"...everyone who has left houses or brothers or sisters or father or mother or wife or children or fields for My name's sake shall receive a hundred times as much and inherit eternal life"* (Matthew 19:27, 29). Following Jesus is an adventure in this life, and as it has been said, "the rewards are out of this world."

Dear God, thank You for creating us for adventure and great stories. Help us to trust You to see us safely through the endeavors set before us. Thank You for the opportunities You give us. Help us to undertake them with all our might...

BY GOD'S STRENGTH, OUR LIVES CAN BE EXCITING.

JULY 14

Affections Above or Below?

"Set your affection on things above, not on things on earth."
— Colossians 3:2

The Bible tells us that we are to believe that we have the promises of God. If God has promised it, it is as good as done and we are by faith to believe that it has come to pass; so in a very real sense, that is biblical. However, the Scripture also tells us that we are not to set our affections on things here below, but are to set our affections on things above.

I remember a young man, like so many today, whose whole life centered on a really great-looking sports car. That piece of machinery had become his idol. He did all but bow to the ground before the car or light votive candles and sprinkle a little incense on the candles in front of it. God has made us for greater things than some pile of metal. In a few years that young man's fancy automobile will be fit for nothing but a junk pile.

God has made you an immortal soul; He has fitted you for the stars. Too many are groveling in the mud flats of materialism. Set your affections on things above—attempt great things for God. You know what? He might just give you that pile of bolts and metal. As C. S. Lewis once put it, "Aim for heaven and you get earth thrown in. Aim for earth, and you get neither." God may be pleased to give you all sorts of things, but your heart should be set on things above.

Dear Heavenly Father, set my heart on things above today. Let my treasure be on things above. Let me truly value the things of Your kingdom. I thank You for my earthly things and ask that, although I possess them, that they not possess me…

BY GOD'S STRENGTH, OUR HEARTS
ARE SEALED FOR HEAVEN.

JULY 15

Self-Confidence or Christ-Confidence?

"Some trust in chariots, and some in horses,
but we will remember the name of the LORD our God."
— Psalm 20:7

One of the best known stories of the Bible is that of David and Goliath. For days on end, the armies of the Israelites faced the armies of the Philistines. And daily Goliath taunted the Israelite army, which cringed before this giant of a man who was nine and a half feet tall. All of their courage and their PMA (Positive Mental Attitude) had fizzled out. Their self-confidence had reached its limit, and it ended up in despair.

Then along came this stripling named David, who went out to take on Goliath saying, *"I come at you in the name of the LORD of Hosts."* There is such a thing as God-confidence, or Christ-confidence, which is infinitely better than self-confidence, though that is better than no confidence at all. With "Christ-confidence," we can do all things. Jesus said, *"…if you have faith and do not doubt… if you say to this mountain, 'Be removed and be cast into the sea,' it will be done"* (Matthew 21:21).

David had practice as a shepherd, slaying a lion and a bear that threatened the sheep. But his real trust was in the Lord, and that is why he prevailed. And so can we—if we trust in the Lord.

Lord Jesus, thank You that I can always trust in You. Make me into such a person as You can entrust with Your work. Help me to never put confidence in the flesh, but in You and Your power and strength…

BY GOD'S STRENGTH, WE CAN
FACE THE GIANTS IN OUR LIVES.

JULY 16

More Than We Ask or Think

"Now to Him who is able to do exceedingly abundantly beyond all that we ask or imagine, according to the power that works in us..."

— Ephesians 3:20

God is the God of "much more." Consider the following verses from His Word. For example, here is 2 Chronicles 25:9 (NKJV): *"And the man of God answered, 'The Lord is able to give you much more than this.'"* "Much more than this" is a favorite phrase of God's Word:

- *"...will He not much more clothe you, O you of little faith?"* (Matthew 6:30).
- *"...how much more will your Father who is in heaven give good things..."* (Matthew 7:11).
- *"For if...we were reconciled to God through the death of his Son, how much more, being reconciled, shall we be saved by His life"* (Romans 5:10).
- *"For if through the trespass of one man many died, then how much more has the grace of God and the free gift by the grace of the one Man, Jesus Christ, abounded to many"* (Romans 5:15).
- *"But the law entered, so that sin might increase, but where sin increased, grace abounded much more"* (Roman 5:20).

And on and on and on the texts go.

Lord God, we pray that You who are the fulfiller of dreams, that You will bring greater achievements for the church of Jesus Christ around the world, according to Your good and perfect will. Give me strength for today to be useful in Your kingdom...

BY HIS STRENGTH, WE WILL EXPERIENCE "MUCH MORE."

AMEN

From Here to Eternity

"Those who are wise shall shine as the brightness of the expanse of heaven, and those who turn the many to righteousness as the stars forever and ever."

— Daniel 12:3

In this verse, Daniel gives a goal to set your heart on. Lift up your eyes. You are not one of the animals of the field to be satisfied with the husks on the ground, but lift up your eyes unto the stars.

Decades ago, I went into a suite of offices for some purpose. I don't remember where it was or why I was there, but I remember one thing: When I got ready to leave and had finished my business, I was in something of a hurry, and I opened a door to the hall and stepped into a 3 x 4 foot broom closet. I instantly stepped out again, shamefacedly closed the door, and looked for the proper exit. I probably was in that broom closet for between one and two seconds.

Wouldn't it be sad if I spent the rest of my life talking about that broom closet where I spent, at most, two seconds of my life? May I say to you, this world to which you give all of your energies and time and thought and effort will be less than two seconds of your eternal life. It has well been said that many people spend more time planning a two-week vacation than they plan where they are going to spend eternity. God has made you for forever. Some people cannot see beyond next year.

God of all creation, give me strength to lift my eyes to the stars, and as I count them, as Abraham did, let my faith and hope grow. Let me be a part of bringing people to righteousness and of imparting Your wisdom to others...

BY GOD'S STRENGTH, WE LIFT OUR EYES TO THE STARS.

JULY 18

Your Philosophy of Life

"For to me to live is Christ, and to die is gain."

— Philippians 1:21 KJV

What is your philosophy of life? You say you don't even have one? Oh, yes, you do. Everyone has one. Some have explicitly stated them or written them down. For most people, however, I am afraid they are more subconscious. These people may not even know they have one, but may I say that the less consciously it is declared, the more fully it controls a person's life—even unbeknownst to them. You have a philosophy of life. What is it?

The world and the kingdom of Christ define success differently. To me, the only success that really matters is that which is of eternal value. Consider the example of Paul. He was not only a great apostle, a missionary, apologist, evangelist, statesman, and preacher, but he was also an unparalleled expert in the art of living. He had discovered the secret of a life worth living. He states it in a very succinct, terse, sententious form: *"For to me to live is Christ"* (Philippians 1:21 KJV). There it is. Seven, simple, single-syllable words: "For to me to live is Christ." There is a divine philosophy of life given to us by our Maker. I do not believe anyone could improve upon it, even if volumes were written.

Here is the great discovery of the secret to a successful life. Paul had discovered the art of living: "For to me to live is Christ." And what does that mean when life is over? He finishes the verse: "…and to die is gain."

Lord Jesus, who is my life, thank You for this beautiful philosophy of life. Thank You for being my life, my light, and my salvation. Thank You that all I need I have in You…

BY GOD'S STRENGTH,
CHRIST CAN BE OUR LIFE.

JULY 19

The Conversion of Paul

"Christ Jesus came into the world to save sinners, of whom I am the worst."

— 1Timothy 1:15

Saul of Tarsus was born into a well-to-do family. His father was a Pharisee, and Saul followed in his footsteps. He was given the finest education. He was sent to Jerusalem to sit at the feet of Gamaliel. There he outstripped all of his countrymen in the religion of his fathers. He was blameless in the sight of men. He had a brilliant and quick mind.

When the crisis of Christianity broke in Jerusalem, he was the one who was going to be their champion. He persecuted Christians, hauling them into jail, torturing and killing them, and causing them to flee from the city of Jerusalem until there was now little fuel left for the martyrs' fires that he wished to start.

He obtained letters from Caiaphas, who was still the High Priest, and set out to find and exterminate these Christians. He was, indeed, going to reverse the Great Commission. Jesus had said to go into all the world and make disciples of all the nations (Matthew 28:19). Saul was going to go into all the world and make sure the Gospel would not be preached to any creature.

Shakespeare says in Hamlet, "There's a divinity that shapes our ends, Roughhew them how we will." Saul was about to discover that Providence as he set out to destroy the church. Christ transformed him on the road to Damascus and changed him into perhaps the greatest missionary ever—the Apostle Paul. When Christ truly changes you, you are not the same anymore.

Lord, You who changed Saul into Paul, thank You for the transforming power You have over human hearts. Thank You for making me Your child and using me in Your kingdom. I pray today for those I love, whose hearts are still unregenerate. Lord, save them…

BY GOD'S STRENGTH,
SINNERS ARE CONVERTED.

The Woman at the Well

"Many of the Samaritans of that city believed in Him because of the word of the woman who testified..."

— John 4:39

When people encounter Jesus, their lives are never the same again. We can see that in the instance of the woman at the well. This well was near Sychar in the region of the Samaritans who were hated by the Jews because they were half-breeds.

Jesus and His disciples were traveling through that region, and the disciples went off on an errand. Jesus met a certain woman at that well. She was a woman of ill repute. You may recall her encounter with Jesus: *"The woman said to Him, 'I know that Messiah is coming' (who is called Christ). 'When He comes, He will tell us all things.' Jesus said to her, 'I who speak to you am He'"* (John 4:25-26). This woman dropped her water pot in amazement. She had confronted the living Messiah, and her life would never be the same again.

Amazingly, He directly told her that He was indeed the Messiah. At that point in His ministry, He generally kept that fact under the radar.

One of the first missionaries for Christ, she rushed to her region and called many of the townspeople to come and meet this amazing man, who was more than a prophet. They came and believed when they heard Jesus for themselves.

Whoever you are, whatever your background, the Lord can use you as a witness for Him. Then, others may also experience the transformation of heart that you experienced after your encounter with Jesus.

Dear Holy Spirit, thank You for Your work in our world. Daily You quicken dead hearts and bring people unto salvation. You call us to repentance and to gather in Jesus' name. May You also use me as a witness to those who do not know You...

BY GOD'S STRENGTH, OUR HEARTS CAN BE CHANGED.

JULY 21

Anti-Christian Persecution

"The Lord said, 'I am Jesus, whom you are persecuting.'"
— Acts 9:5

How did Saul of Tarsus get changed? He was a religious zealot, persecuting the church wherever he could find it. He was committed to its destruction because he thought God wanted him to do this.

One day, as Saul approached Damascus, we are told in the ninth chapter of Acts, suddenly there was a light that shone upon him from heaven as if God turned on a great spotlight with a brilliant, dazzling whiteness that so struck him that he fell to the ground.

He was filled with terror and trembling, and he heard a voice saying, *"Saul, Saul, why do you persecute Me?"* (Acts 9:4). In the Greek text there is an interesting emphasis that does not come out in the English. What it says there is, "Why *Me* do you persecute?" The emphasis is on the word "Me."

That shows us that when anyone persecutes Christians, the apple of Christ's eye, they are persecuting Him—that we are one body. He is the head; we are the body.

Consider Jesus' question: "Why? What have I done to you, Saul? I left My throne in glory. I came down from the ivory palaces into this world of woe. I took upon Myself your guilt and went to a cross, and there I suffered in agony, even the very wrath of My Father, for you. I endured hell for you. Why are you persecuting Me?"

We should pray for the persecuted church—that they would continue to be faithful and that their attackers would be redeemed (as Saul was) or removed.

Jesus, Lord of the church, there are many today who are persecuting You. A new wave of cruelty and barbarism is being unleashed against Your people, and we grieve and ask, "How long, Lord?" before You lift up Your mighty sword and stop Your enemies…

BY GOD'S STRENGTH, THE MARTYRS WILL TRIUMPH.

JULY 22

Blaspheming the Name of Christ

"…and My name is continually blasphemed all day long."

— Isaiah 52:5

We live in an age that is awash with blasphemy. It is grievous to hear the name of Jesus Christ taken in vain, spoken of blasphemously. Why would anyone speak that name in blasphemy? It is the only sin without any motivation other than the pure demonic hatred of the fallen heart of man against God. Why? What more could He do than for you He has done?

God says in the Ten Commandments that He will not hold him guiltless who takes His name in vain. Yet people blithely take God's name in vain all over the place in this culture. They treat it like it doesn't mean anything—and yet their very lives depend on Him, whose name they take in vain. It's hard to turn on the radio or watch TV or a movie and avoid hearing blasphemy.

I would remind every blasphemer, every persecutor, every antagonist of Christianity that they are persecuting the living, risen, glorious Son of God, before whom one day they will stand and give an account of themselves and before whose feet they will bow. For many of them it will be the last thing that happens before they are taken and cast into hell.

God's name is holy. We should not take it in vain in profanity or by using it lightly. Don't ever say, "The Lord told me…" if it really was only your own wishes that told you. The name of God is to be praised, not defamed.

Holy God, we tremble when we think of all the blasphemy of our society. We cringe when we hear even little children swear. Lord, forgive them for they know not what they do. Give us strength for today to always honor Your holy name…

BY GOD'S STRENGTH, WE
CAN KEEP HIS NAME HOLY.

Growing in Christ

"…until we all come into…the knowledge of the Son of God, into a complete man, to the measure of the stature of the fullness of Christ…"

— Ephesians 4:13

Sanctification is just a technical term coming from the Latin that means spiritual growth—that God did not birth us to be merely babies. We are to grow and become little children and older children and then mature adults.

We are the army of Jesus Christ. We sing, "Onward Christian Soldiers," but can you imagine a kindergarten full of little children putting their toy rifles on their shoulders and marching off to war singing "Onward Christian Soldiers"? We would say, "Aren't they cute? Certainly nobody is going to get hurt by that army. That's for sure."

So I would ask you: If you have been born of Christ, have you grown in Christ? You know, it's interesting, you will hear a lot of people say, "I'm a born-again Christian." Now that certainly has a wonderful truth to it. It's saying that we have experienced that life-transforming act where God changes us, and we have a new birth.

But what would you think about a person that you met who is fifty or sixty years old and every time you talked to him, he told about what a wonderful birth he had had—that his mother didn't have a whole lot of pain. It all worked out well, and you keep seeing him and he keeps telling you about when he was born, as if that is the last thing that ever happened to him. God wants us to grow in Christ unto maturity.

Lord Jesus, we repent of our spiritual laziness. We repent of taking the things of You so lightly, while seriously engaged in other pursuits. Give us strength for today, Lord, that we may begin to develop great spiritual maturity…

BY GOD'S STRENGTH, WE CAN AGE GRACEFULLY IN CHRIST.

Are We Winning or Losing?

"Then I looked. And there was a great multitude which no one could count, from all nations and tribes and peoples and tongues, standing before the throne and before the Lamb, clothed with white robes, with palm branches in their hands."

— Revelation 7:9

When Jesus died and rose from the dead, there were some 120 believers who gathered in an upper room to pray, at His command. No one even took note of their existence.

Then Peter preached a sermon, and 3,000 believed. Shortly thereafter, 5,000 more were added to the number, followed by a great multitude of Jews and priests. Next came a time of persecution and when it ended in 313 A.D. with the Edict of Toleration, there were about 10 million professing Christians. By the year 1000, this number had grown to 50 million. By 1800 A.D., the number had grown to 215 million professing Christians. That is an increase of 165 million in 800 years.

In 1795, the modern missionary movement began in earnest with William Carey. By the year 1900 A.D., 100 years later, the number had grown to 500 million professing Christians. That is an increase of 285 million in one century. Jump ahead to today, and we are talking about roughly 2.2 billion professing Christians, larger than any other religion.

There is nothing even vaguely approaching this accomplishment in the annals of human history. When we look at the explosive growth of the Church worldwide, it makes us realize that, by God's grace, we are winning.

Jesus Christ, Lord of the universe, grant us strength today to further Your kingdom on earth. Thank You for letting us be a part of this great multitude who belong to You. Help us to not miss the big picture in our everyday life…

BY GOD'S STRENGTH AND HIS GRACE,
WE ARE ON THE WINNING SIDE.

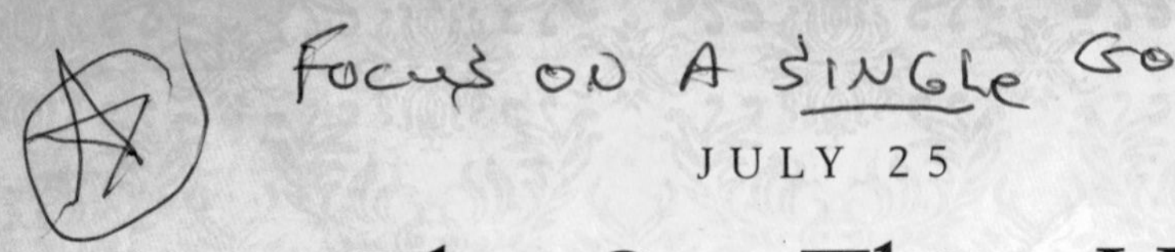

JULY 25

This One Thing I Do

"Brothers, I do not count myself to have attained, but this one thing I do, forgetting those things which are behind and reaching forward to those things which are ahead..."

— Philippians 3:13

Why is it that some people succeed in life while others fail? Is it heredity, environment, luck, circumstances, parentage, money or education? I am sure those factors have contributed toward the success of some, and yet history is replete with examples of individuals who had none of those advantages, and yet they succeeded magnificently. Why?

Since life is fleeting, we should ask ourselves these questions. We should take spiritual inventory and determine what we are going to do and how we might do it better.

What is the secret of success?

Paul says: *"This one thing I do,"* and he makes it very clear that he has a definite purpose in mind. The first great law of success is to have before your mind that goal toward which you are headed. I am convinced that most people fail at the very beginning. The problem is that we jump on our horses and ride off in ten different directions, do we not? If we could just get things in focus, there is no telling what we might do.

The things that are done for Christ and His kingdom may not lead to worldly success. But to be great and successful as a Christian is to be a servant of all.

Dear Lord, we all may wish to be successful, but give us a servant's heart. Help us look for the many opportunities to serve that You give us throughout our lives. Help us to focus on the work You have given us and to stay faithful to You come what may...

BY GOD'S STRENGTH, WE CAN FIND SPIRITUAL SUCCESS.

JULY 26

The Eyes of Faith vs. Unbelief

"Caleb silenced the people before Moses and said, 'Let us go up at once and possess it, for we are able to overcome it.'"

— Numbers 13:3

Joshua and Caleb were among the twelve spies who Moses sent into the Promised Land. But sadly, he and Caleb were outvoted by the other ten who said it was a great land, but it was filled with giants.

Nonetheless, Joshua and Caleb said we are more than able to possess it. *"Let us go up at once and take it,"* they said. They were not men that were filled with fear, timidity, or defeatism. They were positive, they were strong, they were courageous, and they wanted to go up at once.

Now they had also seen the giants. They did not by any means declare that the majority was wrong in its facts of the case, they were just wrong in their conclusions. They had seen the giants and yes, compared to the giants I suppose they were grasshoppers. Ah, but Caleb and Joshua saw the Lord God Jehovah, and compared to Him, the Anakites or Anakim were but ants crawling around on the earth. And so that courage, which is an integral part of true grit, comes from a confidence and faith in God's Word.

Being Christian does not mean that God spares us from facing giants in our lives. What it does mean is *"He who is in you is greater than he who is in the world"* (1 John 4:4). God is much greater than Satan. The Lord can give us victory over all the giants we face. Let us face the problems in life with the eyes of faith, like Joshua and Caleb, as opposed to eyes of unbelief, like the other ten spies.

Lord of hosts, in Your army and in Your company, we are conquerors. Jesus, You who are the Captain of the Lord's army, give us strength for today and courage to face the giants. Thank You for the "weapon" of Your Word, which is the sword of the Spirit…

BY GOD'S STRENGTH, WE CAN OVERCOME THE DARTS OF THE EVIL ONE.

JULY 27

Search the Scriptures

"These were more noble than those in Thessalonica, for they received the word with all eagerness, daily examining the Scriptures, to find out if these things were so."

— Acts 17:11

The Scripture is the final authority in all religious controversies. It is to the Word of God, the oracles of God, not to men, that we are to turn. Down through the centuries people have said, "Well, the minister said this or the priest said that or the church has said this or the Rabbi declares this." But the Scriptures declare it is only in the Bible that we have the infallible Word of God.

I charge you not to take what I say on faith, but to examine what I say in light of the Scriptures. I endeavor to proclaim no novel doctrines, and offer no new religions, but simply to declare that faith which, once and for all, was delivered unto the saints. It is up to you to examine it.

The Bible tells us that the Bereans were more noble than those in Thessalonica because they received the Word with all readiness of mind. In fact, they searched the Scriptures daily to see if this preaching was true. Who was it that was preaching? None other than the Apostle Paul himself. God declares that these people were noble and I would charge you to believe nothing I say without testing it by the Scriptures. If it is contrary to the Word of God, reject it. May God make us good Bereans.

Father, thank You for speaking through Your holy Word. Help us never to reject it to listen instead to man's opinion. Help our churches so that we all boldly proclaim Your Word and not any false doctrine which twists and distorts what You have clearly said…

BY GOD'S STRENGTH, WE CAN BE GROUNDED IN THE WORD OF GOD.

JULY 28

Don't Be Defeated Before You Start

"For as he thinketh in his heart, so is he..."

— Proverbs 23:7, KJV

Paul believed that he could do all things through Christ who strengthened him, and he changed the world. But many Christians today never claim this promise or virtually any other promise in the Word of God. Sadly, they live lives with a trail of many defeats.

In fact, I think it can certainly be said that before any man is beaten at any task, whatever it may be, he first of all is beaten in his own mind. True grit is something that is given to us in part by the spirit of God, something also that must be cultivated.

One psychologist advised keeping the faculty of effort alive in us by a little gratuitous exercise of the soul each day. He says to do something every day that is a little heroic or arduous for no other reason than that you would rather not do it, and, thus, develop your soul. And let no man despise, he says, these unimportant efforts at self-discipline, they forge character. We talk a great deal about bad habits, but there are good habits that need to be cultivated and inculcated in our children. A man who stands by his guns, who stands fast, is generally a man who has learned to do this over a long period of time. God uses different types of people, including those who never quit in what they believe God wants them to do, despite the obstacles.

Lord, give us strength today to do something we would rather not do. Please develop strong Christian character within us. Show us clearly what small act of heroism we can do today and give us the strength to follow through...

BY GOD'S STRENGTH, OUR CHARACTER IS BUILT.

Cultivating Deep Roots?

"…in His law he meditates day and night. He will be like a tree planted by the rivers of water, that brings forth its fruit in its season…"

— Psalm 1:23

The godly man is described in Psalm 1 as one who loves the Word of the Lord and ruminates on it in the morning and in the evening. By being so grounded in the Scriptures, he becomes like a tree with deep roots. But many people do not have deep roots, and so they hardly grow.

The Japanese have a way of taking what ordinarily are large trees and reducing them into tiny little trees and the way they do that is, first of all, cutting off the tap root. Those trees then are only able to use the surface roots, the smaller surface roots of the plant; and so the tree just doesn't grow very much.

And that is the way it is with most people in this world. Their tap root does not go down deep into the Word of God, and so all they have for nourishment are those surface roots that are sucking up the things of this world. Consequently their spiritual growth is badly stunted and they will never show spiritual depth. They will never persevere unto the end and be saved. They will never be like Martin Luther, who could stand before the Diet of Worms and say, "Here I stand, I can do no other, God help me." Therefore, he would not recant anything. Spending quality time in the meditation of the Bible is the key to true spiritual depth.

Lord of the Vineyard, thank You for cultivating and fertilizing and digging around me. Let my roots grow deep past the top soil and down to the nourishing rich soil of Your Word…

BY GOD'S STRENGTH, OUR ROOTS CAN GROW STRONG.

Being Faithful in the Face of Opposition

"...I alone am left; and they seek to take my life."

— 1 Kings 19:14

God can use one man or woman of conviction, even while the rest cower in fear. Think of the great Athanasius who lived in the 300s. At the time, the deity of Christ had come under such enormous attack that it seems that the majority, even within the church, were denying the very deity of Christ. Athanasius, this bold defender of the deity of Christ, seemed to be the only one willing to take a stand. He was even banished from the Roman Empire five times, but he came back. It is possible that without his steadfast stance, we might not even know about our divine savior Jesus Christ.

If it weren't for the boldness of Martin Luther, we might not even know about justification by faith. I think about William Carey, the first Protestant missionary who carried the Gospel to India. Carey said, "One thing I can do is plod," and so with determination he plodded along and he translated the Bible into numerous different languages. One time one of those translations went up in flames, and he had no back up. But what did he do? Quit? No, he plodded with true determination, and he did it all over again.

Elijah thought he was the only one standing for God in the days of wicked Ahab, but God had reserved 7,000 who had not bowed the knee to Baal. May the Lord find us faithful, even if we are in the minority.

Almighty Father, thank You for raising up men and women through the centuries who have stood contra mundum. Raise up people in our time that will stand strong and show the world Your truth...

BY GOD'S STRENGTH, WE CAN STAND AGAINST THE WORLD.

Don't Let Worldliness Cloud Your Vision

"You adulterers and adulteresses, do you not know that the friendship with the world is enmity with God?"

— James 4:4

Friendship with the world can cloud our vision of Christ. Even the old legend of King Arthur teaches that principle.

Knights of the Round Table sought after the Holy Grail, which was purported to be the cup from which Christ had drunk at the Last Supper. The fact that they would spend their whole lives seeking after that cup is difficult for us to see. That was an age of much superstition, but nevertheless there are some truths to be learned from the legend.

There was only one Sir Galahad. According to the original tale, he kept the eyes of his soul upon that goal. By resisting temptation and by resisting a life of ease, he plodded onward until at last it was revealed to him through a great oak tree.

He saw the Grail resplendent in the heavens. He dismounted from his white horse and stood fascinated by the vision, which lighted up his armor. When discussing this ethereal vision later with the King, Arthur wisely noted this vision was for him, but not the others.

There is something to say for those who are pure in heart that they shall see God, and one of the consequences of impurity in our lives is that the vision of God grows dim and fades away. Have you wondered why it seems that God is far away, hard to find? Ah, my friends, upon what have your eyes been feasting? Where have your thoughts been dallying? Blessed are the pure in heart for they shall see God.

Holy God, give me the strength to turn away from the lure of this world and all the vain things that charm me most. "Be Thou my vision, O Lord of my life" and keep my thoughts heavenward so I will not lose sight of You…

AUGUST 1

Spiritual Reproduction

"And you shall be My witnesses in Jerusalem, and in all Judea and Samaria, and to the ends of the earth."

— Acts 1:8

Jesus wants us to tell others about Him, so that they too may come to experience His forgiveness of sins. There is great joy in spiritual reproduction.

I remember the words of Dr. Manford Gutzke, professor of English Bible at Columbia Theological Seminary. He said, "Gentlemen, you can always tell the difference between a real rose and a milliner's rose made in a flower shop. The real rose may be beaten by the winds, it may be eaten by the cat, it may have holes from worms in it, while the milliner's rose may be a beauty to behold. But one thing is certain, the milliner's rose will never produce another rose."

Which are you? The real thing or a fake? A nominal Christian never produces another Christian, but real Christians do. That's one of the easiest ways to tell. So determine that you are going to witness for Christ. I hope you will determine that you are going to witness to someone every week. If you don't know how to do that, you ought to learn how, and there are programs, such as Evangelism Explosion, that are more than happy to train you. But if you can't do that, and until you do, at least invite them to come to church. Ask God to use you to help others follow Jesus.

Lord of the harvest, give me strength for today to be a Christian with a winsome and active witness. May the people I invest my time in know You and love You as I do...

BY GOD'S STRENGTH, WE CAN
BE REPRODUCING CHRISTIANS.

How LONG SHOULD WE SERVE?

AUGUST 2

As for Me

"If it is displeasing to you to serve the LORD, then choose today whom you will serve..."

— Joshua 24:15

Our culture seems to worship youth and warehouse the elderly. But there are many instances in the Bible where God uses elderly people who were committed to Him.

Did you ever stop to think that Joshua was just a young man when he left Egypt? Then 40 years passed by while he was in the wilderness, and then another 50 years or more passed, and by then Joshua was an old man. He was now a man of 110 years and during all of that time he had been faithful and he had trusted in the Lord and believed His promise and with unwavering faithfulness had gone on serving the Lord as God called him to do as a warrior for God.

And so at last the aged Joshua, 110 years old, gathers together the people of Israel at Shechem and there with flowing grey locks, he calls upon them again to renew their faith and to trust in the Lord and to live for Him and he utters those famous words, *"...as for me and my house, we will serve the Lord."* He said that on the very day of his death, 110 years old—and for all of that time he had been doing just that.

Whether you are old or young, don't think that the Lord cannot use you if you commit yourself to Him. May we write Joshua's words on our heart—to actively choose to serve the Lord.

Lord, my heart gives a resounding YES, as for me and my house, we will serve You. Help us to do so faithfully at any age and in all circumstances...

BY GOD'S STRENGTH, WE WILL
SERVE HIM THROUGH ALL OF LIFE.

AUGUST 3

Faithful to the End

"Israel served the LORD all the days of Joshua and of the elders who outlived Joshua..."

— Joshua 24:31

It is interesting that the greatest of saints and the greatest of conquerors in this world have been those who had had grit—they have been willing to go just a little bit farther, a little bit longer for God.

General William Booth, the founder of the Salvation Army, was very enthusiastic in his love for the Lord to the end. When he reached about 80 years of age, he had an operation on his eyes for his failing sight. It was unsuccessful, and he called his son, Bramwell Booth, to his side and his son heard his father say this, "I fear that I shall not have much chance to see objects anymore. God knows best. I have done what I could for my Lord with my eyes; now I shall do what I can for Him without them."

That is true grit, a grit that doesn't quit. Joshua persisted, and there are not many in Scripture about whose character so few blemishes are recorded, as that of Joshua, the son of Nun.

Throughout all of his time leading Israel we find no idolatry, no alliances with the heathen, none of the transgressions that so angered the Lord. It is a virtually perfect example of faithfulness and character and fidelity to the Lord. His epitaph is: Joshua, the son of Nun, the servant of Jehovah. Joshua, a Hebrew name, means the Lord saves—the same name in Greek is Jesus. May we be found to be faithful to the Lord all our days as well.

Faithful Father, grant me the strength to stay faithful to You all my life. Thank You for Your faithfulness to me year after year. Thank You for all You have seen me through...

BY GOD'S STRENGTH, WE CAN REMAIN FAITHFUL AND TRUE.

AUGUST 4

Nehemiah Saw a Need and He Filled It

"Come, and let us rebuild the wall of Jerusalem so that we will no more be a reproach."

— Nehemiah 2:17

Nehemiah was a great man of God and yet a most unusual one. He wrote no psalms, directing the people of God to lifting up their hearts in exaltation and worship as David did. He did not leave us with hundreds of proverbs with which to guide our daily lives as Solomon did.

He wrote no epistles instructing us in the faith so that we may be built up in our spiritual knowledge. He did none of these things. However, what he did was quite unusual: He built a wall. It is most remarkable that the Bible contains an entire book written about the subject of building a wall.

It was, or course, a most important wall; it was the wall that would protect Jerusalem and its temple (which had been rebuilt) from the attack of enemies. Nehemiah well knew that the temple had been destroyed before only after the walls had been breached and broken down. He knew that if the religion of God's people was to continue, there must at least be some hiatus in the singing of psalms and the teaching of proverbs, for there was a practical job to do—the wall must be rebuilt.

God calls His children to do different things. We each have our part in the kingdom of the Lord Jesus. The key is to make sure that we are on track to faithfully carry out what He has called us to do—even if it is to build a wall.

Lord, our protector, thank You for watching over Your people. Help us to protect and preserve that which You have entrusted to us. Let us gladly do the tasks You assign us, whether they are glamorous or menial…

BY GOD'S STRENGTH, WE CAN COMPLETE ANY TASK HE ASSIGNS US.

How May We Know We Are Saved?

"We know that we have passed from death to life, because we love the brothers. Whoever does not love his brother remains in death."

— 1 John 3:14

The scripture commands us to examine ourselves to see if we be in the faith and it makes clear that it is possible because of the deception of our own hearts, to be self-deceived and to be in error concerning our own salvation. I am sure that there are numerous people within the church of Christ who assume that they are saved and yet are not.

In 1 John, he lays down some key principles that help us understand this. He says, for example, *"The one who does righteousness is righteous"* (1 John 3:7).

He also looks at the specific subject of love, especially as the sign and test of our divine sonship. John begins by saying that this is the message that we heard from the beginning that we should love one another. This was the new commandment that Christ gave—that we should love one another, as He has loved us.

It is this commandment that John picks up on at this point and begins to describe to us. Not only was it the new commandment that summed up the ethical teaching of Jesus, but more than that it is the sign and test of whether or not we are part of the family of God. Whether we indeed have been saved or whether we deceive ourselves. How do we know we are saved? We have a love for our brothers and sisters in Christ that was not there before.

God of love, increase our love for You and our love for our fellow Christians. We only love because You loved us first. We pray today that Your love will so fill our hearts that it will overflow to the people around us...

BY GOD'S STRENGTH, WE CAN LOVE ONE ANOTHER.

AUGUST 6

Crossing the Fox River

"Be anxious for nothing, but in everything, by prayer and supplication with gratitude, make your requests known to God."

— Philippians 4:6

When Abraham Lincoln was a circuit rider for the courts as a lawyer, going to wherever the courts were being held in small towns, he had to cross a lot of rivers. That included the notorious Fox River, which, in times of rain, was most turbulent and extremely dangerous.

One night he and a colleague had crossed several rivers in the days before, and his companion had said to him, "If these are this bad, what in the world is it going to be like when we try to cross the Fox?" And it just so happened that that night, as they stayed in an inn, there was a Methodist circuit rider there who had been traveling those parts for almost fifty years. And they asked him if he knew about the Fox River, and he said, "Oh, my, yes. I know all about that. I have been crossing it innumerable times for many years." And they asked if he had any advice about how they might cross it safely. He said, "Absolutely. I have discovered that there is one secret about the Fox River which I never fail to keep in mind." He said, "I never cross it until I reach it."

Well, I think that all of us have faced a great many Fox Rivers that we have "crossed" when we were yet miles away. By the time we have arrived at them, we discover that a drought has come, and the river has dried up. Turn your worries over to God. Instead of worrying, pray and give thanks—and watch God take care of your Fox River by the time you get there.

Dear Lord Jesus, we thank You for taking care of so many of the problems we have worried about. We see Your hand straightening out our path, and we thank You for sending Your angel before us…

BY GOD'S STRENGTH, WE CAN TURN OUR WORRIES OVER TO GOD.

AUGUST 7

Cain Versus Christ

"We should love one another, not like Cain, who was of the wicked one and murdered his brother."

— 1 John 3:1112

In 1 John, the beloved apostle talks about the importance of love. He contrasts that with hate as seen in Cain, who killed his brother Abel.

First, he holds up a picture of Cain and, secondly, a picture of Christ. Cain, the prototype of hatred, and Christ, the prototype of love, stand in stark contrast one to the other and are indicative of the children of the Devil and the children of God.

We will remember that Christ taught that there are two families in this world. There is not a fatherhood of God and a brotherhood of man as some people vainly wish and proclaim. But Jesus said there are two fatherhoods and there are two brotherhoods. There are two families: there is the fatherhood of God and the fatherhood of Satan. There is an antipathy on the part of the family of Satan toward the family of God, which is as long as history and is worldwide and never ending.

Cain was the prototype murderer—the first slayer of men—the one who was to begin the bloodletting that was going to end in a great river, even a great sea of blood, to this very day. Cain was of his father, of Satan, of whom Jesus said that he was a murderer from the beginning. Those born of God do not hate, like Cain, but strive to love, like Christ.

Father God, many claim to want love and world peace, but hatred is strong and seems to be all around us. Thank You that love is more powerful than hate and that one day, love will conquer and You will triumph over all evil...

BY GOD'S STRENGTH, WE CAN OVERCOME HATE WITH LOVE.

Watch Out for Envy

"Not as Cain, who was of the wicked one and slew his brother. And wherefore slew he him? Because his own works were evil, and his brother's righteous."

—1 John 3:12 KJV

Wickedness will sometimes do all it can to suppress righteousness. Jesus said that light has come into the world, but men prefer darkness because their deeds are evil.

Cain was of that wicked one, of Satan, of whom Jesus said that he was a murderer from the beginning and who inspired Cain to his terrible deed of murder. The term that is used in the Greek text for "slew,"—he slew his brother—is an unusual term, and it tells us something about the brutality of the deed that was involved. The term might very accurately be described or translated as "butchered." The original text means to slit the throat, and apparently Cain did a very thorough job on his brother.

Why did he do it? Because his own works were evil and his brother's righteous. We see here a horrifying picture of the evil capabilities of the human heart and of the total depravity of man.

Envy had goaded Cain to such a place, because of the fact that the righteousness of his brother was an indictment against him, that he was brought to the place of even killing Abel. Sadly, virtually everyone has experienced at some time or another in his own life the feeling of envy, which, as someone noted, withers at another's joy, while hating the excellence it cannot reach. Ask God to purify your heart from envy, so it will never take root there.

O Lord, it is hard to understand man's cruelty to man and when we see evil all around us, we are horrified by it. But when we see the dirty fingerprints of Satan even on our own heart, we shudder and run to You for cleansing…

BY GOD'S STRENGTH, WE CAN KEEP ENVY IN OUR HEARTS IN CHECK.

AUGUST 9

Holier Than Thou?

"Do not marvel, my brothers, if the world hates you."
— 1 John 3:13

We often hear people talk about a person who has a "holier than thou attitude." Now if there is anything that we hate it is a holier than thou attitude. But there probably is one thing that we hate even more and that is a holier than thou *fact*; in other words, often we totally forget that there are people who are in actual fact holier than we are.

Justification admits of no degrees whatsoever—there is no one in this world who is more justified than I am, because I am completely and totally justified. I am totally pardoned from all of my sins and accepted as righteous before God. But unlike justification, which admits of no degrees, sanctification does admit of degrees and is greater in one than in another.

So there are indeed in just about any church at any given time people who are at all levels of spiritual growth and sanctification. People who are at all levels of holiness; and if there is one thing that makes many people uncomfortable, it is to be in the presence of someone that is markedly and notably more holy than they are because it is a silent condemnation of their ungodliness and of the remnants of wickedness and worldliness that still cling to their lives. That is why the world sometimes will hate us. May God give us the grace to walk in holiness and to aspire to be more holy.

Holy Father, we wish to be more holy and for Your image to be seen more clearly in us. Grant us to walk in humility and holiness. Let us seek our friendship with those who are holier than we are…

BY GOD'S STRENGTH,
WE ARE MADE HOLY.

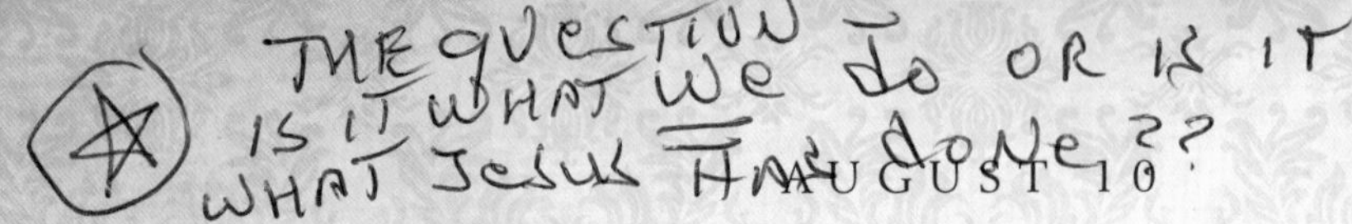

AUGUST 10

False Religion vs. Right Religion

"The Lord said to Cain, 'Why are you angry?...If you do well, shall you not be accepted? But if you do not do well, sin is crouching at the door. It desires to dominate you, but you must rule over it.'"

— Genesis 4:6

In the account of Cain and Abel in Genesis 4, we see a great contrast between true religion and false religion. Of course, in our day when people believe truth is relative, many recoil at such a notion as true versus false religion.

The nature by which Cain's works were unrighteous and Abel's works were righteous was very simply this: Abel held to the right views and practice of religion, while Cain held to false views and practices of religion.

Abel you may recall came before God and brought the sacrifice of one of his flock and offered this sacrifice with the shedding of blood and the giving of a life. Whereas Cain, on the other hand, brought the fruit of the fields from his toil as a farmer and he brought that, and he offered it to God, and he was rejected, whereas Abel's sacrifice was accepted.

Everywhere in the world there is the same picture of Cain's type of religion where man brings the fruit of his own labors and offers it up to God—his own goodness, his own morality and piety and benevolence—and he is astonished and chagrined when it is not accepted by God, and he does not receive that inward peace of knowing that he has been forgiven and accepted by God. Whereas the Christian knows that it is only by the shedding of the blood of the Lamb of God, Jesus Christ, that he is accepted.

Lord God, we see Cain and the chance You gave him to find victory over temptation. Sin is always crouching at the door. Please give us strength for today to overcome it. Help us to please You today…

BY GOD'S STRENGTH, WE CAN OVERCOME TEMPTATION.

AUGUST 11

Jesus Condemns Laziness

"His master answered, 'You wicked and slothful servant!'"
— Matthew 25:26

The Lord Jesus has some unkind things to say about the deliberately slothful person. In the parable of the talents, the Lord lambasts the third man because he was lazy.

The Bible admonishes us to be not slothful in business, but fervent in spirit serving the Lord, and therefore by our fervency in our business we are also serving the Lord. And Paul says that if a man will willfully not work then neither shall he eat (2 Thessalonians 3:10).

And yet we live in a day when these things are being greatly ignored to the detriment of our society. One time some counties instituted a "workfare" program which was to substitute for the welfare program that had been in effect. Sadly, many able-bodied people did not take advantage of this. Too many of them just wanted something for nothing. We are producing more and more people who are being taught by our government in effect that the world owes them a living.

This is a sin and we as Christians need to face up to that. We are producing a generation of slothful, indigent people and it does not portend well for our society.

Furthermore, it does not help the poor, especially since the wealth-transfer systems break the back of the urban family. It is a great tragedy when we as individuals or as a nation stray from God's principles. God's ways still work, and He has designed us for work. Granted, some people in extreme cases cannot. But the exception should not make the rule.

Dear God, thank You for creating us to work. Thank You for the blessings of accomplishments and the joy in a job well done. Help us to do work well and always help those who are unable to do so…

BY GOD'S STRENGTH, WE CAN
DO OUR WORK TO HIS GLORY.

AUGUST 12

Can a Murderer Be Saved?

"Whoever hates his brother is a murderer, and you know that no murderer has eternal life remaining in him."

— 1 John 3:14

John is saying here if we hate our brother, this is murder and that we are a murderer. Now there are many people who cannot even imagine going so far as to murder another person, but he is saying that hatred is like unto murder.

It may be the difference between a mild case and a severe case of the same disease but it is the same infection, the same germ which pervades the body of both. It is the same type of crime, though different in degree. And you know, he says, that no murderer has eternal life abiding in him. The Greek phrase translated as "and you know that no murderer has eternal life" means you know it requires no argument, it requires no demonstration, it doesn't even require reflection. But rather instinctively you know that no murderer has eternal life abiding in him. So if you hate your brethren, it is self-evident by *prima facie* evidence that eternal life does not abide in you.

If you have that desire to do someone in out of revenge, if you harbor that hatred within your own heart, then says John, you are akin to a murderer—even as Cain himself was a murderer, and that type of hatred continues throughout the world.

But there is also something to be said for those who truly repent of their sins, including the sin of murder. The hymn declares, "The vilest offender who truly believes that moment from Jesus a pardon receives." And once saved, let us walk in love.

Lord of life, You give us life and love and the taking of life is not up to us. The germ of hatred is anti-love and leads to death. Thank You that it cannot grow in a heart where Your presence is manifest. Please remove from us any root of bitterness and any hatred…

BY GOD'S STRENGTH, HATRED CAN BE REPLACED BY LOVE.

AUGUST 13

Christ Loves and So Should We

"By this we know the love of God: that He laid down His life for us, and we ought to lay down our lives for the brothers."

— 1 John 3:16

Love is personified in Jesus Christ. Rather than take, He gave…even to the point where He gave His very life that we might be saved. Christ sacrificed His own life out of love for us. And how then should we live, after accepting His love?

We should be ready to lay down our lives for those in Christ. This statement is quite revolutionary in its implications. Even though we might never be asked to actually die for another person, we are asked to daily die to ourselves.

It is important that we do so, knowing that anything that we do less than laying down our lives for our brethren is to fall short of fulfilling the obligation of that love.

This means we could share more than we do. We could give more than we do. We show our love in practical ways. Christ the Savior has shown us the way. If we are to lay down our lives for our brethren, then surely to help others who are poor and who are in necessitated conditions of one sort or another is little to ask. We should help them with the goods of this world. May God give us more grace to live unselfishly.

God of love, give me Your beautiful love in ever greater measure. Help me to live unselfishly, whether I'm giving up a nap or laying down my very life. All small and great acts of unselfish love for someone else come purely from You…

BY GOD'S STRENGTH, WE CAN BE UNSELFISH AND LOVING.

Love In Truth and In Action

"My little children, let us love not in word and speech, but in action and truth."

— 1 John 3:18

Christianity presents an incredible picture of love, the love of God in Jesus Christ. Because its ideals are so lofty and soaring, because its sentiments are so noble and so high, there is a danger that we should love in platitudes, and in ideals, and in emotional sympathies. There is a danger that we should feel that we have paid up our debt to love if we have praised its beauty, if we have felt its charm, if we have experienced its sentiment, then we feel that we have loved.

But John says no, let us not love in word or merely in feeling or in thought or tongue, but love in deed and in truth. We need to love in the practical ways of helping other people who are in need. And he says, *"By this we know that we are of the truth, and shall reassure our hearts before Him. For if our heart condemns us, God is greater than our heart and knows everything"* (1 John 3:19-20). And those two verses have to be read together.

What does that mean *"if our heart condemns us, God is greater than our heart"*? He is saying that if we have lived our life and, because of the love of Christ we have loved our brethren, and we have endeavored to lay down our life for them, then we know we love because He loved us. God assures us in our hearts that we are His because we truly love.

God You who are love, what a miracle it is that any of us are loving at all. It is only Your love in our hearts which makes it so. I thank You for all the love I have received from fellow Christians, especially those closest to me…

BY GOD'S STRENGTH, WE CAN SERVE EACH OTHER IN LOVE.

Is Your Scope In Focus?

"I press toward the goal to the prize of the high calling of God in Christ Jesus."

— Philippians 3:14

The Greek word translated in this verse as "goal" (in the King James it is "mark") is the word from which we get scope, as in telescope, microscope, or in the common phraseology of the day, to "scope out" something. It means "to look into."

Now in a race track the course is marked out very clearly as to where we are to go, but in the course of life there are no chalk lines on either side of us, so therefore it is important that we scope out the goal. In this Christian race, we need not only to run fast, to stretch forward, to press on. The problem with many people is they are going the wrong way. Now they may be going very fast, they may be succeeding and making great advances, but they are just going in the wrong direction.

One husband driving with his wife on vacation came to a crossroads. His wife said they ought to turn left. He chose to turn right. Then he drove the next 50 miles figuring out how he could turn around and go the other way without his wife knowing it.

As Christians we need to make sure we have not lost sight of the real goal. We have a heavenly calling that should guide our lives. We are so bombarded with the material things of this life and the world in all of its secularism, we could totally lose sight of the fact that there is any high calling at all.

Father God, we ask You to help us to keep our focus on You and Your work. Help us not to be distracted by earthly things…

BY HIS STRENGTH, WE CAN
STAY FOCUSED FOR HIS SAKE.

AUGUST 16

Fig Leaf Religion

"...without the shedding of blood there is no forgiveness."

— Hebrews 9:22

Right after sin entered into the world, a dichotomy began—a divergent stream of two different thoughts that ever typify the religions of men. One: God's way—the other: man's. Feeling the shame and guilt of their sin, do you remember what Adam and Eve did as the prototypes of all other lost human beings? They covered themselves with fig leaves. That is a symbolic presentation of all of the religions of the world—they invented fig leaf theology.

Are you a member of the "First Fig Leaf Church"? Here is how you can tell. I think I might give you a bit of a fashion show. The perennial favorite in this fashion parade is probably the choicest fig leaf on the whole tree called "I've done the best I can." Ah, you see people dressed in it everywhere, parading up and down in the street hiding behind that leaf. Or there is also a three-piece fig leaf called "I've kept the Ten Commandments," spoken by people who could not name more than three of them.

But in Eden, God looking upon Adam and Eve's fig leaves, made coats of skins and clothed them. There was that early prototype of the other religion—God's religion—by which an innocent victim had to die and shed its blood because we need to be clothed, as it were, in the skin of that victim. Jesus is the true Lamb of God whose shed blood forgives those who believe in Him.

God our provider, thank You for providing the Lamb for the sacrifice. Thank You, Jesus, You are the Lamb of God who takes away the sins of the world...

BY GOD'S STRENGTH AND BY THE BLOOD OF THE LAMB, WE ARE PURIFIED.

AUGUST 17

Is There Any Cause for Encouragement?

"But many of those who heard the word believed, and the number of the men grew to about five thousand."

— Acts 4:4

Someone asked me, "Pastor, do you think there is any hope for our country? For our world? Things look so bleak that we can't see any hope at all. Do you have any word of encouragement?" "Well, I said, I certainly do. I am greatly encouraged. In fact, I am more encouraged today than I have been for many years about what the Lord is doing in our world."

What is God doing among us? Well, more than most people think. You know, it took one thousand years for the church to grow to the place where it has added fifty million professing Christians to its rolls. But we did that in the last five years when fifty million people were added to the rolls of the church of Christ worldwide. Meanwhile, the church's growth around the world is exploding.

For my own curiosity, I graphed the growth rate of the church down through all twenty centuries to see what has happened. At first, it looked as if the line was almost parallel with the bottom line of the graph, it grew so slowly. The growth of the church for the first five hundred years could hardly be detected in the midst of the population of the world.

But by the 19th and 20th centuries, the rate began to go straight up. So I am very optimistic about what God is doing in the church. God is bringing His will to pass, and we have the privilege to take part in that venture.

Lord of the harvest, bring more workers into the field. Thank You for the growth of Your church around the world. Thank You for this harvesting of the earth. Help us to be willing workers…

BY GOD'S STRENGTH, THE HARVEST IS BEING BROUGHT IN.

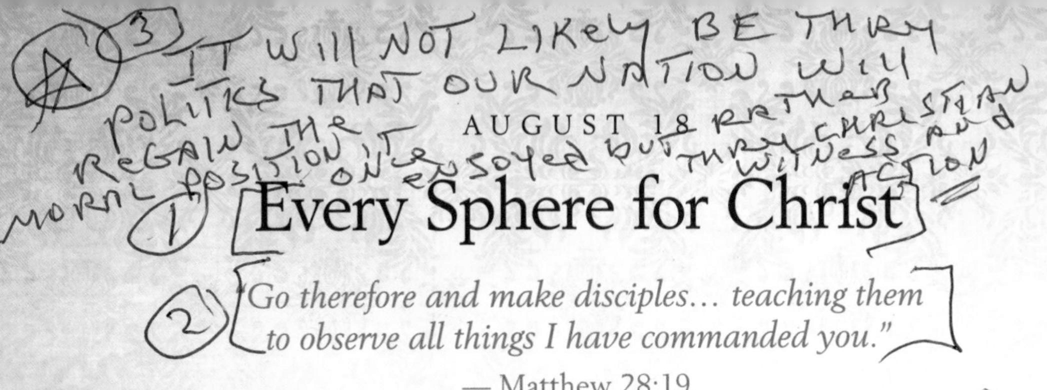

AUGUST 18

Every Sphere for Christ

"Go therefore and make disciples… teaching them to observe all things I have commanded you."

— Matthew 28:19

Piety is great. We need to be holy and devoted to the Lord. But I have a problem with *pietism*, which essentially means abandoning the public spheres of life and leaving these to the unbelievers.

For too long, pietism has hurt the church and it has hurt our nation for the last century or so. Pietism has led to the spiritual retreat of Christians out of all of the spheres of public life into the ghetto of the church—and this has resulted in leaving the rest of the world to unbelievers. We turned over politics to the unbelievers. After all, that was dirty business, wasn't it? Certainly Christians don't want to get involved in that sort of thing.

We abdicated higher education—we left that to unbelievers. And science, and media, journalism, and all of these various fields. We have turned them over to unbelievers and they have wrought havoc in them.

How great it would be for more Christians to be involved in the various spheres of national life. In every sphere of life, whether it be the spheres of law or of government or of education or science, the arts, television, motion pictures, journalism, whatever it is, we Christians need to get in there and we need to make our influence felt. We need to bear our witness for Jesus Christ and bring the teaching of Christ to bear on all of these spheres of life that He might receive the glory. After all, this is His world.

Lord of all, we thank You that the world is Yours and everything in it. We do need to reclaim it for You, and we pray that You will send Your people into every sphere of life. Here I am, Lord. Send me…

BY GOD'S STRENGTH, WE CAN INFLUENCE EVERY SPHERE OF LIFE.

AUGUST 19

Christian Influence In the Public Arena

"Let us break their chains and throw off their shackles."

— Psalm 2:3, NIV

In Psalm 2, the world says of the Lord and of His anointed (i.e., His Christ): "We don't want to be bound by God's rules." So the conflict is set.

There is a growing opposition that is taking place within our own government towards Christianity. Many people do not realize that secular humanism is a religion, which is now doing everything in its power to completely destroy Christian influence in any part of the public order of our nation.

Many decades ago, no one ever heard of secular humanism. A few decades ago it began to make its voice heard. Then it began to become the dominate voice to be heard in the media, in government bureaucracy, in the schools; and now it has taken over almost every one of these spheres completely. Its agenda now is to completely silence the Christian voice in every phase of public life in this country.

After removing all vestiges of it from the public domain, the final solution to the "Christian problem" is then to remove every vestige of Christianity altogether from this nation, both in the public and in the private spheres as well.

Part of the reason this has happened is because for too long we Christians have retreated into our "holy huddles" and have not influenced the world. But Jesus taught us we are to be in the world but not of the world. When we pray "Thy kingdom come, Thy will be done on earth as is it is heaven," we are certainly asking for His presence to be felt in greater ways. Why must Christian influence be squeezed out of the arena that for the most part Christians created in the first place?

O Lord, we see the destruction and silencing of Your church and we ask that You will once again turn our society back to You. We have seen You do it before and we ask humbly for another outpouring of Your Spirit in a national revival…

BY GOD'S STRENGTH, WE CAN HAVE A NEW SPIRITUAL AWAKENING.

A Hand Up or a Hand Out?

"He becomes poor who deals with a slack hand, but the hand of the diligent makes rich."

— Proverbs 10:4

In 1850, two years after a socialist revolution hit Paris, Frédéric Bastiat wrote an excellent book, entitled *The Law*. He said, "The law perverted! The law, I say, not only turned from its proper purpose but made to follow an entirely contrary purpose! The law became the weapon of every kind of greed! Instead of checking crime, the law itself guilty of the evils it is supposed to punish!" Fortunately, the revolution was overthrown. But, of course, those lessons went by the wayside in the 20th century with the rise of many communist states, all of which were violent.

Bastiat said the purpose of the law is single and simple. The purpose of the law, the purpose of government is justice. It is to protect the life, the liberty, and the property of the citizens of that nation. God has given to every person the right to protect his life, his liberty, and his property. And the law is simply the collective enforcement of that right.

Now, since it is unrighteous and criminal for me to take some innocent person's life, since it is wrong for me to enslave another person, since it is wrong for me to unlawfully, unrighteously take their property, it is equally wrong for the government, collectively, to do the same. And that is what Bastiat calls "legalized plunder."

Tragically, in our day we are seeing much "legalized plunder" through government welfare schemes. Charity is great—when it is voluntary. "Charity" by government coercion ceases to be charity. It creates poverty, not riches.

O Lord, so often when we humans do things our way, we mess up so badly. Help us as Your people to be generous and helpful to others without condoning and voting for unlawful gain. Raise up Christian statesmen to govern us…

BY GOD'S STRENGTH AND HIS PRINCIPLES, GOOD GOVERNMENT CAN BE RESTORED.

Statesmen vs. Politicians

"He sat down and called the twelve. And He said to them, 'If anyone desires to be first, he must be last of all and servant of all.'"

— Mark 9:35

When we consider how our fiscal policies in this country are borrowing from the future at such alarming rates, it should not surprise us if our children's children rise up to curse us. We are saddling them with an unpayable debt.

Somebody said well, "It is because of our own greed that we have become ungovernable." We cannot balance the budget of this nation now. Why? Because politicians are scared that they will be voted out of office if they do not pander to the greed of the people. Now, this is not a popular thing to say. But, my friends, somebody has to say it.

This country is going to be destroyed by the twin evils of public greed and a false philanthropy on the part of politicians who are simply buying their reelection by taking money from one group and giving it to another.

The government is instituted for the purpose of administering justice. If you want to know what the government is supposed to do, read the 13th chapter of Romans where God explains what the purpose of government is. And that purpose is justice, not philanthropy. There is a great need for philanthropy and for benevolence but it should come from the private sector where it produces positive results and not from the government sector where it produces chaos and will inevitably bring this nation to destruction. Pray that God would raise up more statesmen who serve the people and instead of politicians who serve themselves.

Lord of the nations, we pray for godly leaders. We pray for public servants, who run for office to serve the people and promote justice and protection. We repent of our national greed and ask for Your help to turn our nation around…

BY GOD'S STRENGTH, THOSE WHO GOVERN US CAN BE PUBLIC SERVANTS.

AUGUST 22

Influencing Our World for Christ

"Be doers of the word and not hearers only, deceiving yourselves."
— James 1:22

We need to be a part of the solution to the problems of this world. James tells us to not just listen, but put into practice what we hear. It is not enough to come to church and sit there for an hour on Sunday morning. We have to hide the Word of God in our hearts and find out what He would have us to be and then begin to influence our world for Christ.

We need to have more Christians in government, in journalism, in the media, in the law, in the courts in order to begin to reverse the tide that has been moving across the country, the tide of atheism and immorality. But it is only going to begin when Christians realize that God has called them to serve Him in every sphere of life—then we can change this nation back for the glory of God.

This is a tremendous challenge to each one of us to be what God would have us to be, to spend time in His Word each day and time in prayer seeking what he would have us to do and then to overcome our fears and go out and serve Christ in the world. It is time to get off the bench; to get out of the bleachers; to get out of the pew; to get into the game and to begin to work for Jesus Christ.

O Lord, we see the need so clearly, but we feel so helpless to do anything about it. Help us to go in Your strength and work for Your kingdom wherever You have put us and to see Your hand in the situation...

BY GOD'S STRENGTH, WE CAN INFLUENCE THE WORLD FOR HIM.

AUGUST 23

The Best of Times, the Worst of Times

"Seek the LORD while He may be found, call you upon Him while He is near."

— Isaiah 55:6

"It was the best of times; it was the worst of times." These familiar words open Charles Dickens' great novel, *A Tale of Two Cities*, which was set in Paris in 1789, just at the beginning of the French Revolution. It was a time of great turmoil in that country. As we consider where our nation is spiritually, I think Dickens' description is apt.

America was unquestionably founded as a Christian nation, as the Supreme Court once admitted, "This is a religious people. This is a Christian nation." Well, that's the way it started. The people in New England, when they got together in the early days of this country, signed the New England Confederation, in which they said, "We all came into these parts of America for one and the same end and aim." Do you remember what that was? They said that one single aim was "to advance the kingdom of our Lord Jesus Christ."

I am sure that many people would be just shocked to hear that, and yet that is where we started. Unfortunately, because we have failed to share the Gospel consistently and frequently, there have been a growing number of people who have not known Christ, who know nothing about His kingdom, have never entered in, and wouldn't even know how. Consequently, the number of unbelievers in this country has grown tremendously, while the percentage of believers has declined.

Let us pray for revival!

Lord of history, we have seen how You have guided nations as well as individuals. We pray for our nation, which started so well. Bring us back to Yourself and give us the gift of repentance...

BY GOD'S STRENGTH,
EMPIRES RISE AND FALL.

AMEN

AUGUST 24

The Foundation of All the Ism's

"For what may be known about God is clear to them since God has shown it to them..."

— Romans 1:19

For the last century, students have been constantly inculcated with the atheistic, humanistic, materialistic view of evolution, which is the foundation upon which every anti-Christian system rests. Every anti-Christian "ism" that has come down the pike for 150 years has found a pseudoscientific foundation in evolution. To wit:

- Communism
- Fascism
- Freudianism
- Nazism
- Humanism
- Behaviorism

Evolutionists have done everything in their power to prevent evidence for creation from being shown. Even if you ask that when the evidence for evolution is taught that the evidence for creation also be taught—that has been defeated in court. There is no other scientific theory in the world where the evidences on both sides cannot be taught. Only evolution is a politically protected "scientific theory." That is not education, dear friends. That is indoctrination.

The late evolutionist Stephen Jay Gould of Harvard said to his colleagues that there had been more than 100 major debates between evolutionists and creationists, and the evolutionists had lost every one of them.

Why do they lose every debate? Because the creationists are such wonderful debaters? Could it be that the evidence is on the side of the creationists? That, Gould could not admit. Everyone knows deep down about the Creator because He has made His handiwork so clear in His creation.

God of truth, You have revealed Yourself and Your creation to us. Help us, Lord, to see truth in the midst of lies. Give us discernment and clear thinking so we may know what is true...

BY GOD'S STRENGTH,
HIS TRUTH WILL STAND

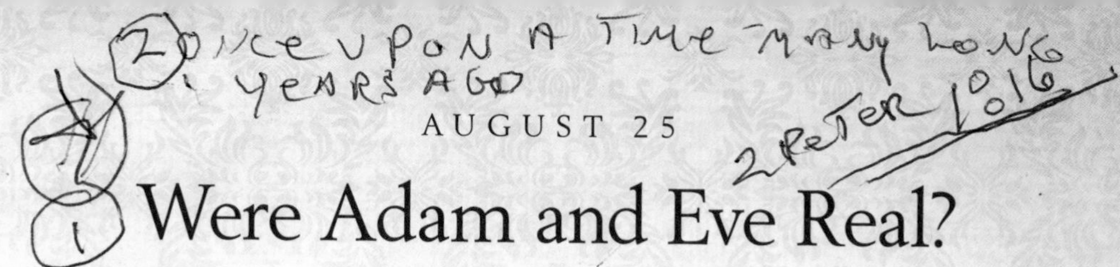

AUGUST 25

Were Adam and Eve Real?

"Then God said, 'Let us make man in our image'…in the image of God He created him; male and female He created them."

— Genesis 1:26a-27b

When you come to discuss Adam and Eve, you immediately run head on into the great wall of evolution. This view has so permeated our society and indeed the society of almost the whole world, that there are few people today who are even willing to give an intelligent hearing on a true Adam and Eve. As well we might examine something from Aesop's Fables, they say, as to examine Adam and Eve.

Well, it is my conclusion after decades of studying the matter, that never has a bigger lie been foisted on the human race with less evidence than that of evolution. Many people suppose that it is a scientific fact that has been established by overwhelming evidence. Well, is that the case or not?

Aldous Huxley—grandson of Thomas Huxley, Darwin's bulldog—admitted that it wasn't science that caused them to believe in evolution. Evolution allowed them to pursue their own immorality. In his 1937 book, *Ends and Means*, Huxley admitted, "We objected to the morality because it interfered with our sexual freedom…The supporters of these systems claimed that in some way they embodied the meaning (a Christian meaning, they insisted) of the world."

Science? It had more to do with sin than science. *"And since they did not see fit to acknowledge God, God gave them over to a debased mind,"* Paul tells us in Romans 1:28. Keep studying and keep seeking the truth, and the God of Truth will reveal it.

Dear God, we wish to be true to Your Word and to read it correctly. Give us the grace to interpret it wisely and not through the lens of popular thinking. Thank You for the scientists who work so diligently at seeking truth. Give them Your wisdom…

BY GOD'S STRENGTH AND
WISDOM, TRUTH IS REVEALED.

AUGUST 26

Arrested Development

"For though by now you should be teachers, you need someone to teach you again the first principles of the oracles of God and have come to need milk rather than solid food."

— Hebrews 5:12

Babies are universally loved and we are drawn to them at whatever their age. But if we visit a newborn and then come back in six months and that baby is still the same size as he was at birth, we know something is seriously wrong. Something is interfering with that baby's development.

I'm afraid there are some people in our churches today who are suffering from arrested development. They haven't grown much. Oh, I think the average church member probably grows to be the equivalent of about a five-year-old. You know, a five-year-old can do a lot of things. He can throw a baseball and run around and ride a tricycle and get into some mischief and talk and do a lot of things.

There are a whole lot of things he can't do. And spiritually I think people sort of grow to about that point. They learn sort of the basics of Christianity. They know the Lord's Prayer and most of the Apostles' Creed and probably at least six of the Commandments and a few selected verses that aren't too long to memorize. Then they decide that now this will get them along and get them by and they forget all about growing at that point. It is a case of arrested development. But that is not what the Bible calls us to do.

Lord, give me strength for today to move beyond shallow spirituality. Thank You for the means of growth. Help me to actively use them. Show me anything in my life that may possibly be holding me back from growing in You…

BY GOD'S STRENGTH, WE CAN MATURE SPIRITUALLY.

AUGUST 27

Don't Believe the Lies

"It is God who clothes me with strength..."

— Psalm 18:32

"You're a dunce." That's what she said. "You're a dunce, and I am going to fail you," and the teacher failed Einstein in mathematics. Who was the dunce?

"I'm sorry, we don't want you in our choir. You can't sing, so don't come back," but Jerome Hines became the greatest *basso profundo* the Metropolitan has ever known.

We believe the lies of our past. Our own failures speak eloquently to us: "You can't do it. Don't you remember? You tried before and you failed. You even tried twice, three times, and you failed. You can't do it." Those are lies.

Walt Disney went broke seven times before he succeeded. Thomas Edison made 10,000 experiments that failed before he developed the incandescent light. Babe Ruth drew up the largest record of failure—of strikeouts—in the history of baseball. Nobody remembers the failures of these people. They remember their successes. Zig Ziglar says that a big shot is just a little shot that kept on shooting.

"I can do all things through Christ." Who said that? Was this small Paul, the apostle, so-called—little Paul with his thorn in his flesh, with his weak eyes, whose bodily presence was weak and his speech contemptible? Yes, that is who it was. And through Christ he changed the world.

May God give us the grace to accomplish that which He wants us to do.

God of truth, we praise You that You have revealed Your truth in Jesus Christ, who is truth incarnate. Forgive us for believing lies that cause us to be on the sidelines of life when we should be out on the field. Lord, give us strength for today to believe Your truth in a world that rejects it...

BY GOD'S STRENGTH, WE KNOW THE TRUTH IN A WORLD OF LIES. AMEN

AUGUST 28

Priorities

"But seek first the kingdom of God and His righteousness, and all these things shall be given to you."

— Matthew 6:33

I always remember the admonition of Charles Spurgeon who said that Christ never told us to seek the kingdom of God. He is right. Christ never told us to seek the kingdom of God. He told us to seek it *first*.

Instead of being worried about "all these things," that is, what to eat, what to wear, providing basic necessities, Jesus tells us to make His kingdom and righteousness our top priority.

When we get so consumed with all "these things" to the point that we put the kingdom of God way down on the list, then the result is 1) we don't begin to have all of the things that God is more than willing to give to us, and 2) we miss out on the blessings of seeking the kingdom of God.

As we consider how to engage in "spiritual purposing," so that His kingdom really is our true priority, then consider ways to spend more time with Christ—time reading His Word, time going to Him in prayer. That quiet time is the essence of the Christian life. Without that, you will never grow in God's kingdom. I would urge you this day to determine that starting now you are not going to let a day go by that you don't spend some time in His Word and in prayer. That has been a goal of mine for virtually my entire Christian life. I hope you make it yours if isn't already.

God, our King, we are citizens of Your kingdom and we are so grateful for being included and accepted by You, our rightful King. Give us the grace to put You first and seek to advance Your kingdom every day...

BY GOD'S STRENGTH, HIS KINGDOM GOES FORTH.

A Bankrupt Future If We Don't Repent

"The rich rules over the poor, and the borrower is servant to the lender."
— Proverbs 22:7

We have given up the free enterprise economy the founders of this nation gave to us. We have followed the socialists, albeit a number of paces behind them, down that disastrous road. We are suffering the consequences right now. But we haven't even begun to see the consequences that will be coming one day.

Our politicians are recklessly spending money like there is no tomorrow. The federal government spends regularly more than we take in. But if we just took the figure of $1.4 trillion (which is smaller than the amount of our federal spending) and you stacked it up in dollars, it would reach 88,000 miles—one-third of the distance to the moon. This is incredibly selfish because the government has no money of its own.

Author Rus Walton put it very well when he said: "Government is not a producer; it is a taker, a taxer, and a spender. Every dollar spent by the public sector is a dollar the government must take from the private sector, from the workers and earners and investors. The dollar taken by government cannot be spent or invested by that productive private sector."

What is happening is that too many Americans are living off of the public trough—they are living off of the sweat and labor of their fellow Americans. And who will pay for all this? Our children and our children's children. Because we have turned our back on God, our national greed is destroying the future.

Pray for revival.

Dear God, help us to get our national house in order and to stop spending money we don't have. Thank You for what You have given us and help us to be good stewards of that which You have entrusted to us…

BY GOD'S STRENGTH,
WRONGS CAN BE RIGHTED.

Does the Bible Teach Socialism?

"All the believers were of one heart and one soul, and no one said that what he possessed was his own. But to them all things were in common."
— Acts 4:32

Some people like to say that early in the book of Acts we see an early form of socialism. The early Christians shared what they had, in some cases even by selling their houses and sharing the proceeds so no one had need. But I believe a close look at that passage will reveal that it is in fact antithetical to socialism.

A husband and wife team, Ananias and Sapphira, decided to sell their property, but they kept back a part of the price, told the disciples that they had sold it for more, and then *"brought a part of it and placed it at the apostles' feet." "Then Peter said, 'Ananias, why has Satan filled your heart to deceive the Holy Spirit and keep back part of the proceeds of the land? While it remained unsold, was it not your own?* [There you have an apostolic confirmation of the right of private property.] *And when it was sold, was it not under your authority?...You did not lie to men, but to God'"* (Acts 5:2-4). Both husband and wife dropped dead because of their sin of lying.

Not only the property and the means of production, but the results of that production were in the couple's power, not in the power or the hands of the state. Furthermore, you will notice, that this action was voluntary. And where was the money given? To the church—why that's enough to give Karl Marx apoplexy! Socialism may sound Christian, but in reality it is anything but.

Lord Jesus, You who are the Giver of all good gifts. Thank You for what You have given me and help me to be generous in sharing, especially with Your people. Help us to be honest in all our dealings with money and to give freely...

BY GOD'S STRENGTH,
WE CAN BE GENEROUS.

AUGUST 31

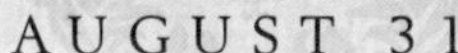

Turning the World Right Side Up

"These men who have turned the world upside down have come here also."

—Acts 17:6

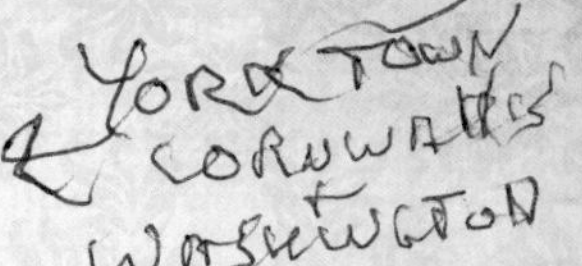

The apostle Paul and Silas had been preaching in Philippi (in modern day Turkey) where many people had been converted. There was a great tumult and they were cast into prison. Finally released, they went on to Thessalonica (in Greece), where they went into the synagogue and preached the Gospel with great power.

Numbers of the Jews were converted to Christ. A great multitude of devout Greeks also were converted, as well as a number of the notable women, so that some of the Jews, being moved with envy gathered together some lewd fellows of the baser sort. They gathered a company and they came to the house of Jason, where Paul and Silas had been. They were going to drag them out, but they could not lay their hands on them.

They took Jason and some of the brethren and brought them before the rulers of the people and they said: *"These who have turned the world upside down have come here also."* I love that description. Wouldn't it be wonderful to have inscribed on your tombstone: "Here lies one who turned the world upside down." That is what Christianity does.

As we see it from the proper perspective, the world is already turned upside down. What we are trying to do is turn it right side up. It was the pagan conception of turning the world upside down. Certainly we live in a world that desperately needs to be turned right side up in our time—and the Gospel of Jesus is the answer.

Lord Jesus, thank You for coming into this world to turn it right side up. As Your followers we ask for strength to work on this task with You. Help us to have a positive influence on the world around us…

BY GOD'S STRENGTH, THE WORLD CAN BE TURNED RIGHT SIDE UP.

SEPTEMBER 1

Who Owns the Children?

"You shall teach them [God's words] diligently to your children..."

— Deuteronomy 6:7

Several years ago the State of Nebraska jailed seven fathers for a supposedly heinous crime. These seven fathers spent Thanksgiving in jail. They spent Christmas in jail. They spent New Year's in jail. What had they done?

They placed their children in a Christian school to receive a Christian education. The bone of contention was that this was a church school that refused to be licensed by the state or to have its teachers accredited by the state. And in an example of the exercise of raw power, the state clamped down, padlocking the church and the school, throwing the pastor in jail and imprisoning seven fathers and then with warrants for their arrest, causing the mothers to flee out of the state with their children.

Now, it cannot be said that the state is interested in the educational achievement of the children because two independent testing organizations came into the school and ascertained that the children were two to two and a half years ahead of the children in the public schools in the state of Nebraska. No. It is simply a determination to repress Christian schools, to establish precedents, which can be used all across the country so that there can be no competition to the completely atheistic, secularistic, humanistic education that is being forwarded in our public school system today.

There is a battle today over who owns the children—the parents or the state? The Bible says the parents, specifically the fathers, are responsible for their children's education. It is to God we must ultimately give an account.

God our Father, we thank You for letting us be parents and we desperately need Your wisdom and guidance. We see the state taking upon itself more and more authority, and we pray for Your help in educating and rearing godly children...

BY GOD'S STRENGTH, WE CAN REAR GODLY CHILDREN.

SEPTEMBER 2

The Four Horsemen of the Godless Apocalypse

"The fool has said in his heart, 'There is no God.' They are corrupt, they do abominable deeds, there is none who does good."

— Psalm 14:1

There are "four horsemen" of the godless apocalypse, who have done so much to intellectually create the society in which we live today. It begins with philosophy, then impacts the culture, and then moves to everyday people and to the politicians.

Freud's views of man totally changed the thinking of the vast majority in our modern age and gave a picture of man totally at odds with the previously held biblical picture. Marx, the second horseman, through his writings brought so much evil upon the world—leading to the deaths of more than 100 million people in his effort to create "the worker's paradise."

Of course, there was Darwin, whose views of the origin of the species and biology affected not only biology, but all of the sciences, then all of the social sciences, and then almost all of life itself. The Nazi Holocaust was based on their interpretation of Darwinism, leading them to try to create a "Master Race"—killing millions of the supposed inferiors in the process.

Then finally there was Nietzsche and his book *Übermensch (Superman)*, which also added fuel to the super race notion of Hitler. Nietzsche coined the phrase "God is dead."

But those four horsemen have largely been thrown to the ground. All of these men built their philosophy on practical atheism, but those who deny God only show themselves to be fools.

O Lord Jesus, even though these "four horsemen" have been largely discredited, we see pagan religions and Islam coming in like a flood. Only You can give our society another chance to return to You…

ONLY BY GOD'S STRENGTH, CAN THIS POST-CHRISTIAN SOCIETY BE TURNED BACK.

AMEN

SEPTEMBER 3

The Thud of "Christless Feet"

"So he cried out, 'Father Abraham, have mercy on me, and send Lazarus to dip the tip of his finger in water and cool my tongue. For I am tormented in this flame.'"

— Luke 16:24

It bothers me greatly to see so many people, blithely on their way to eternal perdition.

There was a young man named William C. Burns of Scotland. He was a very compassionate and effective minister for Jesus Christ. But when he was only sixteen years old, he was simply Billy Burns. He grew up on a farm, a long way from any town. He probably had never seen fifty people in his lifetime. He had never been to a big town. Never.

But his mother took him, at the age of sixteen, to Glasgow. As they were walking down the crowded streets of Glasgow, his mother suddenly noticed that Billy was gone. She called for him. She turned around and in panic began to retrace her steps down the street looking for him anxiously. Finally, she came to an alley and there back in the alley, seated on the ground with his back against the wall, his knees up before him, his arms around his knees, and his head on his knees, he was sobbing uncontrollably. She ran up to him and said, "Billy, Billy, what is the matter? Are you all right? Are you all right?"

He looked up at her with a tear-stained face and said, "Oh, Mother, Mother. The thud of all those Christless feet is breaking my heart!" He was not only moved with compassion, he grew up to do something about it. I pray you will, too. May God give us a greater love for the lost.

Lord God Almighty, we are so grieved by all the ungodly people who are so very lost and have no idea how serious their situation is. Only You are mighty to save and we ask humbly to be used by You to gather people to Yourself…

BY GOD'S STRENGTH, AND BY HIS POWER SINNERS ARE SAVED.

SEPTEMBER 4

The Old Man and the New

"He who was seated on the throne said, 'Look! I am making all things new.'"

— Revelation 21:5

The great Dutch theologian, Abraham Kuyper, who was the only theologian I know of to ever rise to the position of Prime Minister of his country, had this to say: "But in regeneration a change took place. By this divine act, our person is in principle detached from his former ego in the old man… Our person is no longer identified with the old man, but opposes him. Even though he succeeds in enticing us again to sin, even in the yielding we do not what we will, but what we hate. Only hear what St. Paul says: *'For the good that I will to do, I do not do; but the evil I will not to do, that I practice'* (Romans 7:19 NKJV)."

A new man has been created, and the believer must consciously be more and more separated from the old nature, which must be more and more mortified and slain. We must identify more and more with the new nature. Only in thus being so identified, will our prayers be pleasing to God and will they be answered.

Say "yes" to the new man and "no" to the old man. If you are in Christ, you have received a new nature. However, as long as you are alive, you still have within an old man. Which of the two will you cater to? Which will you feed? Which will you starve? That will determine your spiritual progress.

Lord Jesus, we struggle with the two natures within and look in longing for the day You will forever remove our sinful nature, and we will be glorified, without even a possibility of a sinful thought. Hasten that day, Lord…

BY GOD'S STRENGTH, WE CAN FIGHT THE SINFUL NATURE.

Saved Unto Good Works

"For we are His workmanship, created in Christ Jesus for good works, which God prepared beforehand, so that we should walk in them."

— Ephesians 2:10

Most Americans have it backwards when it comes to salvation. They think they are going to be saved by their good works. We know that is not true. We are saved by grace through faith. Yet the problem is that there are many church members who think they have the problem all solved. They don't do anything because they assume they are just saved. We are not saved *by* good works, but we are saved *for* good works, as Ephesians 2:10 says.

So, let me ask another question. What have you accomplished for Christ? Many people resolve to do nothing and succeed perfectly.

What is the proper relationship between faith and works? We are saved by faith and after that we live our lives in thanksgiving to God by doing His will. If there were no work for us to do, God could just take us home as soon as we got saved. But He has left us here in this world to do good works, which He has prepared and planned for us to do. These works have nothing to do with our justification, but they help along our sanctification, they glorify Him, and they benefit our fellow man.

Lord Jesus, thank You for entrusting me with good works for me to do for You. Help me to do them well and in joyful gratitude to You…

BY GOD'S STRENGTH,
WE CAN DO HIS WORK.

SEPTEMBER 6

You Get What You Give

"Give, and it will be given to you: Good measure, pressed down, shaken together, and running over will men give unto you."

— Luke 6:38

Do you have many friends? Or have you, like so many people, never really learned the secret of how to make friends? We make friends by becoming a friend. In some ways, we receive back that which we give. Look at these Scriptures:

- *"Judge not, that you be not judged. For with what judgment you judge, you will be judged. And with the measure you use, it will be measured again for you"* (Matthew 7:1-2).
- *"Therefore, everything you would like men to do to you, do also to them, for this is the Law and the Prophets"* (Matthew 7:12).
- *"But this I say: He who sows sparingly will also reap sparingly, and he who sows bountifully will also reap bountifully"* (2 Corinthians 9:6).

Think, speak, and act positively, and lovingly and you will find that you receive in turn loving and positive thoughts and words and deeds. In the physical world, it is Newton's Third Law of Motion: For every action there is an equal and opposite reaction. But, it is just as true in the psychological and spiritual world. In fact, the speech research unit of Kenyon College proved through many tests that if a person is shouted at, he almost always shouts back.

Ask God to help you to be more loving, more generous, more kind, more Christlike.

God, You are the Giver. When we give it is in imitation of You. Help us to be givers with a thankful heart, not to give in order to get something back but because we wish to share Your bounty.

BY GOD'S STRENGTH, WE CAN LEARN TO LIVE GENEROUSLY.

SEPTEMBER 7

Blessed Assurance

"And without faith it is impossible to please God, for he who comes to God must believe that He exists and that He is a rewarder of those who diligently seek Him."

— Hebrews 11:6

Faith in Jesus is the only ship that sails for Paradise. Faith is the only door to heaven. Faith is the only key that opens the mansions above. Faith is that upon which we rest our heads when we come to the end of this life. Surely it is sad that millions of people in America have never learned the great foundational truth that salvation is by faith alone. Consequently, they have never come to the place where they know assuredly that they are going to Paradise.

Some professing Christians do not realize that they can have the assurance of salvation. But the Bible says it emphatically of those who truly believe in the Son of God: *"These things I have written … that you may* ***know*** *that you have eternal life"* (I John 5:13) [Emphasis added]. You don't need to guess, surmise, or speculate. You can know for sure. That is the wonder of faith, and that faith is faith in the crucified and risen Christ. It is faith in the only Redeemer of the world, the only One who has taken our sins and paid for them all, and now offers to receive us freely into His kingdom above.

Suicide bombers of radical Islamic groups blow themselves up and kill others because they think by doing so they will end up in paradise. They are wrong; they will end up in hell. But we as Christians should rejoice in the blessed assurance that we can know we have eternal life.

God of my salvation, thank You for the firm assurance of eternal life. Thank You that I belong to You both here on earth and later in heaven. This is a "foretaste of glory divine"…

BY GOD'S STRENGTH, WE ARE SAVED FOR ALL ETERNITY.

An Unusual Purpose of the Pulpit

"Woe to you, when all men speak well of you, for so their fathers spoke of the false prophets."

— Luke 6:26

One purpose of the pulpit is actually to drive members right out of the church as part of the continuing purging. The operation of the keys of the kingdom of God is coordinated with the whole matter of church discipline.

As the truth is preached and some unregenerate church members hear the truth, it tromps on people's toes. And their ungodliness and impenitence and wicked lies are exposed and their heresies are blasted. They leave and the church continues to be purified.

Of course, one of the tragedies of the church today is that too many preachers are afraid to step on anybody's toes. They will have to answer to Christ for that.

As the truth is proclaimed, God's own people will be drawn unto Him and the tares will be repulsed. That is the inevitable consequence of preaching the truth. Of course my greater desire is that everyone would repent and come to Christ and that none would be driven away.

Ah, my friends, but that shall never be—for we are a savor of life unto life for some and death unto death for others, and that is part of the calling of every minister and of everyone who names the name of Jesus Christ. What is true of me is true of you as well in your witness for Christ. We need to persevere unto the end, for those who persevere unto the end will be saved.

Pure and holy Lord, we wish that none would turn away from You, but we have promised to work for both the purity and the peace of the church. Help us to never water down Your Word or accept heresy because we want peace and unity…

BY GOD'S STRENGTH, THE CHURCH CAN BE PURIFIED.

SEPTEMBER 9

Advantages of Wealth

"Wealth makes many friends, but the poor is separated from his neighbor."
— Proverbs 19:4

Proverbs has much to say about practical living, including the advantages of wealth and the disadvantages of poverty. Saint Francis indeed might have taken poverty for his bride, but the wisdom of the book of Proverbs does not recommend it. For example, it says, *"The rich man's wealth is his strong city; the destruction of the poor is their poverty"* (Proverbs 10:15).

Like Francis, there have been those of a more mystical bent who have glorified poverty, and yet this is not what wisdom would have us see. As far as this book of the Bible is concerned, the destruction of the poor is their poverty. Indeed, poverty can be a devastating thing, and there are those in our cities today who know full well the truthfulness of this ancient wisdom.

Proverbs tells us that the rich man gains many advantages through his power of giving gifts. It brings him before great men. It procures for him universal friendship, such as that friendship may be, and it enables him to pacify the anger of an adversary—for a gift given to an angry man pacifies anger, we are told. Not only does his wealth make for him many friends, but it also secures positions of influence and authority over those who are not wealthy. It enables him to rise to positions of prominence, to hold places in parliaments or obtain governorships or other such offices as this. Above all, the Bible says to trust in God and not in uncertain riches.

Lord, You give us what we have. Help us to be content and at the same time improve our income when we are able. Your kingdom goes forth through funding, including that from the affluent. Help us to use what we have for Your honor and glory…

BY GOD'S STRENGTH, WE CAN USE
OUR RICHES TO BUILD HIS KINGDOM.

SEPTEMBER 10

The Church and Society

"You are the salt of the earth. But if the salt loses its saltiness, how shall it be made salty? It is from then on good for nothing but to be thrown out and to be trampled underfoot by men."

— Matthew 5:13

The church needs to awaken after many decades of lethargy and sleep. When this happens, I believe we will see many of the most unfortunate and godless decisions that have been made in this country in the past few decades reversed, and America will be restored again to a godliness—the kind of godliness that made us great.

This isn't going to happen overnight. Christians need to have far more influence in public elections. I believe that if we mobilized properly we could be the dominant force in elections in this nation. Those who would flaunt their disregard for moral and ethical standards would then find it increasingly difficult, and finally, impossible to be elected to high office in this nation.

I believe the church will also need to exercise more responsibility for the needy. As the nation retreats from the socialistic path it has been on for some time, the obligation will again be returned to local organizations and to the church. We will need to more fully exercise our responsibility and opportunity to minister to the poor, as the church at one time did. That will, indeed, give us the opportunity of bringing to them not only the physical needs of food and clothing, but also the Gospel of Christ, which can feed their souls and clothe them in the white robes of righteousness. Meanwhile, I am grateful for those already involved in this process. Take away the church and their feeding programs and a lot more people would do without.

Lord Jesus, give me strength for today to find a need and to fill it in Your name. Thank You for the incredible way Your people all over the world feed the hungry and clothe the naked. Lord, help us to make a difference for righteousness' sake in this country…

BY GOD'S STRENGTH, THE CHURCH OF CHRIST CAN BE TRUE SALT AND LIGHT.

Do Christians and Muslims Worship the Same God?

"Yes, the time is coming that whoever kills you will think that he is offering a service to God."

— John 16:2

Religion-wise, the greatest competitor to Christianity for hearts and souls for all eternity is Islam. Some people like to say we all worship the same God, just with different names. How naïve they are.

Islam has been violent for the bulk of its fourteen-centuries-long existence. From the very beginning, Islam gained much of its territory by wielding the sword. By about 1000 A.D. half of what had been Christendom was conquered by Islam.

All of the churches to which Christ sent letters in the book of Revelation were in territories now dominated by the Muslims. Much of the New Testament was written in and to places now in Muslim hands. This includes the books of Galatians, Ephesians, and Colossians. The Christians were first called Christians in a place (Antioch) now under complete Muslim control.

The radical follower of Islam does not represent the views, life, actions of all or of most Muslims. But taking jihad seriously is one of the teachings of the Koran, and those who do it are considered good Muslims.

The difference between Christianity and Islam is enormous. Mohammed said that people were to give their sons for Allah. The Bible says that God gave His son for you and me.

Oh Lord, as we see the spread of Islam and its violence and its persecution of Your saints, we tremble at the terror with which they are flooding the world. But we thank You that You only allow evil to seemingly triumph for a limited time…

BY GOD'S STRENGTH, WE CAN STAND AGAINST EVIL.

SEPTEMBER 12

The Bible and Laziness

"Yet a little sleep, a little slumber, a little folding of the hands to sleep—so will your poverty come upon you like a stalker, and your need as an armed man."

— Proverbs 6:10-11

Proverbs contrasts the diligent one who will succeed with the sluggard who will fail. By a person's diligence, his indefatigable keeping at his tasks, his lack of slothfulness, his rising early, and his attending to the minute details of his affairs, he gains for himself and for his family wealth.

The one who deals with a slack hand, one who by design is lazy, will not have what he needs. Now there are those that might look at some who are profligate in their great wealth and spend their money luxuriously and foolishly, but the Bible says that the poor man who is slothful is a brother to the man who is a great waster. The Bible says further that the sluggard will not plow by reason of the cold, therefore he shall beg in harvest and have nothing.

The desire of the slothful kills him for his hand refused to labor. The drunkard and the glutton shall come to poverty and drowsiness shall clothe a man in rags. The slothful man says there is a lion in the streets, so he can't work. As the door turns upon its hinges so does the slothful man upon his bed. Another thing about the slothful man we are told is that he obstinately refuses to be corrected and because he refuses to be corrected, he does not improve, and he continues in his poverty and his misery. May God give us the grace to work diligently to not only provide what we need and to generously provide for others. May he also make us teachable.

Lord, You told us to go to the ant and be wise. Like these little creatures we should work hard and plan for the future. Help me to be diligent today in all my tasks...

BY GOD'S STRENGTH, WE CAN PRAY FOR THE FUTURE AND ENTRUST IT TO HIM.

SEPTEMBER 13

Manna and the Sabbath

"...This is what the LORD has said, 'Tomorrow is the Sabbath, a holy Sabbath to the LORD. Bake that which you will bake today, and boil that which you will boil, and all that which remains over lay up for yourselves to be kept until the morning.'"

— Exodus 16:23

In the days of Moses, when His people were wandering in the wilderness, God provided for them daily bread in the form of manna. On the day before the Sabbath, however, they were to gather enough for two days. Then next day, on the Sabbath day, there was none on the ground. If the manna was left overnight on any of the other days, it would have worms and stink, but on that seventh day it would not corrupt or gather worms, and it would be good the next day.

How amazing God is! This reminds us of the fact that if we will remember His Sabbath, God will provide for us. Working on the Sabbath is something to avoid if at all possible. I think of one man who told me years ago that he had to work on the Lord's Day to gather up money for some unusual expenses. I knew at the time that would not work out, and, lo and behold, the day came when he lost his primary job and had a severe financial setback. I believe that if he had obeyed God that would not have happened to him.

Jesus taught us that the Sabbath was made for our good. Indeed we do better when we rest for a day. The Sabbath day is a "day of sacred assembly," according to Leviticus 23:3 (NIV). As much as is possible, we should set aside the Lord's day for worship and for rest.

Lord, give me strength for today to rest on Your day, to gather with Your people and worship You in Spirit and in truth. Thank You for the gift of a day off, the gift of Your re-creation in our lives...

BY GOD'S STRENGTH, WE CAN HONOR THE SABBATH AND BE REFRESHED.

SEPTEMBER 14

Taking from the Government

"Now we command you, brothers, in the name of our Lord Jesus Christ, that you withdraw yourselves from every brother who walks in idleness and not according to the tradition that he received from us."

— 2 Thessalonians 3:6

After trillions and trillions of dollars in wealth transfers, was the result that there is not a single poor person left in this country? Would that that were so! The result was that millions of people who could work are no longer working. Millions of Americans are receiving food stamps.

Americans and Christians need to realize that there is no morality in the government's coming with a gun and taking money from you and giving it to the poor. I am amazed at how many people speak about these things as if there were a moral and spiritual matter involved. Does anyone attempt to justify Robin Hood on spiritual and moral grounds?

God wants people who are willing to voluntarily give of their money to help the needy and not people who have it taken away at the point of a gun. But if you don't think it is taken away at the point of a gun, just try and not give it, and you will find very quickly that you will end up in jail.

We have a very perverted sense in this country today, and I believe that it is going to result in the emasculation of the American civilization. I think we as Christians all too often have been more than willing to take anything we can get out of the government, and we have had our own complicity in this whole thing. It is destroying the moral fiber of the American people.

Lord, give me strength for today to provide for my family. Forgive me for ever being "generous" with other people's money. Help us to be genuinely concerned about and generous toward the poor and the down and out…

BY HIS STRENGTH, WE CAN BE PART OF THE SOLUTION, NOT THE PROBLEM.

Transformed Lives

"He who was seated on the throne said, 'Look! I am making all things new.'"

— Revelation 21:5

In the 19th century, in Britain, there was a skeptic who said to a converted drunkard, "Surely you don't believe those Bible miracles, such as Christ turning water into wine." The ex-drunkard replied, "If you think that's a miracle, come to my home and I'll show you how Christ changed beer into carpets, chairs and even a piano."

Christ had come to dwell in the heart of that converted drunkard and had transformed his inward life and his outward circumstances as well. From His time to the present, Jesus Christ has been active in the supernatural work of transforming human hearts.

In the Gospels alone, we see a few examples of lives changed by Jesus:

- Mary Magdalene, from whom Jesus had cast out seven demons (Luke 8:2), was privileged to be the first to see Jesus after He had been raised from the dead.
- The greedy Zaccheus, who gave away half of his income after meeting Jesus, had formerly been involved in a dubious but lucrative position, which he forsook for the sake of following Christ.
- Simon Peter, an impulsive man who often acted before he thought—was changed into a powerful Christian leader and the Lord used him despite his impetuous nature.
- Two brothers, John and James, known as "sons of thunder," presumably because of their explosive tempers became loving disciples.

So too, we become new creatures in Christ, who makes all things new.

Lord, give me strength for today to live fully committed to You. Thank You for the change You have made in my life. Help me to give You all the praise and glory for making all things new, including me…

BY HIS STRENGTH, WE CAN EXPERIENCE NEW LIFE IN CHRIST.

SEPTEMBER 16

Testimony of a Former Evolutionist

"In the beginning God created the heavens and the earth."

— Genesis 1:1

If we get the subject of origins (creation-evolution) wrong, what else do we miss? Nonetheless, the assumption of so many today is that science has somehow disproved God. Consider the testimony of the late Dr. Dick Lumsden, biology professor and former dean of Tulane Graduate School.

Dr. Lumsden dogmatically taught evolution to his classes until one day a student politely asked him a number of pointed questions. She asked him questions such as: "How does evolution fit with the fundamentals of information theory?" "Aren't the odds of random assembly of genes mathematically impossible?" "Last month you showed us how mutations were genetic disasters. How, vis-à-vis natural selection, could they randomly produce new and better structures, improved species?" "Where exactly, in the fossil record—the evidence for progressive evolution, the transitional forms between major groups?"

Initially Lumsden dogmatically defended evolution, trying his best to answer her questions. But after an honest evaluation of the issue, he concluded that evolution was scientifically bankrupt: "I realized that the origin and diversification of life by evolution was a mathematical, physical, and biochemical impossibility, that the evidence for it was at best circumstantial, and a lot of what we really knew about biology was outright contradictory to the hypothesis." Dr. Lumsden became a reluctant creationist first and later a Christian. For those willing to look at the evidence, creation is the better explanation of origins.

The opening sentence of the Bible says it all. And if God did that, then can He not do the rest?

Lord, give me strength for today to be a witness for You. We praise You that all of creation shouts out, pointing to Your creative power. We praise You that You can transform even a skeptical college professor…

BY HIS STRENGTH, WE CAN RECOGNIZE
WHAT HIS HANDS HAVE MADE.

SEPTEMBER 17

The Bible and the Constitution

"When the righteous are in authority, the people rejoice; but when the wicked rule, the people mourn."

— Proverbs 29:2

The United States' Constitution was signed September 17, "in the year of our Lord," 1787. Today, we are often led to believe that it was a product of secularism. But that is not true.

Before the founding fathers ever sat down to write a Constitution, they had behind them more than 150 years or so of constitution-making of sorts by various Christian settlers of this country. The Mayflower Compact of 1620 was the first such example. The Pilgrims put on paper a political charter based on the biblical concept of covenant. This was the first of about 100 or so charters, compacts, frames of government, paving the way to the Constitution. In 1639, a Puritan colony produced the Fundamental Orders of Connecticut, which mentions the importance of "the Gospel of our Lord Jesus." That document was inspired by a sermon and was a key step on the way to the U.S. Constitution. That is why Connecticut prides itself as being "the constitution state."

A study of the 55 founders who met in Philadelphia in 1787 and produced what has been called "the miracle in Philadelphia" found that at least 52 of them were men in good standing with Trinitarian churches. These were not secular men, but Christians. While John Adams was not present during the proceedings, he nonetheless played a pivotal role in the nation's founding. He said, "Our Constitution was made only for a moral and religious people. It is wholly inadequate to the government of any other." Pray for America to get back on the right track.

Oh, Lord, help us to live our lives pleasing to You, so that we, too, may influence the people around us and build something strong and lasting in Your name…

BY GOD'S STRENGTH, WE CAN HELP RETURN THIS NATION TO HIM.

SEPTEMBER 18

Wealth Can Be Uncertain

*"He who trusts in his riches will fall,
but the righteous will flourish as a branch."*
— Proverbs 11:28

While the book of Proverbs encourages diligence and honestly earning wealth, it also has some warnings against putting one's hope in untrustworthy riches.

First of all, it says that it is always insecure. If a man places his dependence on wealth, it will in due time fail him, and only in his imagination is it a sure defense. Proverbs 23:5 says, *"Will you set your eyes on that which is not? For riches certainly make themselves wings; they fly away as an eagle toward heaven."*

The Bible says also that if it is obtained in any other way than by honest labor it is useless, even worse than useless. So if it is obtained by falsehood, by tricks, by misrepresentations in business, for example, it is likely to be, according to the Bible, as a vapor driven to and fro. Wealth obtained that way will never rest until finally it makes its way into the hands of the righteous.

The Bible also says that there are certain spiritual and moral dangers in the pursuit of wealth and that one needs to pursue it with caution. Paul says the love of money is the root of all evil, and those that would hasten to be rich are going to indeed fall into a snare. And if that seeking of riches involves any deviation from the uprightness which God requires of us, then it is worse than death. Better is a little with righteousness than great treasure without it.

Lord, give me strength for today to see through the deceitfulness of wealth. Please purge away any money-love in my heart. Help me to work diligently and wisely for that which You provide…

BY HIS STRENGTH, WE CAN TRUST
IN HIM, NOT OUR BANK ACCOUNT.

SEPTEMBER 19

Wesley's Wisdom on Wealth

"Go to the ant, you sluggard! Consider her ways and be wise. Which, having no guide, overseer, or ruler, provides her bread in the summer, and gathers her food in the harvest."

— Proverbs 6:6-8

John Wesley had a saying: You should make all the money you can, save all the money you can, and give all the money you can.

As a Christian leader, Wesley was referring to making money in ways that please God. Any money-making venture that steals from others displeases the Lord. We do well to earn as much as we can, especially during our productive years. The Scriptures also encourage us to save for a rainy day. We cannot presume upon tomorrow.

As to giving all we can, I must say that my ministry has been significantly blessed by some productive, wealthy Christians who invested in the kingdom.

It is certainly a fact that there are those who have been extraordinarily industrious and creative in the making of wealth and the building of businesses and great enterprises, and God has blessed them abundantly. God has used such men as this in an incredible way in the work of the kingdom of God.

We need to see money in its proper perspective. I think when we see money for what it is, simply an opportunity to do good for the kingdom of God, then we can see it in an entirely different perspective. May God grant each one of us such diligence in the affairs of this life that we may be able to do just that.

Make all you can. Save all you can. Give all you can.

Lord, give me strength for today to do my part in bringing in income, to save for a rainy day, and to generously bless those around me in need. Thank You for all the opportunities You provide for us, even in unexpected ways…

BY HIS STRENGTH, WE CAN VIEW MONEY AS A MEANS, NOT AN END.

SEPTEMBER 20

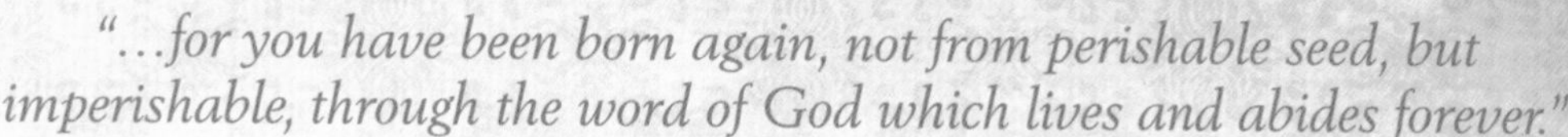

Jesus Can Change Anyone

"…for you have been born again, not from perishable seed, but imperishable, through the word of God which lives and abides forever."

— 1 Peter 1:23

Jesus can change anyone. Malcolm Muggeridge of England was a witty journalist and the editor of the English satirical magazine, *Punch*. He became a convinced socialist during the days of Stalin. In the words of author Lloyd Billingsley, Muggeridge felt that the USSR "had a future, whereas Britain and the West had only a past." He became the Moscow correspondent for the liberal British newspaper, *Manchester Guardian*. Before leaving for the "worker's paradise," he and his wife "cheerfully burned their bridges" destroying diplomas and their marriage certificate and other vestiges of bourgeois society, as they embraced Communism. But when they arrived in "Utopia," they were disillusioned. Eventually he realized that man cannot bring utopia on earth, Muggeridge became a Christian and used his writing skills to bring glory to Christ.

Through the years, I've seen thousands of people come to Christ. All of them have a story to tell in one way or another. Some stories are more dramatic than others, but as long as they truly come to Christ, they are on their way to heaven. I think of a man whose whole family rejoiced when he was converted. His daughter told my wife: "I've got a new daddy. And I like him better than the old one."

Of course, among the finest testimonies are those of individuals who grow up in a Christian home and love and serve the Lord faithfully all their lives, without ever going on the path of the prodigal son. It doesn't matter how you come to Christ—what matters is *that* you come to Christ.

Lord, give me strength for today to walk with You in the new life You bring. Thank You, Jesus, that You make all things new and have changed our hearts of stone into hearts of flesh…

BY HIS STRENGTH, WE CAN
EXPERIENCE THE NEW BIRTH.

SEPTEMBER 21

How Diligent Are We, Really?

"The hand of the diligent will rule, but the slothful will be put to forced labor."

— Proverbs 12:24

The Scriptures teach that we should be diligent in all areas of our lives. You know we say that it's wonderful that certain people have certain gifts and they can play, they can sing, or they can paint or do whatever it is. Yet it is because these people have been diligent, whereas we have been slothful. While we have been just lazy and relaxing, they were applying themselves to improve the talents and gifts that God has given them.

Isn't it wonderful there are some people who are tremendously effective soul winners in personal evangelism? Well, they have been working at it. Isn't it great that there are people who are great apologists for Christ and can take on the skeptic and deal with him at his level? But it just didn't happen that way.

The same is true in the spiritual world. I am sure that it would impugn the very character of the kingdom of God to suppose that the tender plant of God's grace can flourish in the garden of a sluggard. God calls us to diligence. May we be so in our study of the Word of God, in our prayer, in our determination to try to improve in the various qualities and characteristics of our lives.

We should pray He blesses us with more diligence. In all things it is by His grace. But in all of these things by His grace He gives us certain abilities and certain gifts and then He expects us to exercise them diligently.

Lord, give me strength for today to be more diligent in life, using my gifts and talents for Your honor and glory. I ask Your forgiveness for any laziness on my part…

BY HIS STRENGTH, WE CAN USE OUR GIFTS AND DEVELOP OUR TALENTS.

SEPTEMBER 22

Obscuring the Gospel

"For God did not send His Son into the world to condemn the world, but that the world through Him might be saved."

— John 3:17

Unfortunately, throughout the ages, the devil has distorted Christianity so much that the Gospel has often been obscured. Sometimes even church-goers don't have a clue what real Christianity is all about.

Sometimes, the "Christianity" being attacked by our culture today is such a false, twisted caricature that it bears little resemblance to the true faith. Indeed it ought to be attacked.

Recently, a lesbian who claimed to be a Christian came "out of the closet," declaring war on historic Christianity—the religion of the cross. It turns out that as a child she had been placed naked on a cross by an adult for some twisted, religious reason. Today she resents and rejects the cross of Christ as the means of salvation.

Woe to the person who did this terrible misdeed for it has caused her to reject a "straw man" of Christianity, not the real thing. But God's timeless truths about the salvation He offers us in Christ are not made null by the sins of professing Christians. Even if the entire official Church were to become apostate, that would not nullify the Gospel.

The true Gospel is a beautiful message. It is good news. But to understand the good news, we must come to grips with the bad news. We are all sinners before a holy God, who will not accept us as we are "…'til on that cross, as Jesus died, the wrath of God was satisfied," as the hymn "In Christ Alone" notes. That is good news.

Lord, give me strength for today to proclaim Your pure and simple Gospel. Thank You for preserving the true faith through centuries of wrong. Thank You for keeping and preserving me…

BY HIS STRENGTH, OUR
FAITH CAN BE PRESERVED.

SEPTEMBER 23

The Elevator to Paradise

"For by grace you have been saved through faith, and this is not of yourselves. It is the gift of God, not of works, so that no one should boast."

— Ephesians 2:8-9

Mankind inveterately seems to want to do something to earn salvation. They say, "Oh, that is too easy."

I think of a minister in South Africa who went down into the depths of a mine at lunch time to preach the Gospel to some of the workers there.

When the foreman heard the message of salvation, he said, "Oh, I don't believe that. It's too easy. We have to do our part."

As they got into the elevator at the bottom of the shaft, the preacher asked, "What do we have to do to get to the surface?"

"Nothing. I just push this button."

"Surely you have to do something to help pull yourself up."

"Of course not. The elevator does it all. It was difficult to build, but it lifts us up in just a few seconds. There is nothing we have to do but push the button."

When God provided for us that "elevator" to Paradise, He did it at infinite cost, a cost which caused Him to bore a hole into the very pit of hell where Christ suffered and died and endured the wrath of God in our place. An infinite price has been paid. But for us, it is free; for us it is easy. It was not easy for Christ when He paid the price. We simply have to get in, and believe, and He will lift us to heaven by faith.

Lord, give us strength for today to treasure the Good News in our hearts. Help us to share it with joy and gratitude. Thank You that You did all the heavy lifting in our salvation...

BY HIS STRENGTH, WE
CAN RECEIVE HIS GIFTS.

SEPTEMBER 24

Angels—Named or Otherwise—God's Servants

"I heard a man's voice between the banks of Ulai, which called, and said, 'Gabriel, make this man understand the vision.'"

— Daniel 8:16

Daniel is the only Old Testament book in which any angels are named, and two of them are named in that book. They are Gabriel and Michael, and both are mentioned in the New Testament. Gabriel announced the virgin birth to Mary. In Jude, we learn that Archangel Michael did battle with Satan, with Lucifer.
We do have the name of that fallen angel (Lucifer) who did not keep his first estate, but other than those three, the names of angels are unknown to us.

We see in Daniel 8 that Gabriel came in the form of a man. God spoke to Gabriel, and Gabriel came and appeared to Daniel.

Daniel's response to Gabriel is worth noting. When he came near, Daniel was afraid and fell upon his face. Apparently, this knocked him out because it says in the next verse that he was in a deep sleep. Now keep in mind of whom we are speaking. We are speaking of Daniel—one of the godliest men who has ever lived. This is Daniel who was not afraid to stand up to the likes of Nebuchadnezzar; Daniel who was willing to be cast in among the lions; Daniel who would not defile himself for any cause. This holy man, Daniel, we now find, is approached by Gabriel, and he is so overwhelmed that he literally passes out at the experience.

Angels are God's special servants to help further His kingdom. They are not to be worshiped, even though they are awe-inspiring.

Jesus, King of angels, we thank You for these ministering spirits which You send to serve those who are to inherit the kingdom. Thank You for sending us angels to aid us, even without our being always aware of it...

BY HIS STRENGTH AND WILL,
ANGELS MINISTER TO US.

SEPTEMBER 25

God Rules in History

"There is no wisdom nor understanding nor counsel against the LORD."

— Proverbs 21:30

How wondrous it is when we see all of the anti-God powers of this world crumble before the power of our Lord. It is amazing as we see God working in history and how so often when evil systems and empires and powers have seemed to rise to the very zenith of their power that suddenly they wither and crumble away.

So it was with Egypt in the days of the Exodus, as it would be later in Assyria, as it would be in Babylon, as it came to be in Rome when the barbarians came and knocked upon the eternal city of Rome. So it was with the Nazis, as they moved across Europe and then suddenly their power seemed to be broken and they, like a wounded octopus, drew their tentacles back to themselves to die in the mix of the rubble and ruin. So it was with the vaulted claims of fascism.

Then in our own recent time, so it was also with many of the nations in the grip of communism. When it seemed that there was nothing that could stop its inexorable march across the world, suddenly, it seemed almost overnight to begin to crumble and collapse everywhere. God is sovereign and God is faithful and will protect and cause those who are His own to persevere.

Persecutors of the church have down through the centuries discovered that God fights for His own. He is rarely early but never too late, as the Israelites discovered at the Red Sea when the Egyptian army bearing down on them—just before God destroyed it. How wondrous is our Lord!

God of history, thank You for ruling in the affairs of men. Thank You that evil is only permitted for a given time and then will be stopped. Thank You for Your wonderful plan for the world…

BY HIS STRENGTH, ALL HIS ENEMIES WILL BE A FOOTSTOOL FOR THE FEET OF CHRIST.

A Major Theme in Revelation

"They overcame him by the blood of the Lamb and by the word of their testimony..."

— Revelation 12:11

In today's world it doesn't seem as if the Christians are winning. It seems that unbelievers have the victory; they have taken over the machinery of life. They run the government and the media and the schools and most everything else. But things are not necessarily what they seem, as the book of Revelation points out.

At different points in that book Satan's forces appear to be victorious. The beast makes war against Christians and kills them. They rejoice over their dead bodies lying in the street for three and a half days. And yet their rejoicing is premature and at last God breathes new life into them, and they stand upon their feet and soon have dominion over the world with Christ, the King of kings.

Christ is ever pictured throughout the entire book, over and over again, as the victor. He is the victorious One, and because He is victorious, we who are in Him are victorious also in spite of everything that may seem to be the other way around.

Are believers in great tribulation? They shall come out of it. Are they killed? They shall stand upon their feet. Are they persecuted? They shall stand victoriously upon Mount Zion. Are their prayers not heard? Their prayers shall set the judgments in motion, and they will rule the world.

Jesus, the King of kings and Lord of lords, will one day inherit the nations, as He's been promised. It may look like that could never happen, but God is on the move—and His plans will stand.

Jesus, King of kings, we praise and honor You for being the Ruler of the nations. Thank You for revealing what is to come. Thank You that we will be victorious with You and that evil will one day be completely uprooted...

BY HIS STRENGTH AND AUTHORITY, CHRIST WILL RULE THE NATIONS.

SEPTEMBER 27

Work Out Your Salvation

"Therefore, my beloved, as you have always obeyed, not only in my presence, but so much more in my absence, work out your own salvation with fear and trembling."

— Philippians 2:12

What exactly does Paul mean here in this verse? We know that the Bible repeatedly teaches that salvation is not something that we work for, but rather it is a gift: *"...the gift of God is eternal life through Jesus Christ our Lord"* (Romans 6:23). It is not something that we obtain by our merit, for the Scripture says that it is by grace that we are saved, through faith, not of works, *"so that no one should boast."* (See Ephesians 2:8-9.)

Philippians 2:13 holds the key: *"...for it is God who works in you both to will and to do for His good pleasure"* (NKJV). God plants the desire within our hearts, and then He gives us the strength and the ability to do that which we now desire to do. In the same way that Christ said to Lazarus, "Lazarus, come forth," Lazarus got up and came out and Jesus made him alive. Lazarus did nothing at all until God worked it in him and made him alive.

I've often said that God just put a screwdriver in my "wanter" and turned it upside down, and suddenly to my astonishment, I found myself wanting to do things that I had never wanted to do before, and not wanting to do things which I had always loved to do before. Working *out* our salvation is not the same as working *for* our salvation.

Beautiful Savior, give us the strength to work out Your salvation in our lives, knowing that You will one day hold us accountable. Keep us from backsliding or being negligent in our spiritual disciplines...

BY HIS STRENGTH, WE WILL REACH HEAVEN, OUR HOME.

God's Part, Man's Part

"Nor do I count my life of value to myself, so that I may joyfully finish my course and the ministry which I have received from the Lord Jesus, to testify to the Gospel of the grace of God."

— Acts 20:24

Some people think of trusting in God as if they don't need to do anything else—just sit back on their lazy chair, watch TV or read a book, while God does all the work. Instead, we should take that guarantee of God, *"I can do all things through Christ who strengthens me"* (Philippians 4:13 NKJV), and trust in Him. Let me point out to you that doesn't mean that you just rest and wait for God to drop all of these blessings down the chimney. It means that you work harder.

Look at the Apostle Paul as an example. He was an indefatigable worker, and he never stopped. God used Paul in absolutely great ways because he was so committed to the task at hand. He was a tentmaker, and he refused gifts from many churches because he didn't want to be a burden to them. But he was most concerned about the kingdom of God and the glory of Christ and the salvation of men and women.

Where do those things rank in your list of priorities? Only you and God know. Taking God at His guarantee involves taking Him as Lord and Savior and Master. This is the One who died in agony for your sins, the One who loves you eternally and infinitely, the One who has redeemed you, the One who adopted you into His family and made you His heir. This is the One, Jesus Christ. Let Him use you for His glory and others' good.

Lord, forgive me for my spiritual laziness. Give me strength for today to serve You diligently. Thank You that in Christ we can do all things You set before us…

BY GOD'S STRENGTH, WE CAN BE USEFUL TO GOD'S KINGDOM.

SEPTEMBER 29

The Necessity of Humility

"The meek will He guide in judgment, and the meek He will teach His way."

— Psalm 25:9

Among the pagans, humility was not a virtue, it was a vice. I think of a man who described himself as a complete pagan. He scorned humility and all Christian virtues as being beneath the dignity of the pagan mind. His name was Adolf Hitler.

I remember one time debating a modern humanist atheist on a radio show, and someone called and asked what they should do to become a Christian. I said at first you need to get down on your knees and repent of your sins and accept Jesus Christ as Lord and Savior of your life.

Well, the host interrupted and said, "No, you should stand on your feet, be proud." Well that's the humanist motto, "Be proud." You know it is hard when you're pretending to be a god to be humble, and that's of course what humanists believe that they are.

Lowliness of mind and humility, those are two virtues that are not seen very often. I recall reading about two men who were arguing, and finally one of them despairing of ever changing the mind of the other said, "I can see that I am going to do nothing today to change your mind, but I would prayerfully ask you to prayerfully consider if there might just be a possibility that you could be wrong."

A constant theme of the Bible is that God opposes the proud, but gives grace to the humble. Paul asks a great question that helps encourage humility: *"What do you have that you did not receive?"* (1 Corinthians 4:7).

O Lord God Almighty, You are so high and lifted up and yet You dwell with the humble of heart. As I walk with You, please develop in me a true humility that only You can bring.

BY GOD'S STRENGTH, WE CAN ACQUIRE TRUE HUMILITY.

Christ and Humility

"Let nothing be done out of strife or conceit, but in humility let each esteem the other better than himself."

— Philippians 2:3

When Paul wrote the church in the Roman outpost of Philippi (in modern day Turkey), he had many positive things he commended them for. But Paul realized that the only flaw that he saw in the Philippian church was a tendency to divisiveness, a tendency which ultimately was going to be destructive to that church. But he did his best to point out to them the danger, the rocks that lay submerged in the path of the ecclesiastical ship at Philippi.

In order for them to be of one mind and one accord they had to acquire humility. He wrote to them, *"Let each of you look not only to your own interests, but also to the interests of others. Let this mind be in you all, which was also in Christ Jesus..."* (Philippians 2:4-5).

Jesus humbled Himself by becoming a man. The Second Person of the Trinity took on human flesh. So He was fully God and fully man. Then He humbled Himself in complete obedience, living a perfect life. Finally, He humbled Himself by dying on the cross. This was a degrading form of execution reserved only for slaves and non-Roman citizens. But God raised Him from the dead and vindicated Him completely. One day every knee shall bow and every tongue confess that He is Lord.

Humility comes before honor. Christ has shown us the way.

Lord, You who humbled Yourself so completely and received the name above all names, help me to have a true picture of You and, thus, a true picture of myself, resulting in humility...

BY GOD'S STRENGTH AND BY HIS LIGHT,
WE CAN SEE OURSELVES CLEARLY.

OCTOBER 1

A Song in the Heart

"The LORD is my strength and song, and He has become my salvation."
— Exodus 15:2

When we see that God delivers us, and He becomes our strength and our salvation, then He creates within us a song. Divine strength and spiritual song always go together. Nehemiah said *"...the joy of the LORD is your strength* (Nehemiah 8:10), and so assurance and deliverance leads to rejoicing, and rejoicing leads to strength for holy living.

This is why Paul says that we are to rejoice in the Lord always because in rejoicing we find strength. If you are not rejoicing, you are not going to have strength for the journey in the Christian life. Is there joy in your heart? Is there joy in your home? Is there singing in both? There won't be unless you know that God is your God and has become your salvation. The enemy of our souls cannot stand the praise of God. If you ever feel overwhelmed by evil or discouraged, start singing, even if you don't feel like it. A song of praise will lift your heart and soul to God, and evil will flee.

God inhabits the praises of His people. The Christian religion has always been a singing religion. When you ever find yourself getting low, turn to the hymnal and sing to the Lord a new song. We sing because the Lord is our strength and our salvation.

Lord God, You created music, and You put a song in my heart. I thank You for this "heavenly language" that You gave us. I will praise You and sing unto Your holy name...

BY GOD'S STRENGTH, WE CAN
LIFT OUR VOICE IN PRAISE.

OCTOBER 2

And a Teenager Shall Lead Them

"Uzziah was sixteen years old when he began to reign, and he was king in Jerusalem for fifty-two years."

— 2 Chronicles 26:3

Today it seems to be the heart's desire of every teenager that on his sixteenth birthday he receives a car, preferably a long, low, sleek one with a lot of painting on it and several mufflers. Well, the ancient Jewish leader Uzziah had more than his heart's desire when he became sixteen. They gave him the whole kingdom, and he became the king of Judah.

"Woe to you, O land, when your king is a lad" (Ecclesiastes 10:16) says the Old Testament writer. At the time Luther was brought before Philip of Spain, a young man who had just ascended to the throne, the placards that the supporters of Luther raised around the Diet of Worms cried out the message, "Woe unto that nation whose king is a child."

And yet, surprisingly enough, to every rule there are some exceptions, and Uzziah proved to be the exception and followed after the Lord. He walked in all of the ways of his father and according to the teachings of the prophet Zechariah. As long as Zechariah was there, Uzziah sought God, and God caused him to prosper greatly. He reigned longer (for 52 years total) than any of the other kings of Judah or Israel, save one. Sadly, he did not remain faithful after the prophet died. May God give us grace to serve Him faithfully, no matter what our age may be and no matter how others may react to the Lord.

Lord, our King, in one sense it does not matter who governs us at any level because You are sovereign. We ask, however, that You would bless us with good and godly governors and with Your servants who follow the counsel of Your Word.

BY GOD'S STRENGTH, OUR GOVERNORS CAN BE GODLY.

OCTOBER 3

Promotion is From the Lord

"And he [Uzziah] did what was correct in the eyes of the LORD as everything his father Amaziah had done. And he sought after God in the days of Zechariah, the one who instructed him in the fear of the LORD. And in the days that he sought after the LORD, God caused him to succeed."

— 2 Chronicles 26:4-5

Success is of the Lord. The Bible teaches us that promotion is from above. Now this is very contrary to the attitudes of people today who think they can force themselves up the ladder of success. The Bible tells us that promotion is from above—that it is God who blesses or withholds His blessing, and because of Him kings and nations and individuals prosper and succeed or fail to do so. Obviously, as we have opportunity we should strive to do our best with the resources God has given us to better our lives and the lives of those around us.

And we read in this passage that as long as King Uzziah sought the Lord, God made him to prosper. With his heart he sought after God, and the Lord caused him to prosper.

Those who would tell you that the Scripture calls us to be totally unconcerned with our own well-being do not understand the message of Scripture, in my opinion. But what the Bible calls us to do is to seek our wellbeing at the hand of God. That you will find from one end of the Scripture to the other, and the Bible says that God will bless us. Now in the Old Testament those blessings always appeared here in this life because these things were done for an example unto us. In the New Testament era, sometimes those blessings appear in this life, sometimes in the next. Either way, in the long run God's blessings follow obedience.

Jehovah-Jireh, our Great Provider, thank You for sustaining our lives. Thank You for the spiritual riches You have bestowed on me. Lord, give me strength for today to praise and thank You, whether You do or do not increase my worldly goods…

BY GOD'S STRENGTH, WE CAN LIVE IN CONTENTMENT.

OCTOBER 4

Blessings in This Life and the Next

"Now these things were our examples to the intent that we should not lust after evil things as they lusted."

— 1 Corinthians 10:6

What happened to people in the Old Testament provides lessons for people of all time. The fact that God will bless us and cause us to succeed and prosper if we seek and obey Him is seen clearly in the Old Testament. If the blessings or the cursings had come into the next world, which is invisible to our eyes, there could have been no example unto us at all, for we would not have known whether they had been blessed or not. And we may well have supposed that those who lived wickedly were blessed in the future life, and those that lived godly were not.

I think that one of the greatest decisions every person in this world has to make is to decide: What is the source of blessing and success and prosperity? I also think that every Christian should seek those things—and I am not talking about worldly success and prosperity per se, though God may be pleased to grant that to you, but that our life should be a success. By that I mean, we will accomplish that for which God created us for we have been made for His glory. Everyone must answer this question in his own heart: Where is the source of my blessing and my success? James tells us *"Every good gift and every perfect gift is from above and comes down from the Father of lights, with whom is no change or shadow of turning"* (James 1:17).

"Come Thou Fount of every blessing, tune my heart to sing Thy praise. Streams of mercy never ceasing call for songs of loudest praise." Thank You, Jesus, my Fount of every blessing. Let me always be grateful for what You give me…

BY GOD'S STRENGTH, WE ACKNOWLEDGE HIM AS THE SOURCE OF EVERY BLESSING.

By Grace Alone

"Watch out for dogs, watch out for evil workers, watch out for those who practice mutilation"
— Philippians 3:2

The Apostle Paul warned the Philippian Christians about evil workers, whom he called dogs. What they were doing was an attempt to add something to the Gospel. These are the kind of people that Paul condemned in Galatians 1.

In Galatians 1 he is talking about those who are calling them to some other kind of Gospel. This is a Gospel that is antithetical to the grace of God, the grace of Christ. This is the Gospel that always has to add something more. Well, yes, salvation by grace through faith is good and nice—BUT it is not enough. You have to add circumcision, you have to add the Mosaic ritual or you have to add baptism or you have to add some kind of sacramentalism, or you have to have the baptism of the Spirit—you have to have something in addition. They are never satisfied with simply the pure Gospel of the grace of Christ.

In this text, Paul is talking about the same Judaizers. They were claiming that Gentiles could be saved through faith in Jesus—as long as they added to it circumcision ("mutilation" in Philippians 3:2). We can add nothing to the finished work of Christ on the cross. It is the Gospel of Christ as it was proclaimed by the Apostle Paul, as it was enunciated by Augustine, as it was systematized by Calvin, and it is the purest expression of the Gospel of grace that there is—salvation by grace alone.

"Oh to grace how great a debtor, daily I'm constrained to be." Yes, Lord, Your grace is all sufficient and never ending. I thank You and praise You that You have poured out Your grace on me…

BY GOD'S STRENGTH, HIS GRACE HAS SAVED US.

Rejoice in the Lord

"Rejoice in the Lord always. Again I will say, rejoice!"
— Philippians 4:4

Paul's letter to the Philippian Christians is an epistle of joy. The words joy, rejoice, and rejoicing appear over and over again in this epistle. In the final chapter, Paul gives this command. It is an imperative: Rejoice in the Lord! Now we generally tend to say to people," Well, I hope you will be happy." Paul never said that. He said, "Rejoice!" That's a command, an imperative in the Lord.

Why is that important? We tend to look upon that as some peripheral issue of not too much importance. But Paul obviously felt it to be a very important matter. I think the secret of why this is important can be found in the fact that in Nehemiah 8:10 we are told that the joy of the Lord is our strength. One thing that is true of all strong Christians, they enjoy the Lord. And so consequently they spend much time with Him, in His word, in prayer and in service to Him, and it shows in their countenance.

A great resource for the Christian is found in the hymnal. Here we have centuries of beautiful psalms, hymns, and spiritual songs written by Christians throughout the ages. As one of the hymns says, "I sing because I'm happy. I sing because I'm free." Jesus has made me free. With His joy you will be able to serve. With His joy, you will be able to be a good soldier of Jesus Christ. Therefore, rejoice!

Lord, You are my joy and You are my song. I thank You that I can rejoice before You today. When my day is hard and my song stilled, then will I praise You and You will fill my heart with Your presence and joy…

BY GOD'S STRENGTH,
WE CAN ALWAYS REJOICE.

OCTOBER 7

A Good Memory Leads to Thanks

"I will remember the works of the Lord;
surely I will remember Your wonders of old."
— Psalm 77:11

The word "thank" comes from the same root as "think." People are not thankful usually because they are not thoughtful. They don't think about things that have been done for them and so they don't thank people for doing that.

We are not going to be glad and joyful over something and thankful for it if we don't think about it, and so we need to constantly remind ourselves. That's why the Scriptures and Christ over and over said, "Remember." "Remember." "Remember!" We are to remember and think about these things in order that we may be thankful for what Christ has done in coming into this world for us: what He has already accomplished; what change He has made in our lives; what He has done for us over the years; how He has provided for us; what He has promised; and what we have to look forward to. We should remember all these things and thank Him for them.

It is only as we think about those things and recognize them as God's blessings that thanksgiving grows in us. Unthankful children are always glum, down in the mouth. When you see a person whose mouth is turned down, who has a downcast, dog look on their face, they are not thankful. They are just sorry for themselves, they are miserable, and they don't think about anything that God has done for them. Unfortunately, there is a little bit of that in every one of us, and, therefore, the Bible tells us to remember what God has done.

Dear Jesus, give me the strength of mind to remember the good and to dwell on what You have done for me. You have cared for my body and soul. You have secured my eternal salvation through Your blood. Give me strength for today to remember Your goodness...

BY GOD'S STRENGTH, WE CAN
REMEMBER ALL HIS BENEFITS.

OCTOBER 8

Listening to Jesus

"But one thing is needed. And Mary has chosen the good part, which shall not be taken from her."

— Luke 10:42

The late motivational speaker Zig Ziglar once made an interesting comment about focus. He said suppose you took an outside stack of old newspapers, papers that would easily go up in flames with the right input and a magnifying glass on a sunny day. If you took that glass and you slowly moved it around in an unfocused way, nothing would happen. But if you carefully allowed the magnifying glass to stay at the same place—in a focused way—it could easily cause a fire (if that was your goal). We accomplish little if we remain "wandering generalities" as opposed to becoming "a meaningful specific."

It's easy to get distracted by many things. In modern times, we are over-stimulated, over-exposed, and over-saturated—often with wordy things. In such a context, it is easy to forget what truly matters—listening to Jesus. In this passage, Martha and Mary have Jesus over as a dinner guest. Martha gets frustrated that she is doing all the work, while Mary is just sitting there listening to the Master. So Martha asks Jesus to tell Mary to help her. Instead, Jesus commends Mary for simply listening to God's Word. We need to focus on what God has to say for us. We need to focus on His purpose for us, which may be different during different phases of our lives.

Whatever pressing activities we may feel obligated to do, it is most important that we always center our lives by spending time with Jesus. Remember this: If you're too busy to pray, you're too busy.

Lord, thank You for inviting us to sit at Your feet and listen. Forgive us for being slaves to "the tyranny of the urgent." Instead, help us to focus on that which is important, beginning with spending time with You…

BY GOD'S STRENGTH, WE CAN FIND TIME TO LISTEN TO HIM.

OCTOBER 9

Just the Product of Change?

"If Christ is not raised, your faith is vain; you are still in your sins."

— 1 Corinthians 15:17

Are we just random accidents, with no future hope beyond the grave? Evolutionists essentially believe we are. Listen to what British atheist Bertrand Russell (1872-1970) said in his book, *Why I Am Not a Christian*: "…man is the product of causes which had no prevision of the end they were achieving…" Evolution says we're here by accident.

Continues Russell: "…his origin, his growth, his hopes and fears, his loves and his beliefs, are but the outcome of accidental collocations of atoms; …no fire, no heroism, no intensity of thought and feeling, can preserve an individual life beyond the grave…" The grave stops it all.

Death not only overtakes us all, but everything else, too, says Russell: "… all of the labour of the ages, all of the devotion, all of the inspiration, all the noonday brightness of human genius, are destined to extinction in the vast death of the solar system, and that whole temple of Man's achievement must inevitably be buried beneath the debris of a universe in ruins…"

He concludes, "Only within the scaffolding of these truths, and on the firm foundation of unyielding despair, can the soul's habitation henceforth be safely built." Begin with the premise that life is meaningless and then you can build meaning into it, says Russell. What a phrase, "the firm foundation of unyielding despair." What a contrast God gives us in His Word—we have a firm foundation of truth because Jesus definitely rose from the dead.

O Lord, give us hearts of compassion for those around us whose lives have no meaning and no purpose and no Savior. Help us to be shining lights in their darkness. May the light from the empty tomb dispel the darkness…

BY GOD'S STRENGTH,
WE SERVE A RISEN SAVIOR.

OCTOBER 10

A Nation in Need of Prayer

"If My people, who are called by My name, will humble themselves and pray, and seek My face and turn from their wicked ways, then I will hear from heaven, and will forgive their sin and will heal their land."

— 2 Chronicles 7:14

Every once in a while a national tragedy takes place. For a short time, it jolts many people into returning to church or looking to God for help. Then fairly soon after, many go back to business as usual.

It is tragic that such horrible things as what took place in Columbine would be necessary to awaken an apathetic people to the need for this country to return to God. Solzhenitsyn, the great author and intellectual of the Soviet Union, said that when he was but a young man, he heard an old peasant farmer speaking to a friend, summing up the whole situation in the Soviet Union in a very simple, single sentence. He said: "We have forgotten God and we have destroyed ourselves." We are in the process of doing that very same thing.

Dear friends, things can change. I am quite sure it won't take many more national tragedies for the American people to begin to say, "Enough is enough." And I want to say to those members of the Supreme Court who have given this nation this hellish milieu of ungodliness and immorality, "You had better get on your knees because you are going to have to answer to God for what you have done." God promises to heal our nation, if we humble ourselves, repent from our wicked ways, and seek His face. Ours is a nation in great need of prayer.

Lord God, You have been so gracious and so good to us, and we turned away from You. Let it not be too late for our nation to return unto You. Lord, we deserve Your wrath, but we ask for Your mercy…

BY GOD'S STRENGTH, OUR NATION
CAN RETURN TO THE LORD.

OCTOBER 11

Unanswered Prayer

"Do not abandon me, O LORD; O my God, do not be far from me."
— Psalm 38:21

Unanswered prayers—the bane of every Christian's life—is the distressing problem of the children of God down through the centuries. It is, in fact, the cause of spiritual retrogression.

It is because of unanswered prayers, perhaps more than any other reason, that Christians pray less, and when they pray less, their lives are less changed by God and their prayers are consequently less answered. The result is that having begun their spiritual career with great joy as they spend time with the Savior, over the years, things changed.

Many Christians have discovered that their prayers have become tedious. They have often felt that their prayers have not risen any higher than the ceiling. Their lives seem to be unaffected by their prayers—not only their lives personally, but the circumstances in which they live. God's timing is not ours. Our prayers are heard, and God will answer. Often it is a matter of surrendering our will to His. Sometimes we might not be praying according to His will.

There is one prayer that God will always answer, "Thy will be done." When we ask for God's will to be done in our lives, He will do it. We often find great, positive changes in our lives when we submit to God in prayer. God delights in answering our prayers. Don't let your prayer life become a tedious listing off of rote items. Instead, recognize it for what it is—communing with the Almighty Creator of the Universe.

O Lord, You who answer the cry of the heart of Your children, You see the long-time prayers that we have laid before You over and over. Give us strength for today to persist in prayer, to be faithful in our prayers, even if the fulfillment takes place after we're gone…

BY GOD'S STRENGTH, WE CAN
PRAY "THY WILL BE DONE."

Christopher Columbus

"...And the Gospel must first be preached to all nations."

— Mark 13:10

Christopher Columbus used to be a hero. Today, he is politically incorrect and unjustly blamed for many of the bad things done in the wake of his historic voyage.

His name, Christopher, means "Christ-bearer." *Pherein,* the second part of his name, means "to bear"—the one who bears Christ.

Interestingly, the pilot of the Niña, one of the three ships made famous by Columbus, drew a map of the known world. At the top of the map is a drawing of St. Christopher carrying the Christ child across the Atlantic Ocean to the New World, and the features of St. Christopher are unmistakably the features of Christopher Columbus, who, his son tells us, was a tall man with blonde hair and blue eyes. His hair turned white at the age of thirty. He was a gentle man who hated swearing and blasphemy and tried to live a godly life.

The word "Columbus," coming from the Italian *colon,* means "a member." Christopher Columbus liked to say he was a member of the body of Christ and would carry Christ to the New World. He himself said, "I am a most unworthy sinner, but I have cried out to the Lord for grace and mercy and they have covered me completely...No one should fear to undertake any task in the Name of our Savior, if it is just and if the intention is purely for His holy service." Opening the New World for the rest of the earth to come and begin to Christianize was no small task.

Lord of the Universe, we thank You for the bravery and great daring of Christopher Columbus. We ask for Your grace to do what You call us to, whether great or small...

LORD, GIVE ME STRENGTH FOR
TODAY TO SAIL UNKNOWN SEAS.

Getting Prayers Answered

"This is the confidence that we have in Him, that if we ask anything according to His will, He hears us."

— 1 John 5:14

In dealing with unanswered prayer, note that all of Jesus' prayers were answered. *"Father, I thank You that You have heard Me"* (John 11:41), Jesus said. Now why was this? It was not simply because of His divine nature, but because like a good Son, He was committed to His Father. He is the one who could say, *"…for I always do those things that please Him"* (John 8:29). *"This is My beloved Son, in whom I am well pleased"* (Matthew 3:17), said His Father. In effect, His prayers were the desires of His Father, and so they were answered.

Consider any parent and child. All parents have some ideal or idea in mind about what they want their child to grow up to be. They have some ideal for their child's education, morality, safety, and physical well-being. Consequently, when a child comes to a parent and makes a request, it is filtered through the ideal the parent has in mind, consciously or subconsciously.

If it is contrary to what the parent feels is ideal for that child, (if the parent has any backbone at all) it will be denied. Since God has no lack of backbone, those requests made to Him that are contrary to His ideal for us are invariably denied. When we submit ourselves to His ideal and His plan for our lives, it can be nothing other than that which is good. Mercifully, God does not answer all of our prayers. In retrospect, we can be glad for that.

Father, help us to pray more effectively. Forgive us that often we just hasten into Your presence with a "Gimme, Gimme, Gimme" attitude. Help us to praise You, to confess our sins, to thank You, and to lay our concerns before You. Thank You for Your care for us…

BY GOD'S STRENGTH, WE ARE ADOPTED CHILDREN WHO BRING OUR REQUESTS TO OUR FATHER.

OCTOBER 14

Key Elements in Prayer

"Therefore pray in this manner:
Our Father who is in heaven, hallowed be Your name."
— Matthew 6:9

In our day of short attention spans, it is often hard for people to learn how to pray effectively. Too often we come to God with all sorts of petitions and intercessions like, "God bless Uncle John and Aunt Sue and Grandma," and we are sending prayers all over the place, yet the sender is broken down. We have no ability to have prayers answered because we ourselves are often not right with God. Of course, there is more to prayer than petition. We should include in our prayers, prayers of:

- Petition, which is asking something for yourself,
- Adoration, which is praising God for what He is,
- Thanksgiving, thanking God for what He has done,
- Intercession, praying for the needs of other people, and many others.

I like to use the ACTS formula for prayer. First is Adoration—to spend time in praise of God. Second is Confession of sin. Third comes Thanksgiving. Fourth comes Supplication, which includes petitions and intercessions.

In the Lord's Prayer, Jesus teaches us to begin in praise, then to petition God for His will to be done. Next comes a request for our daily needs. After that is a request for forgiveness of sins, along with a commitment to forgive those who have sinned against us. Next comes a very important petition that we not be led into temptation, but delivered from the evil one, that is, from Satan, is the best translation. Finally, it closes as it opened—with praise and adoration, for our God is great.

Lord, give me strength for today to spend meaningful time with You in prayer. Forgive me for my mind wandering. Thank You, Jesus, that You are seated at the right hand of the Father, and You are even interceding on our behalf. Help us to always remember that...

BY GOD'S STRENGTH, OUR PRAYERS CAN AVOID BEING MERE BABBLING.

OCTOBER 15

God At Work Around the World

"I tell you, there is joy in the presence of the angels of God over one sinner who repents."

— Luke 15:10

God is at work throughout our world in great ways—often in ways we do not hear about.

Christianity is no longer a Western religion. It is a world religion. In fact, the growth of non-Western missions is now reported to be five times the rate of growth of Western missions. Christianity is becoming a Third World religion.

What is behind all these incredible developments? Well, for one thing, a greater commitment to prayer. For example, since 1989, when a "global prayer strategy" was initiated, millions of Christians from 180 nations have been involved in daily prayer for revival across the world. They spend at least five minutes when the sun rises in their area to pray for the spread of the Gospel. Prayer warrior David Bryant says, "As the sun moves across each time zone, the torch of prayer is being passed around the clock, around the world."

In the last 50 years of the 20th century we saw the rise of active ministry of the lay person. Increasingly, tens of millions of lay people around the world have begun to share their faith in Christ. They have been equipped, trained, emboldened, and encouraged to go out and share the Good News with others. This is another reason for the great explosion of converts around the world.

Let God use you where you are, regardless of your level of theological training, to let others know about Jesus. There is a great deal of joy when someone becomes a true believer in Jesus. Even the angels rejoice.

Dear Lord, thank You for how You are actively at work around our world and drawing many people to Yourself from a variety of backgrounds. Thank You for the millions of Christians praying and the millions of Christians, including laymen, sharing the Gospel...

BY GOD'S STRENGTH, WE CAN JOIN IN THE WORLDWIDE HARVESTING.

OCTOBER 16

Daily Cleansing

"If we confess our sins, He is faithful and just to forgive us our sins and cleanse us from all unrighteousness."

— 1 John 1:9

"Who may ascend the hill of the LORD?" (Psalm 24:3), the psalmist asks, and he answers this question by saying, *"He who has clean hands and a pure heart"* (v. 4). How shall we come into the presence of God, about whom the prophet said: *"Your eyes are too pure to look on evil, and You cannot look on wickedness"* (Habakkuk 1:13)? We must first come to be cleansed in that fountain that flows from Calvary's hill.

We must come and ask God to cleanse us in every part of our being. Many people forget that even their memory is tainted by its intimate connection with the old self. All manner of sin has been brought into the sanctuary of the mind. This memory needs to be cleansed. Did you ever ask God to cleanse your memory from all of the evil stored there? Your affections need to be cleansed and purified. Our wills need to be cleansed.

We need to realize that only through the blood of Christ is there cleansing for sin. "What can wash away my sin? Nothing but the blood of Jesus." If we are going to come into the presence of God and expect Him to hear and answer prayer, we dare not come into His presence besmirched and befouled and tainted with our sins. "Cleanse me, O God." That means, of course, that we are going to confess our sins and repent of them as well as ask to be cleansed from them.

Forgive us, Lord, for our many sins. Forgive us that we keep repeating them, sins of commission and sins of omission. Thank You for Your cleansing blood, Jesus, the only means by which sin is forgiven…

BY GOD'S STRENGTH,
WE CAN BE WASHED NEW.

Life in Christ Is Not Boring

"... And He said to them, 'Follow Me, and I will make you fishers of men.'"

— Matthew 4:19

Are you living an adventure, or are you living a humdrum monotony? When it comes to truly following Christ, life is one of the most thrilling and most exciting adventures the human spirit can know. What is an adventure? It would be interesting to have people answer that, wouldn't it? It may be something very different than you might think.

Actually, "adventure" comes from the Latin words *ad* and *venire*, which mean to "come to," which are exactly the same roots from which we get the word "Advent." An Advent means the "coming to" this world by Christ. An adventure is a "coming to." It is a coming to Christ.

The Christian life is a supernatural life. The spiritual man was dead, and only as the Holy Spirit, the giver of life, comes and quickens our lives will there be the slightest stirring in the garden of our soul.

We need to pray that the Spirit would fill us and enliven us, that He would bring us to spiritual life and joy that only God can give, and that He would empower us to live for Him, to overcome temptation, and to serve Him throughout our lives. It is the work of God's Spirit to sanctify us in this way. Life is never the same after that.

Lord, forgive us for ever believing Satan's lie that following You is boring, while rebelling against You is exciting. Thank You so much for the Christian adventure. Lord, give me strength for today to follow the prompting of Your Spirit...

BY GOD'S STRENGTH, THE CHRISTIAN LIFE IS AN ADVENTURE.

Guide Me, O Thou Great Jehovah

"He leads me in paths of righteousness for His name's sake."
— Psalm 23:3

Did you ever think about the fact that we were born to be led? Now that sort of goes cross-grain for many of us because there are many people who would much prefer to think of themselves as leaders than the led. But if we are Christians, we are born to be led because we are sheep—and sheep must be led. We all profess such: "*The LORD is my shepherd; I shall not want. . . He leads me beside still waters...*" (Psalm 23:1, 2).

I remember riding in a bus down from Jerusalem to Jericho years ago and seeing on the left side of the road a great flock of animals with a man right in their midst. Half of the animals were in front of him, and half of the animals were behind him, and they were all moving gradually up the hill. Our perceptive guide said, "If you will note carefully, you will perceive that all of the animals in front of the shepherd are goats, and all of the animals behind him are sheep because, you see, sheep will naturally follow, but goats have to be driven with a stick or a whip."

Whose agenda are you following today? Is it yours, or has it been submitted to the Spirit of God that He might lead you? You will find that as the Spirit of God guides and leads your life, you will live a life more exciting and adventurous than ever you dreamed the Christian life could be.

Heavenly Father, thank You for making us sheep and not goats. Help us to follow Your leading and not to get ahead of You and away from You. Help us to faithfully complete the task well that lay before us now...

BY GOD'S STRENGTH, WE CAN ENJOY HIS CLEAR LEADING.

OCTOBER 19

Who Is the Lord?

"Why do you call Me, 'Lord, Lord,' and not do what I say?"
— Luke 6:46

How sad it is that there are many professing Christians who think of God as some sort of a genie in a bottle who is there to help them fulfill their plans. They call upon God when they want to, when they need help to do what they want to do.

Thus, Christ is their servant and they are the masters. The Scripture makes it plain that we are the bondservants of Christ. He is our Master and, therefore, we need to be available to Him. The greatest ability the Christian needs is availability. Are you available to God? Are you available to Him today and each day to use you?

Offer yourself each morning to God, to Jesus Christ as Master and Lord of your life, and you will be amazed at what will happen and the opportunities for service you will have that will make the end of your day a glorious thing. As you lie down at night, you will know that God has used you, that your life has had eternal significance.

People will be brought into your presence who have deep needs, those who have need of Jesus Christ, and you will have the pleasure of pointing them to the Savior. Your life will begin to bud and blossom and bring forth fruit abundantly to the glory of Jesus Christ, if you are available to Him and if you sincerely pray, "O God, use me today." This is a prayer He will answer.

Forgive us, Lord, for too often playing church. Forgive us for treating prayer like a spiritual vending machine, where we insert our coins and out comes the product. Lord, You are our master, not our genie. We submit to You today with gratitude...

BY GOD'S STRENGTH, WE CAN SUBMIT TO JESUS OUR LORD.

New Beginnings Start With the New Birth

"Jesus answered him, 'Truly, truly I say to you, unless a man is born again, he cannot see the kingdom of God.'"

— John 3:3

The spiritual life is in some ways analogous to the physical. In our physical lives we are born, we grow, and we die. In the spiritual world it is also necessary for us to be born and to grow, but we never die. Jesus said, "...*whoever believes in Me has eternal life*" (John 6:47).

The Christian life begins with a new birth. Jesus declared it as the great imperative. He said, *"You must be born again"* (John 3:7). I think of an evangelist who came to a town and preached on that very text, and he said, "You must be born again." The next night the crowd regathered and he preached "You must be born again." And the third day again, "You must be born again."

Finally, one of the elders said to him, "Sir, why do you keep preaching on the text "you must be born again"?

He replied, "Because you must be born again."

Have you? Have you experienced that life-transforming change that only God by His Spirit, through faith in Jesus Christ can bring about? As the Bible says, *"Therefore, if any man is in Christ, he is a new creature. Old things have passed away. Look, all things have become new"* (2 Corinthians 5:17). That is what is meant by the "new birth." That is the new beginning of the Christian life.

Dear Lord, it is such a privilege to be born again, to know that although I have messed up, I can be forgiven and can start afresh. Thank You that the old is gone and the new has come...

BY GOD'S STRENGTH, WE CAN SEE THE KINGDOM OF GOD.

OCTOBER 21

Growth Must Follow Regeneration

"I will give you a new heart, and a new spirit I will put within you."
— Ezekiel 36:26

For those who truly believe in Jesus, God promises a heart transplant. This is what being born again is all about—the old has passed away and in Christ all things are made new.

When we come to understand the glorious Gospel of His grace—that totally undeserved, unmerited, unworked for grace—that Christ came and did it all: He paid the penalty for our sins upon the Cross; He endured the punishment of Hell; He purchased for us a mansion in paradise; and He offers all of it to us freely if we will but place our trust in Him and receive him into our hearts as Lord and Savior. Only then, in that day you will find a new you looking at you in the mirror and you will have reached the starting gate.

Some people seem to think that this is the final goal. No, it is just the beginning. I'm sure that many a twenty-two year old or so, after having worked arduously for four years in college and more years before that, finally is handed a diploma and told, "This is the commencement." They would like to think that this is the end and that now they can retire and rest. So too, the Christian life begins with a new birth. Growth is absolutely essential in any kind of life—how much more so the Christian life. Reading the Bible, praying, fellowship with other believers, corporate worship, and sharing the Gospel are some of the means of that growth.

Father, thank You for taking my heart of stone and giving me a heart of flesh. Thank You for the gift of regeneration and of justification. Now I ask that You may help me in the process of sanctification, of growing in You. Don't let anything hold me back...

BY GOD'S STRENGTH, WE CAN DAILY ACCESS THE MEANS OF GROWTH.

OCTOBER 22

A Fairy Tale for Adults

"Claiming to be wise, they became fools."

— Romans 1:22

We know that many a young man or woman has lost his or her faith because they have come to believe that evolution is a proven fact. This is tragic—especially when you consider the scientific evidence itself. Micro-evolution (small changes within kind) is proven. But macro-evolution (all creatures can be traced back to one common ancestor) is fraught with assumptions and contradicts the evidence we have, such as the fossil record.

One time a scientist from France made a remark about the idea of common ancestry through biology, remarking: "Evolution is a fairy tale for adults." And that is precisely what it is.

The number of fables and stories and fictional novels that have been spun out of evolution must be counted in the tens of thousands. It is a fairy tale for adults. In fact one noted evolutionist recently wrote this, "We may weave stories, we may create scenarios, it all depends on…" On what? How do you think he finished that sentence? On the scientific facts? On the indisputable evidence? No. He said, "It all depends on the extent of our imagination and the credulity of your audience." You can make up any kind of story you want, and they are forever weaving stories on the least thread of evidence at all—their fairy tales for adults.

In the text above, Paul summarizes the state of those who have rejected God who has made Himself manifest in His creation—professing to be wise, they became fools.

God of wisdom and might, teach us Your wisdom that we may not become fools. Keep our minds clear and focused that we may not believe false and incorrect teachings…

BY GOD'S STRENGTH, HIS TRUTH WILL SHINE FORTH.

OCTOBER 23

The Real King of Kings

"In the days of these kings the God of heaven shall set up a kingdom which shall never be destroyed. And the kingdom shall not be left to another people, but it shall break in pieces and consume all these kingdoms, and it shall stand forever."

— Daniel 2:44

Shelley, in one of his sonnets, tells of meeting a traveler from Egypt who, in a trek across the desert wasteland, came upon the remains of a marble statue. All that remained on the pedestal were two feet and the lower part of two gigantic legs. Lying in the sand was the cracked remnant of what had been the head.

When the traveler rubbed the sand away from the pedestal, he found this inscription: "My name is Ozymandias, king of kings: Look on my works, ye mighty, and despair!" He turned and looked and as far as the eye could see, there was naught but the sifting sand. Whatever kingdom and glory he once realized had all disappeared.

Daniel was shown things about some of earth's kingdoms, including ancient Babylon, the Medo-Persian Empire, the Macedonian Empire, and Rome as well. The rulers of these kingdoms boasted great things, but soon they passed away and they became nothing more than a chapter in a history book.

What is the Babylonian empire today? What is the Medo-Persian empire today? What is the Macedonian empire today to anyone? Simply historical points of interest on the continuum of time.

However, in the days of the Roman emperors, the God of heaven established a new kingdom, that of our Lord Jesus, which will never be destroyed. It continues to fill the whole earth to this day.

Jesus, King of kings, give us strength and insight and clear thinking today so that we might see You as You really are—the King of all kings, the Ruler of the nations. Open our eyes that we might see You on Your throne…

BY GOD'S STRENGTH, WE CAN BOW THE KNEE TO THE TRUE KING OF KINGS.

OCTOBER 24

Ultimate Success

"His lord said unto him, Well done, thou good and faithful servant..."
— Matthew 25:21, KJV

We only have one life. We have to make it count. But count for what? What is the purpose of life?

We are deluged with positive thinking types of messages these days. Some of them are outwardly Christian. However, if you dig a little deeper, often you find essentially a humanistic message with a Christian veneer.

The key question is this: In whom is our trust? Ourselves or God? Positive thinking beats negative thinking. But best of all, is sanctified positive thinking.

Americans are consumed with success. However, what is the ultimate success? Is it not making it to heaven? To be successful in this world only and then be cast into eternal hell is ultimate failure. True success means not only going to heaven, but helping others to get there also by spreading the Gospel.

The world tells us repeatedly to trust in ourselves, to have self-confidence. Our goal instead should be to have Christ-confidence. Are we putting all our emphasis on this life only or the next? It's an important question.

On the one hand, some worldly success can actually be counter to God's purposes. On the other hand, it is a sin to bury our talents. God has given them to us that we may glorify Him in all we do.

To achieve real success in life, we should strive to serve the Lord so diligently that one day He will look us in the face and say, "Well done, good and faithful servant."

Lord Jesus, please help me to do the right things for You as a thank You for the salvation You have earned by Your blood. If there is anything in my life that would keep You from saying "Well done" at the end of my life, please prune it away...

BY GOD'S STRENGTH, WE CAN SO LIVE
AS TO BE COMMENDED BY CHRIST.

OCTOBER 25

Work Together or Prepare to Lose

"...be eager to keep the unity of the Spirit in the bond of peace."
— Ephesians 4:3

In Philippians, Paul tells us that we are to stand fast in one mind and one spirit, striving together for the faith of the Gospel. The word striving together in Greek is the word from which we get athletics, and in fact it would be a team sport, probably team wrestling. The Greeks had a form of wrestling where one team of 5 or 6 people would line up here, and the other team would line up there, and at a signal they would all leap at each other and there would then be a mass of individuals wrestling.

Well, we are to strive to wrestle together for the faith of the Gospel, for the propagation of the Gospel of Christ. You know there is nothing that will solve church problems more than an outward look at the enemies that are all around us.

The early church had to deal with the Roman pagans who thought Christians were atheists because they didn't have idols. They had the Greek sophists there around them. They had the Jews who were persecuting them. They had all sorts of problems out there, so generally they wouldn't be fighting among each other.

The problems of the peace time army are notorious, and that's what happens. The church is involved in a warfare. I assure you one thing, if you had 5 or 6 men on a wrestling team wrestling with others, they no doubt had some differences among them, but I assure you they would learn to work together—or they would quickly lose.

Dear Lord, forgive us that Your church on earth is fraught with factionalism. Forgive us for any way in which we contribute to this disunity. Give me strength for today to be a positive force for unity in Your body...

BY GOD'S STRENGTH, WE CAN STRIVE TO BE A UNIFYING FACTOR IN THE BODY OF CHRIST.

OCTOBER 26

Dealing With Persecutors

"Do not be frightened by your adversaries. This is a sign to them of their destruction, but of your salvation, and this from God."

— Philippians 1:28

When Paul wrote the Philippian Christians in the first century, Christianity was illegal for the most part. In fact, during the Roman Empire, there were ten waves of serious persecution against the believers. Sometimes hot, sometimes cold—but always there.

One of the incredible things about the Christians, which the Romans noted, is that they weren't afraid. I remember reading a dialogue between a Christian who was chained to an iron bed, which was being heated red hot and he was being killed. They were still threatening him and calling upon him to recant, and he was laughing at them and saying in effect: Do your worst. You can do nothing but send me into the presence of Christ the sooner. You can do nothing but transfer me into paradise. I am not afraid of you.

This was terrifying to them. It was a token to them of their own perdition. They realized that this was the true God that these people worshiped. Are you terrified by the adversaries? Some Christians never even see an adversary because they do not speak boldly for Christ, they don't really encounter them. Oh they may see the adversaries of Christ, but the adversaries of Christ never see them. They are focusing on those Christians who are active, those Christians that are involved in the struggle. May God give us grace to boldly and lovingly speak His truth in our own day, as anti-Christian bias is continuing to heat up.

Dear Lord, we are reminded of the hymn which says, "The body they may kill. God's truth abideth still." Forgive us for any fear when facing death at the hands of persecutors. Thank You that Your kingdom advances, even sometimes through martyrdom...

BY GOD'S STRENGTH, WE CAN FACE THE OPPOSITION OF MEN.

OCTOBER 27

Same Empires, Different Views of Them

"Daniel spoke and said: I saw in my vision by night…Four great beasts came up from the sea, diverse from one another."

— Daniel 7:2-3

In the book of Daniel, two dreams are described. The first is Nebuchadnezzar's and the second is Daniel's. In these two dreams the same four earthly kingdoms are described.

In Daniel 2, Nebuchadnezzar had a dream of a great image whose head was of gold and whose shoulders and chest were of silver, loins of brass and its feet and legs of iron mixed with clay with ten toes. Scholars believe this was a vision of the four great world kingdoms that were to ensue. Babylon being the first, the head of gold, to be followed by the shoulders, the Medo-Persian empire, and then the Grecian empire, or Macedonian, if you will, of Alexander the Great, followed by the Roman Empire and its ten rulers.

In Daniel 7, we find a similar picture of the same forthcoming world empires. In each case these were to be succeeded by the kingdom of Jesus Christ, which would have no end.

Nebuchadnezzar saw these kingdoms in terms of their outward glory. Daniel, with spiritual eyes, saw the same kingdoms as beastly.

We are in the world, but not of the world. Jesus is the King of kings and Lord of lords. God is sovereign over the nations, and one day Jesus will inherit the nations. The God we worship is not only the great Creator, but He rules over the world.

Jesus, Ruler of the Nations, we praise You that You are sovereign over all of history. You raise up and You tear down whom You will, but all for the greater good of the advance of Your kingdom. Help us not to fear men, but only to fear and reverence You…

BY GOD'S STRENGTH, WE CAN BE
ON THE RIGHT SIDE OF HISTORY.

Daniel's Vision of the Winds and Great Sea

"I saw in the night visions, and there was one like a Son of Man coming with the clouds of heaven. He came to the Ancient of Days and was presented before Him…His dominion is an everlasting dominion…"

— Daniel 7:13-14

Daniel had a dream in which he saw the rise of four nations, symbolized by four beasts, which came up from the Great Sea, which had been stirred up in great tumult by the four winds of heaven.

So we see that first of all, looking at the origin of four kingdoms (the Babylonian, Medo-Persian, Greek, and Roman) that they are earthly in nature. They rise up from the sea and are contrasted with the kingdom of Christ, which is a kingdom that comes down from above. Christ's kingdom is given by God the Father.

Secondly, we see here that these kingdoms are tumultuous in their nature. They are usually brought about by force, by revolution, by war, by usurpation of one sort or another, or by conquest. By contrast, the kingdom of the Son of Man is given to Him.

These earthly kingdoms rise and fall. But when Christ's kingdom is established, it is an everlasting kingdom, which extends from generation to generation on into the endless ages of eternity and it has no ending whatsoever. As Christians, we can be grateful to be a part of the kingdom that will never fail.

Sovereign Lord, we praise You that the nations are like dust on a scale before You. We praise You, Jesus, for Your eternal kingdom, which began in such a small way but is a mountain that will one day fill the whole earth…

BY GOD'S STRENGTH, WE CAN JOIN CHRIST'S EVERLASTING KINGDOM.

Daniel and the Four Beasts

"These great beasts, which are four, are four kings which shall arise out of the earth."

— Daniel 7:17

Daniel had a vision of four beasts which succeeded each other. They represented four worldly kingdoms—each one being brutal in its own way. They are not lifting up their eyes to God, but they are looking downward as the beast does. This is always true of godless politics. It always acts in a beastlike manner and, therefore, it is destructive of human life. It tramps and stomps on people; it devours much flesh; it kills millions of human beings.

We think of the Persian Empire (the second kingdom prophetically described by Daniel), which later sent an army of two million men to attack Greece. History shows us that some of the battles of antiquity that these nations engaged in were enormous battles with armies that included two, three, and four million soldiers, and the number of the people that were killed was absolutely astronomical.

These beast-like kingdoms are all different from each other, whereas the kingdom of Christ, which arises in the days of the last of them (the Roman Empire), is the same, and it continues on from generation to generation and still remains the same.

The truth is much simpler than error; goodness is simpler than evil. If you want to see something that is extraordinarily complex, try to follow the plot line of a soap opera. Evil is quite contorted and convoluted and extremely complex, but God offers something that is so much simpler: Good triumphs over evil.

Lord, give me strength to live in the simplicity of the Gospel, to crave Your simple truths, and to live by them. You know, Jesus, that simple is not the same as easy, but Your grace is all sufficient...

BY GOD'S STRENGTH, WE CAN RECOGNIZE THAT HE RULES THE NATIONS.

OCTOBER 30

Satan Preys on Our Failures

"…as far as the east is from the west, so far has He removed our transgressions from us."

— Psalm 103:12

We need to avoid a trap of Satan—to so dwell on our failures that we can't move forward. Our sins can disable us because every time we sin Satan has the same message for us, "Ah hah! Now you've done it. You've blown the whole thing. Certainly Christ has no more need and use for you!"

We need to forget those failures. We need to forget those sins, which are buried in the depths of the sea never to be remembered against us anymore. We need to forget the hurts of the past. In the Christian life—and especially I can also say in the Christian ministry—though it is filled with many blessings, it is also filled with many hurts. I think sometimes people must suppose that ministers have the hide of an elephant, and nothing that they can do or say to them is going to hurt them. That is not true. I feel sometimes as if I have a thousand cuts where my brethren have cut me, from which I am bleeding.

If I were to believe some of the messages, then I would certainly conclude I have never done anything worth any value at all in the ministry and I ought to give it up. Well, those things can hurt and those things can cut and those things can distract us, but Paul says those are the kinds of things that we are to forget. Let's move forward, forgetting what lies behind and pressing on, in Christ.

Jesus Christ, I come to You with my hurts today. Let me lay them at the foot of the cross…

BY HIS STRENGTH, WE CAN RELEASE OUR HURTS TO JESUS.

Don't Get the Buggy Before the Horse

"For by grace you have been saved through faith…not of works…For we are His workmanship, created in Christ Jesus for good works…"

— Ephesians 2:8-10

Suppose that you lived in the country 100 years ago, when horses and buggies were common. One day you came into the city and discovered that most people were putting the buggy in front of the horse and saying, "Giddy-ap, horse. Push, push," and somehow they couldn't get the horse to push the buggy at all.

You would think to yourself, "How incredibly stupid can these city folk be?" And you would be right. Yet the vast majority of people in America today have the Gospel just that backwards.

The Bible contains two basic elements, like a horse and buggy. It contains the law and the Gospel, and unless we get these in the proper relationship it never will work.

The proper relationship between the two—as taught by the early church and by Augustine—is the great rediscovery that Martin Luther made and proclaimed to the world on October 31, 1517. It has dramatically changed the world. D.T. Niles said that in all other religions, good works are "in order to," whereas, in Christianity, good works are, "therefore." We're not saved by good works. But when we're truly saved, good works will naturally follow.

Even in the Ten Commandments, God said, *"I am the Lord your God, who brought you out of the land of Egypt, out of the house of bondage."* Therefore, He decrees, *"…you shall have no other gods before Me"* (Exodus 20:2 3). Having first been brought up and brought into God, therefore, we do good works.

Lord, You are our righteousness. Thank You for raising up people throughout the centuries who shine the light on the true Gospel for all to see. Thank You for the clarity of salvation by faith, with works of gratitude to follow…

BY GOD'S STRENGTH, HE SAVES US.
IN HIS STRENGTH WE DO GOOD WORKS.

The Biggest Organization Worldwide

"...you also, as living stones, are being built up into a spiritual house as a holy priesthood to offer up spiritual sacrifices that are acceptable to God through Jesus Christ."

— 1 Peter 2:5

One day two men were sitting together on an airplane. One was a businessman. The second man was a representative of a worldwide organization. "You must work for Coca Cola," said the first. "No," replied the second, "We have far more field representatives, more employees and more customers, if you can call them that."

Now, the first man was definitely intrigued. "Microsoft?" "Bigger." "The U.N.?" "Again, much bigger." "Tell me." I am a minister in the Church of Jesus Christ.

Think about it. The kingdom that contains more citizens than any country on earth, the association that has the most members is the Church of Jesus Christ. Not any one denomination, but the collective body that professes to believe in the Son of God comprises the largest group of people on the globe. The members of Christ's Church are in every country and of every race around the globe. There's simply no other group, institution, or fellowship even remotely similar.

If you are in Christ, you are part of the largest family in the whole world. Despite all the setbacks, the Body of Christ is the most successful "organization" ever.

Lord Jesus, Head of the church, we ask You to give us strength today so that we can live our lives worthy of the family name, Christian. Thank You for this worldwide enterprise. We are grateful for any job you give us within Your kingdom. Help us to serve You well...

BY GOD'S STRENGTH, WE CAN REJOICE AT BEING IN HIS FAMILY.

NOVEMBER 2

Pray for the Persecuted Church

"Yes, and all who desire to live a godly life in Christ Jesus will suffer persecution."

— 2 Timothy 3:12

Humanly speaking, persecution against Christianity began with Jesus Himself being spitefully treated and then crucified. It continued with the persecution, torture, and murder of the disciples, and then of many other followers of Christ. It went on in greater ways in the entire Roman Empire during ten huge waves of persecution. For almost 300 years, persecution swept across that kingdom, and millions of Christians died. Then the Edict of Toleration was issued and the persecution ceased—at least for a while. Then it broke out again and again and again and again.

Still today, persecution continues. In the 20th century, more Christians were persecuted and killed for their faith than in any other century. Stalin killed ten million or more. Hitler killed six million Jews; also six million other people, most of whom were Christians. The Korean Communists came into churches, sprayed gasoline on the congregations, and turned flamethrowers on them. In recent years, mostly in Muslim countries, but also some in the remnant communist countries, Christians are being imprisoned, they are being beaten, they are being tortured, they are being crucified by the hundreds, they are being skinned alive, they are having their eyeballs plucked out, and they are beheaded. This is happening in our world in our times.

Pray for the persecuted church. Pray that they will be faithful through it all. Ask that God would take the persecutors and redeem them or remove them.

Heavenly Father, we thank You that You are sovereign and though You allow persecution, one day You will avenge Your enemies. Hasten that day, Lord…

BY GOD'S STRENGTH, WE KNOW THAT CHRIST WILL EVER GET THE VICTORY.

NOVEMBER 3

How Christ Got My Attention

"I know one thing: I was blind, but now I see."

— John 9:25

At one time, I was far away from God, immersed in the sin and pleasures of the world. But one Sunday morning, after having attended a party late the night before, I was awakened by a preacher on my radio alarm clock, whereas there had been music on that radio station the night before. Not interested in spiritual things, I was about to spring out of bed and change the station.

But he said a few things that caught my attention. The preacher declared that the Bible says, "The wages of sin is death...but...the gift of God is eternal life through Jesus Christ our Lord." I will never forget that first day I heard that incredible statement. I was astonished that he had the audacity to say that God wanted to give me heaven as a gift. I thought the man must be mad. Being, of course, a great authority on theological matters, at the age of 24, I figured that he didn't know what he was talking about. After all, who was he but a doctor of theology, a pastor of one of our nation's great churches with a worldwide radio ministry? As to me, why, I could even find my Bible—given enough time.

I realized I must find out if these things are so. Within a week, as I read about Jesus Christ and His sacrifice in my place, I found myself on my knees, in tears, asking God to forgive me. My life has never been the same ever since.

Lord, give me strength for today to share the good news with others that they, too, might receive Your free gift of heaven. Thank You for taking the punishment of my sins on Yourself on the cross...

BY HIS STRENGTH, WE RECOGNIZE OUR WEAKNESS AND NEED FOR A SAVIOR.

NOVEMBER 4

Suffering for Christ

"For to you it was granted on behalf of Christ not only to believe in Him, but also to suffer for His sake…"

— Philippians 1:29

In this verse, Paul is saying that suffering for Christ is of grace—it is a gift given unto you, first of all to believe in Christ and secondly to suffer for His sake. I think of one writer who points out that belief brings life, and suffering brings muscles. It is a freely given weight-set given by God to you to develop your spiritual muscles as we suffer for Him.

May I ask you this, have you suffered for Christ's sake? Now you know a lot of people think that suffering for Christ's sake is having a headache, or having arthritis or something like that. That's not suffering for Christ's sake; everybody suffers that way, Christian, non-Christian, all alike.

Suffering for Christ is very different. Suffering for Christ is something that we endure because of our witness for Christ, and we are called upon to suffer for Him as well as to believe in Him. And we are to rejoice in that, as Jesus told us Himself in the Sermon on the Mount: *"Blessed are you when men revile you, and persecute you, and say all kinds of evil against you falsely for My sake. Rejoice and be very glad, because great is your reward in heaven…"* (Matthew 5:11-12a).

And we grow in faith when we are willing to suffer for Him. If we want to have spiritual muscles, then we need to realize and accept the gift, both of believing in Him and suffering for Him.

Dear Jesus, give me the strength to suffer gladly and patiently for You. Help me not take on a burden You have not asked me to carry. But when the time comes to suffer for Your name's sake, give me the grace to endure…

BY GOD'S STRENGTH, WE ENDURE,
EVEN WHEN SUFFERING FOR HIM.

NOVEMBER 5

More Christians Are Needed in Politics

"When the righteous are in authority, the people rejoice; but when the wicked rule, the people mourn."

— Proverbs 29:2

Slowly but surely, more and more we see that Christians are beginning to take their proper place in every sphere of life in our society. You may recall that one of the most important founders of this country was John Jay, and he said, "Providence has given to our people the choice of their rulers, and it is the duty as well as the privilege and interest of our Christian Nation to select and prefer Christians for their rulers."

Now who was this John Jay? Was he some sort of extremist? He was the first Chief Justice of the first Supreme Court, appointed by the first President of the United States, George Washington. He also wrote some of the Federalist Papers.

Well now, what he said we ought to do is being done. At one point, not too long ago, only five members of the House of Representatives could be found who were evangelical Christians. Most of them were probably nominal. But that number went up a decade later to 100, and then up to 125. Lord-willing, evangelicals in the political realm will be even more visible in the years to come.

So often we hear that no one should impose their morality on anyone, but the reality is that someone's morality is always being legislated. It is not a question of "if," but of "what" and of "whose."

Dear Lord, You have said we should not put our trust in princes. Even the best of them can let us down. Help us to trust You alone. Meanwhile, we do pray that You would raise up more godly leaders. Help Your church to regain its role as salt and light in society…

BY GOD'S STRENGTH, THE CHURCH CAN BE THE CONSCIENCE OF THE NATION.

NOVEMBER 6

God and War

"The Lord is a man of war; the Lord is His name."
— Exodus 15:3

This verse in the Song of Moses, celebrating God's victory over the Egyptians in the Red Sea, sounds strange to our ears. God—a man of war? The liberals have had a field day with this text. God is love, they say, and nothing but love and the idea that the Lord is a man of war is an outworn ancient barbarian concept and certainly is not fitted for Christians to consider and it is obviously not spiritual. It's a sinful idea that God is a man of war.

Well, before we go too far with that and talk about how unholy and ungodly and unchristian that is, let me call your attention to the last book of the Bible: *"They sang the song of Moses, the servant of God, and the song of the Lamb, saying: 'Great and marvelous are Your works, 'Lord God Almighty! Just and true are Your ways, O King of saints!'"* (Revelation 15:3). The Song of Moses is reaffirmed in the New Testament.

God has many facets to Him. He is a God of love preeminently, He is a God of grace and mercy and kindness and longsuffering, but He is also a God of holiness and justice and righteousness. In the original Song of Moses (Exodus 15), He justly punished Pharaoh's army, as they tried to attack the Israelites. He is a God of wrath against sin, and we cannot do away with that aspect of Him—otherwise we create an idol of our own mind, something other than the true God.

Lord, God Almighty, give me strength to embrace all aspects of Your character. I also tremble when I consider that Your justice will not sleep forever. Thank You for Your holiness, Your justice, and Your righteous anger against evil...

BY GOD'S STRENGTH, WE SEEK WAR ONLY
AS A LAST RESORT AND ONLY WHEN IT IS JUST.

Obey God in the Little Things, Too

"It pleased Darius to set over the kingdom one hundred and twenty officials, so that they would be over the whole kingdom, and over them three presidents, of whom Daniel was first..."

— Daniel 6:1-2

In this verse, Daniel is preferred among all of these other key leaders of the great Medo-Persian empire, as he was among the Babylonians. Why? Because an excellent spirit was in him. Here is a man in his late 80's, and we cannot help but harken back to that time when he was in a cell as a teenager, confronted with a temptation to disobey God in some small ceremonial law of his religion. At the time, you will recall, there was something that Daniel did which was to affect his entire extraordinary career for all these seventy some years that were yet to come.

"But Daniel purposed in his heart that he would not defile himself with the portion of the king's food, nor with the wine which he drank" (Daniel 1:8). The matter at hand may seem trivial to some. But he determined to obey God in all things, even what he ate and drank. Daniel obeyed God in little things and was able to obey Him in big matters, too.

I hope perhaps that the tremendous implications of that statement might become even more apparent now that he is an older man, who has been obeying God all along. That he determined that he would not defile himself before God, that the one all consuming passion of his heart was to refrain from breaking even the least of the laws of his God. What a tremendous determination. I hope that same determination is yours.

Heavenly Father, give me strength to obey You in the big and seemingly insignificant details of my life. Lord, let me live my life to please You in all things and do all my work to the satisfaction of anyone over me and to Your glory...

BY GOD'S STRENGTH, WE CAN OBEY GOD EVEN IN THE DETAILS.

Character Matters

"Then this Daniel was preferred above the presidents and officials because an excellent spirit was in him, and the king thought to set him over the whole realm."

— Daniel 6:3

Observing Daniel in the lions' den passage, we see a godly man standing out in an ungodly place. We see growing here in the midst of this degenerate, pagan, idolatrous, polytheistic, licentious court, a most beautiful white flower. And I think that one of the first lessons to be learned in this is that such a beautiful character does not depend upon the circumstances in which it is raised.

You see, there are some things that you cannot grow in certain soils because they don't provide the nutrients. But here you do not find the human soul draws from the environment around it. If it is a believing soul, it is grounded in God and it draws its spiritual nourishment from Him and it matters not what is around. In fact it is strangely true that some of the most beautiful of Christian characters have come forth in the midst of the most degenerate circumstances.

Yet how many times have we heard it said, "Well, if only circumstances were different; if only I didn't have that miserable, wretched boss, always riding on my back, always on my case, I could be a much better Christian at work." "Ah me, what a wonderful Christian I could be if I had a different husband or a different wife, or my children weren't so rebellious." "Oh, if I just didn't have so many physical problems I could be a great Christian." But Daniel gives a lie to it all. Here, blossoming in this incredibly pagan court is this character of Daniel.

Oh, Lord, give me the strength today to grow in godly character. Let my inward and outward life be beautiful to You. Help me not to resist Your inner work within me...

BY GOD'S STRENGTH, WE CAN EXHIBIT GODLY CHARACTER, REGARDLESS OF OUR ENVIRONMENT.

NOVEMBER 9

Being Envied for Righteous Living

"Then the presidents and officials sought to find occasion against Daniel concerning the kingdom..."

— Daniel 6:4

Sometimes, people can hate us, not for doing anything wrong, but rather, for doing everything right. Shakespeare said, "Envy doth merit, as its shade [shadow] pursue." Envy pursues after merit, even as our shadow pursues us everywhere we go. And so if you would be meritorious, if you would rise so much as an inch or two above the common herd, you will find that envy will be hard on your heels and breathing down your neck and blowing its hot flame breath singeing the hairs on the back of your neck. And so it was with Daniel and so it has ever been.

Daniel was preferred. Daniel had an excellent spirit. Daniel was envied and Daniel was conspired against to pull him down.

One theologian noted that there is a certain tendency in evil that always wants to pull that which is good down to its own level. Evil is egalitarian. Evil men want to make everyone else just as evil as they are.

If we are first place, a price has to be paid. If that primacy is as faithful and righteous as Daniel, it must be doubly paid for. The leveling demands of evil are for a democracy of being. Evil men seek to make all things evil. Men who are failures demand a universal failure, and men unable or unwilling to rise above their low estate seek savagely to raise all eminence into a common democracy of mediocrity and defeat. Daniel had done nothing wrong, but he was hated all the more.

Oh, Lord Jesus Christ, give me the strength only You can give that I might stand against evil. Thank You for Your protection and Your peace in the midst of trouble. Keep me safe, Lord, and keep me strong...

BY GOD'S STRENGTH, WE CAN STAND FIRM EVEN WHEN ENVIED FOR BEING GODLY.

NOVEMBER 10

True Freedom

"You shall know the truth, and the truth shall set you free."
— John 8:32

The world boasts about its freedom all of the time. For example, there is a poem that starts like this:

It matters not how straight the gate,
how charged with punishments the scroll,
I am the master of my fate.
I am the captain of my soul.

Hogwash. Luther put it much more accurately when he said that the will of the unregenerate man is like a dumb jackass ridden by the devil who turns it whithersoever he will. Or to change the metaphor, he is like a man chained to the oars below deck while Satan steers the ship laughingly over the precipice into the churning chasm beneath.

But the Christian has been set free…free to serve Christ, free to follow Christ, free to do great things for Christ because those shackles have been broken at Calvary.

It begins with repentance, a determination to turn from sin and to follow Jesus Christ. *"As you have received Christ Jesus the Lord, so walk in Him"* (Colossians 2:6)—which is a continual repenting of sin and determining to follow Christ in all the ways of new obedience.

Somebody said, "There are just so many people in me. If I only knew which one I was, I would know what I ought to do." But if we set in our hearts on the determination to love God with all our being and to love our neighbor as ourselves, then we are fulfilling the greatest command. True freedom is the choice to do what is right.

Oh, God of Truth, give us the strength today to live in the freedom which Your truth provides. Thank You for our freedom in Christ Jesus to live our lives in service and in truth. Let the truth continue to bring freedom and let us be faithful bearers of truth…

BY GOD'S STRENGTH, WE CAN
WALK IN FREEDOM FROM SIN.

The Blood of the Soldier, the Blood of the Savior

"When they had mocked Him, they took the purple robe off Him and put His own garments on Him. Then they led Him out to crucify Him."
— Mark 15:20

November 11 is Veterans Day. It marks this day in 1918, when the Armistice was signed, ending four years of bloody battles in Europe at the close of World War I. It was initially called Armistice Day but eventually was changed to Veterans Day, when in 1954, President Ike Eisenhower signed a bill changing Armistice Day to Veterans Day.

It is a day to remember the thousands who have died for the liberties we enjoy in this country, as well as to remember all of those who were maimed and wounded and still carry, sometimes decades later, the signs and evidences of their combat.

War should be avoided if at all possible. But in this evil world, that is not always possible.

Edmund Burke once said, "The only thing necessary for the triumph of evil is for good men to do nothing." We are so good at doing nothing, aren't we? Not many more than half of us vote. Few of us work to elect decent candidates or do anything to advance the cause of virtue and morality in America.

Freedom is not free. It was paid for by the blood of the soldier. Spiritual freedom is not free. It was paid for by the blood of the Savior, which is of infinitely greater value.

Jesus Christ our Savior, give me strength for today to continue to fight evil. Help us to not take for granted either our salvation or our freedom. Help us to be grateful, knowing these were purchased with blood…

BY HIS STRENGTH, WE CAN DO SOMETHING TO OPPOSE THE TRIUMPH OF EVIL.

Samson Was Strong, Yet He Was Weak

"So the woman bore a son, and she called him Samson. The boy grew, and the LORD blessed him."

— Judges 13:24

Samson was the strongest man that ever lived, as the makers of certain luggage have attested. They named it in his honor. It's indestructible because it's Samsonite.

Now Samson was a real man, he was not the idol of Homer's mind, living on Mount Olympus. He was a humble son of Manoah and his wife, he was of the tribe of Dan in Israel, and God had gifted him remarkably.

His birth was announced by an angel. He was given a high calling and purpose to deliver the people of God from the 40-year-long tyranny of the Philistines, and he was given a consecration.

He was to be a Nazarite, one separated unto God. He was to be one whose separation was seen by the fact that no razor was to touch his head and no strong drink was to touch his lips. He was truly a remarkable man. Not the kind of fellow you would want to arm wrestle with, I assure you, regardless of how big you are.

He judged Israel for 20 years. He heard their cases, he judged them, he bore with their problems, he led them in battle, he fought with them and for them, and yet all we remember is Samson and Delilah. He fell because of his relationship with Delilah, a Philistine woman. All young preachers take note. All the rest is forgotten in the tragedy of his fall.

Oh, Lord, my strength and my shield, give me strength today to lean on You. Make me a muscular Christian. Let me go forth in Your strength, never depending on my own ability. Thank You, Jesus, that You are my strength and salvation…

BY GOD'S STRENGTH, WE CAN MAKE SOMETHING OF OUR LIVES.

NOVEMBER 13

Be Not Unequally Yoked

"I find more bitter than death the woman whose heart is snares and nets, and whose hands are fetters. He who pleases God escapes her, but the sinner is taken by her."

— Ecclesiastes 7:26

The name Samson was derived from the Hebrew word for sun, and he certainly was the light of day for not only his parents, but for all of the people of Israel who had been suffering under the grinding tyranny of the Philistines for so long.

But he also had a great weakness: he had an eye for women—the wrong kind of women. His calling was to deliver the people from the Philistines, and yet he couldn't deliver himself fast enough to them. He saw this one that pleased him well, and he asked his parents to go get her for him. But they remonstrated: *"Are there no women among your relatives, or all of our people, that you are intending to take a wife from among the uncircumcised Philistines?"* (Judges 14:2).

He replied, *"Get her for me, for she pleases me well"* (verse 3).

Strange unbelieving flesh, and so we see that every such woman he went after betrayed him—every one. And how many Christians have gone after unbelievers, men or women, and found that their lives have been destroyed by such betrayal because at the very heart of the marriage there is a great divide that cannot be covered over?

Lord Jesus, give me strength to stay faithful to You and to my loved ones. Help me to never form an adulterous relationship. Help me teach this truth to others to keep them from eternal harm. I pray today for the people I know who are unequally yoked that You would save the unsaved…

BY GOD'S STRENGTH, WE CAN MAKE OUR EARTHLY RELATIONSHIPS COUNT FOR THE KINGDOM.

Never Flirt With Evil

"Therefore let him who thinks he stands take heed, lest he fall."
— 1 Corinthians 10:12

Did you realize that virtually no drunkard on skid row ever thought he would end up there? They all flirted with sin. So did Samson in the Bible.

Now if any man ever had the right to be self-confident, certainly Samson did; as the strongest man in the world, he was not impressed by anyone. You remember that one time when the Philistines came upon him, he had no weapon but the jawbone of an ass, and with that one jawbone he killed a thousand Philistine soldiers and he boasted about it.

The word confident comes from *con-fide*, literally "with faith." We should all have faith, but the world tells us that we should have faith in ourselves. The Bible tells us that we should have faith in Christ.

Well, Samson thought he had enough strength to have confidence in himself, and, unfortunately, it was that confidence that caused him to dally with sin—ultimately in the form of his dalliance with Delilah.

When you have self-confidence and you deal with normal problems and you overcome them, it can lead to self-conceit and pride. When you run into a problem big enough, it leads to despair and fear. But in the case of confidence in God, there is nothing bigger than God.

Supposing in their self-confidence that they are never going to fall, some Christians have flirted with alcohol or drugs or tobacco or whatever kind of sexual sin it might be, quite confident that they are never going to become an addict. This can lead to tragic endings. Don't dabble with sin.

Dear Lord Jesus, give me strength today in order to build Christ-confidence. Help me to rely on You and not myself. Help me in humility to know that I am not strong enough to withstand temptation. I put my trust in You…

BY GOD'S STRENGTH, WE CAN RESIST TEMPTATION AND NOT DALLY WITH SIN.

NOVEMBER 15

The Miry Pit of Sin

"After this Samson loved a woman in the Valley of Sorek, whose name was Delilah. The Philistine rulers came up to her and said, 'Trick him!'"

— Judges 16:4-5

How many people have flirted with sin only to find they have fallen into a miry pit? I think of a man who was away on a business trip, and he saw a very attractive prostitute on the same side of the road. He stopped his car and picked her up. A man who had never done anything like this before in his life. A man who had a wife and two or three kids at home. A man who was a respectable businessman, but now he was far from home. He picked her up.

When he woke up the next morning and he went into the bathroom, disgusted with himself, to wash his face. There on the mirror written in lipstick were the words "Welcome to the world of AIDS."

Samson foolishly dabbled with sin by seeing the Philistine woman, Delilah. She was offered large sums of money by her people if she would discover the secret of his strength. She began to entice him and provoke him and tried to get him to reveal where his great strength lay, but he would not reveal it—at least initially.

Sounds like some young people today: "Honey, if you really loved me, you will do it." "Buster, if you really loved me you wouldn't ask," is the proper response, girls.

Finally, Delilah wore Samson down, he revealed it, and they captured him and blinded him. Giving in to sexual sin was the weakness of the world's strongest man.

Dear God, give me strength to withstand temptation. Keep me pure and holy and let me never flirt with sin. Keep my family from falling also. Lord, let me never disgrace your church and never bring shame to Your holy name…

BY GOD'S STRENGTH, WE CAN AVOID THE MIRY PIT OF SIN.

You Can Trust the Bible

"…and Jehoiachin king of Judah went out to the king of Babylon, he, his mother, his servants, his princes, and his eunuchs. The king of Babylon took him in the eighth year of his reign."

— 2 Kings 24:12

Higher critics have done their best to destroy trust in the Scriptures. Yet, all of their efforts only confirmed the reliability of the Bible for those willing to look at the facts.

For the last 150 years, archeologists have excavated thousands of sites in the Near East, sometimes with great animosity toward the Scripture, attempting to disprove it. Yet virtually every time they turned over their spades, they discovered another confirmation of the Bible.

For example. One of the last kings of Judah, Jehoiachin, was taken by Nebuchadnezzar into Babylon and thrown into where he and his family languished for 37 years. Then we read that a later king lifted up the head of Jehoiachin king of Judah out of prison, spoke kindly to him, gave him new clothes, caused him to sit at his table, and he provided him with an allowance for the rest of his days.

Well, the critics had a field day with that—no Babylonian king would ever treat anybody so graciously as that. But in the hanging gardens of Babylon, 300 clay tablets have been found. These were written from 595 to 570 B.C., and they list many of the nations that were brought captive into Babylon, including Judah. One of these tablets is called the Jehoiachin tablet. The Jehoiachin tablet confirms exactly what the Bible has said all along.

God Almighty, Lord of the kings of the earth, grant me strength today to trust You in all things. Thank You for the reliability of Your Word. Thank You for the trustworthiness of all You say.

IN GOD'S STRENGTH, WE CAN TRUST HIS ETERNAL WORD.

The Bible and Angels

"And He was there in the wilderness for forty days, tempted by Satan, and was with the wild beasts. And the angels ministered to Him."

— Mark 1:13

We seem to be living in the time when angels are getting much attention, even in movies or television. One of the most common myths is the idea that an angel was once a human being and now is in process of earning his wings by returning to earth and doing good things. But an angel never was and never will be anything other than an angel. And a human being never was and never will be anything other than a human being. They are separate orders of creation.

All of the angels were made at once. They did not descend from original parents as we did, but they were all created at the same time and they do not procreate.

Angels are far superior to us in almost any way that you can imagine. They are wiser, they are holier—at least those who have kept their first estate and are not fallen angels. The devil and demons are all angels. They are fallen, sinful angels that took part in a rebellion and now are loosed upon this earth, but they are still fallen angels.

Angels are also much more powerful than we are. We realize that in the Old Testament we read of one angel who destroyed 185,000 Assyrian soldiers in one night. The Bible makes it very plain that you are not to take on the devil in your strength, and only by Christ do we have any possibility of winning any contests that we may have with him.

Jesus, King of the Angels, give me strength today to know my place in creation, a little lower than the angels, but crowned with glory and honor. Thank You, Lord Jesus, for having dominion over both Your angels, the ministering spirits who do Your will, and the fallen angels who seek to cause us harm. Thank You for Your angels who do Your will...

BY GOD'S STRENGTH, WE CAN WELCOME THE HELP OF HIS ANGELS.

Lessons From Belshazzar's Fall

"Then they brought the golden vessels that were taken out of the temple of the house of God which was at Jerusalem... They drank wine and praised the gods of gold and of silver, of bronze, of iron, of wood, and of stone."

— Daniel 5:3-4

The grandson of Nebuchadnezzar, Belshazzar was the king who held a great pagan feast, using the goblets stolen from the Jewish Temple some decades before. Belshazzar went white when he saw God's literal handwriting on the wall against him.

Now that story of Belshazzar the king and the astounding events of that night of his great feast have lessons which are as fresh today as they were when they were first given:

1. Here is a picture of the foolishness of those who trust in merely the things of this world. How foolish was Belshazzar to trust in the impregnable walls of Babylon—the walls that were so easily breached by diverting the river Euphrates.
2. It reminds us that those who will not study history are doomed to repeat it. Belshazzar had a tremendous lesson from his grandfather of humbling oneself before God. Nonetheless, Belshazzar went on his way to his unexpected destruction.
3. Belshazzar's sin was not just drunkenness and debauchery, but the super-abounding sin of impiety and blasphemy.

Lord, God of history, teach us to heed those who have gone before us and give us the strength to live a godly life in the midst of a blasphemous people. Help us to remember that all who mock Your name and flaunt their sin in Your face will be called to account and that it is Your people who will triumph...

BY GOD'S STRENGTH, WE CAN LIVE AN HONORABLE LIFE.

NOVEMBER 19

God Can Turn Things Around in an Instant

"Why, my soul, are you cast down? Why do you groan within me? Wait for God; I will yet thank Him, For He is my deliverance and my God."

— Psalm 42:11

From the depths of the psalmist's sorrow, he calls out unto the depths of the mercy of God, knowing that help shall come, so he has put his hope in the Lord. Consider how many times God has turned things around in a sudden way. Who would have thought:

- In the hour when Lazarus lay stinking in his tomb, that soon he should be rejoicing around the table with his Redeemer?
- When Jonah was in the depths of the sea that soon he would be preaching at Nineveh?
- When Nebuchadnezzar, the mighty monarch of Babylon, was out munching on the grass in the forest, that one day soon he would again be sitting upon the throne in Babylon?
- When Joseph was deep in the prison in Egypt, that soon he would be prime minister of the greatest nation in the world at that time?
- When Job was sitting there on a dunghill scraping off his sores in the midst of his sorrow, that soon he would be rise up and be richer and more blessed in everything in this world?

Put your hope in God, despite your circumstances. As the hymn notes, "Hast thou not seen how thy desires 'ere have been granted in what He ordaineth?"

Heavenly Father, give us strength today to praise You in the midst of trouble to wait upon You and to remember that our lives are in Your hands and You will turn all things to benefit my soul and Your kingdom...

BY GOD'S STRENGTH, WE CAN RECOGNIZE THAT GOD CAN TURN THINGS AROUND IN AN INSTANT.

Wisdom Seeking

*"O you simple, understand wisdom, and you fools,
be of an understanding heart."*

— Proverbs 8:5

Certainly, we should be seeking wisdom. But in one sense the Bible presents wisdom as seeking us. We can see this is the great wisdom chapter of Proverbs 8.

In the first eleven verses we see an introduction of Wisdom personified as a woman standing at the gate calling forth boldly for all to come and hear what she has to say. She sets forth her reasons why men should trust in her in contrast to the seductive, sinful women who are described in the preceding chapters.

Then in verses 12-21, Wisdom displays her various excellencies and points out what she has accomplished and what she continues to accomplish in the lives of those who have sought after her.

In the second half of Proverbs 8, we see that Wisdom is to be sought after and acquired. By seeking Wisdom, we are seeking God. We see here an adumbration, a foreshadowing, of the incarnate Christ. We see that there is something more here than just a human wisdom, but here is the One by whom God created the universe. The creation poem found in verse 22 and following is similar to the Logos passage in John 1.

Finally, in the last few verses of Proverbs 8, again Wisdom articulates the duty of all to harken to her instructions. By Wisdom, God created the world.

God is the source of all wisdom, and He wants us to walk in His wisdom.

Lord Jesus Christ, give us strength today to live in Your wisdom. Help us to see that the wisdom of this world is foolishness to You. Grant us Your wisdom that we might know Your thoughts and practice right thinking…

IN GOD'S STRENGTH, WE
CAN WALK IN HIS WISDOM.

NOVEMBER 21

Never Give Up

"...the race is not to the swift, nor the battle to the strong..."
— Ecclesiastes 9:11

It is the victory of faith that enables us to go on in the final count. When you think of Abraham Lincoln, what qualities come to your mind? Would it be compassion? Concern for the little man? Justice? Humor? I think if we really knew Abraham Lincoln, we would know that the overriding quality of his character was nothing other than perseverance. He was simply a man who persevered to the end.

Abraham Lincoln was a failure. He was a miserable, wretched, repeated failure. As a young man, he ran for the state legislature and was overwhelmingly defeated. He then went into business, failed completely, and spent the next seventeen years paying off the debts of a no-good partner. Although he did win a Congressional seat once, he was not able to successfully return to Congress. After that, he tried to get an appointment to the U. S. Land Office and was turned down.

He then decided that what he ought to do was to run for the Senate of the United States and he was pounded into the ground. He was defeated here, and he was defeated there; he failed in this, and he failed at that; he was overwhelmed here, and he was overwhelmed there; he was a loser, until he ran for the presidency of the United States and became one of the greatest men this world has ever known.

The character of a loser is that he quits. Deep down, Abraham Lincoln was never a loser at all because he never quit.

Lord, give me strength for today to persist in doing what I believe You have laid on my heart to accomplish. Even if I have to plod along and deal with one setback after another, help me to persevere in the end. Spiritually, I thank You that You have promised to finish in me what You have started...

BY GOD'S STRENGTH, WE CAN OVERCOME ONE SETBACK AFTER ANOTHER.

NOVEMBER 22

Is There a Purpose for Suffering?

"We had the sentence of death in ourselves, so that we would not trust in ourselves, but in God who raises the dead."

— 2 Corinthians 1:9

"Sweet are the uses of adversity." At least so said the bard from Stratford-on-Avon. I am afraid, however, if actually put to the test of a vote, there would be an almost unanimous disagreement with Mr. Shakespeare on that point. "Bitter" is the word. Crushing, wracking, wrenching, discouraging, heartbreaking, and faith-shattering are the uses of adversity. This, I am sure, would be the attitude of most people.

Several years ago I received a call from a woman who was an atheist. Several times in the midst of her conversation she referred to one tragedy or another, always to be followed by the comment: And where was God then?

I suppose there is nothing that causes more people to stumble in the matter of faith than the problem of suffering, because none of us is exempt in this fallen world. We all face it at one time or another in our lives.

But God uses troubles in our lives to clear away the dross. He lets us undergo suffering that we might be of comfort for those undergoing similar problems. Most important is that we will never be like Jesus without the crucible of Jesus, the most desirable person who ever lived, who was portrayed as a *"man of sorrows and acquainted with grief"* (Isaiah 53:3). If we would be like Jesus, we will have to pass through the valley of the shadow.

Dear Lord, give me strength for today to not lose hope in You whenever I suffer. Help me to realize that You are purifying me. Also, help me to weep with those who weep and to be a comfort to those around me who are suffering…

BY GOD'S STRENGTH, WE CAN PERSEVERE EVEN THROUGH SUFFERING.

NOVEMBER 23

The Risen Christ

"Now it happened, as I journeyed and came near Damascus at about noon, suddenly a great light from heaven shone around me."
— Acts 22:6

Consider the resurrection of Jesus in the conversion of Saul of Tarsus, who became Paul, the apostle. By seeing the risen Christ, Saul knew in an instant, Christianity was true after all.

In that instant on the road to Damascus, the whole world of Saul, the Pharisee, was changed. He had believed quite emphatically that with the ignominious death of Jesus the "Imposter" upon a cross, the true God had conquered, and the end of that life was sealed forever. He believed that Jesus was exposed for the fraud that He was, and God had put His seal upon the truth of the religion of the Jews.

Now, suddenly, everything was turned topsy-turvy. God had obviously raised Jesus from the dead, for He was alive and He was glorified. He was evidently the Son of God as He had said, raised from the dead. He was, indeed, the Living Messiah, as He had claimed. Paul's world was completely changed. In that brief moment the life of Saul was transformed. Now he knew the truth.

Paul had believed, like so many persecutors of the church, that he was doing God a favor. He believed that the Christians were wrong and that he was doing God's will. Then Jesus revealed Himself, and in an instant Saul realized he was wrong.

The resurrection of Christ changes everything

Lord Jesus, we praise You that although You died for the sake of our trespasses and sins, You were made alive by Your Father. We praise You that in an instant You can change the hearts of even the most antagonistic of souls...

BY GOD'S STRENGTH, WE CAN SEE LIFE THROUGH THE GRID OF THE RESURRECTION.

Pilgrims, Old and New, Give Thanks

"In everything give thanks, for this is the will of God in Christ Jesus concerning you."

— 1 Thessalonians 5:18

"In the Name of God" begins the "birth certificate of America," as it is called. The Mayflower Compact was the first step leading to the creation of the Constitution.

Every Thanksgiving we have an annual holiday reminding us to give thanks to God, just as the Pilgrims did in their long physical and spiritual journey.

"In the Name of God" is where America began, and I trust that today, though they have been long dead, the Pilgrims may still speak to us through this national holiday that we might learn something of those grand ideals, those spiritual truths, that so gripped their lives and so changed the world. Though their voice has oft been silenced by the cacophony of secular voices in our time, I think Thanksgiving should be a time to take a few minutes to thank God for His many blessings. That would include our fathers and mothers who brought forth this good land.

The Pilgrims based their colony on the Bible. They were fair in their dealings with all. They began as a church in England, where there was no religious freedom, so they moved to Holland, where there was toleration. Eventually, they came to America to worship Jesus according to the dictates of their consciences.

The Pilgrims dealt with unbelievably difficult circumstances. Half their number died that first winter, but through it all they thanked God. They provide a model of giving thanks to God in all circumstances.

Lord God, we do give thanks to You for all Your blessings. Give us Your strength in hard times to continue to give thanks and praise to You. Help us to honor this holy day by true thanksgiving to You…

BY GOD'S STRENGTH, WE CAN THANK HIM EVERY DAY OF THE YEAR.

Don't Confuse Mercy and Justice

"Not by works of righteousness which we have done, but according to His mercy He saved us, by the washing of regeneration, and renewing of the Holy Ghost…"

Titus 3:5, KJV

This world does not operate on grace; it operates on the basis of merit, on the basis of justice. Quid pro quo, this for that; you do this, you get that. That is the way the entire world operates—on the basis of justice or equity.

Early in my ministry, I went to preach in a jail, and a man snapped at me that all he demanded was justice. I said if he got justice, the floor would open up and send him to hell.

What we need is mercy, not justice.

Consider the trial of Julius and Ethel Rosenberg, the famous couple accused of being Soviet spies who gave away our atomic secrets. They were convicted for espionage by the jury and were sentenced to death. Their lawyers said to Judge Kaufman, "Your honor, all my clients ask for is justice."

Judge Kaufman replied, "What your clients have asked for, this court has given them. What you really mean, is what they want is mercy, and that, this court is not empowered to give."

But that is precisely what our God—the Judge of all of the earth—is able to do: grant us mercy. That is the wondrous news of the Gospel.

While none of us is perfect, and none of us has lived up to God's standard, and all of us have fallen short, Jesus Christ came to do what we are unable to do. In His mercy, He saved us by His blood.

Lord, thank You for Your mercy and grace, which alone saves us through faith in You. Forgive us when we presume on Your mercy. Thank You, Jesus, for paying a debt You did not owe at a price that we could never pay…

BY GOD'S STRENGTH, WE CAN RELY ON GOD'S MERCY.

Daniel Foresaw the Roman Empire

"After this I saw in the visions at night a fourth beast, dreadful and terrible, and exceedingly strong. And it had great iron teeth. It devoured and broke in pieces, and stamped the rest with its feet. And it was different from all the beasts that were before it, and it had ten horns."

— Daniel 7:7

Hundreds of years before it arose, Daniel foresaw the Roman Empire. The same ten horns in this verse are like the ten toes of the image described in Daniel 2, believed to represent ten rulers of the Roman Empire.

This beast (verse 7) is not given a name. It is more dreadful than any of the previous beasts and is exceedingly strong with great iron teeth. The beast devoured and broke in pieces and stamped the residue with its feet. It was different from all of the rest.

When Rome came onto the scene, it was a republic, which made it different from all of the monarchies that had come before until finally Caesar Augustus made himself emperor.

I don't know that we can be dogmatic about our interpretation here. But I believe we see here a prediction of the long war against God that took place during the Roman Empire. Their rulers blasphemed greatly and had themselves called gods. They waged war against the saints. But eventually, God judged the wicked empire and toppled it. Also, Rome was a picture of the war against God that was to come. Though His kingdom has many enemies, even today, they are destined to fail.

Sovereign Lord, grant us the strength today to see clearly Your work in history. Help us to understand how the rulers and kingdoms of this world topple and fade away, while Your kingdom is eternal. Let us fear You alone and no earthly ruler, no matter how powerful they may become…

BY GOD'S STRENGTH, WE RECOGNIZE HE IS SOVEREIGN OVER HISTORY.

NOVEMBER 27

Christ the King

"He has delivered us from the power of darkness and has transferred us into the kingdom of His dear Son."

— Colossians 1:13

There are those whose theology does not allow them to admit that Jesus Christ has a kingdom today. They believe that His kingdom is not to be established until He returns a second time. Therefore, they cannot allow that the stone cut out without hands landed upon the Roman Empire (in Daniel 2:34-35), and that it depicted Christ coming to establish His kingdom. They cannot allow that it is a picture of Christ coming to establish His kingdom in the midst of the Roman Empire, and which brought down the empire. They have to see it as something in the future.

Now they give a number of theological reasons for their views, but none of them allow that Christ already has a kingdom. In fact, I have heard people refer to Christ as our Prophet, Priest and *soon coming King*. But according to the Reformers and the Reformed churches in general, He is King.

So does Jesus Christ have a kingdom today? That is a question worth asking. When Paul wrote the sentence above to the Colossians, it says that He transferred us—past tense. It is an accomplished fact. We have been translated/transferred into the kingdom of His dear Son. I am thoroughly convinced that Jesus Christ is presently a King, that His kingdom is already established. Of course, the day is *yet to come,* when the world will see the fullness of His kingdom. Regardless of our theological differences, there is no doubt that it is Jesus who is the King of kings and Lord of lords and no one else.

Our Father in heaven, give us strength and wisdom today to read Your Word correctly. Thank You that You are a king, Lord Jesus—not only a king, but the King of kings—the eternal King of Your kingdom in which You have placed us. Thank You that You have set us in Your kingdom of light...

BY GOD'S STRENGTH, WE HAIL AND HONOR CHRIST THE KING.

Government Can Be the Great Persecutor

"...and the same horn was warring with the saints and prevailing against them"

— Daniel 7:21

In Daniel 7, the prophet, who lived about 500 years before Christ, had a vision in which he foresaw one pagan kingdom after another arise. They were like beasts. The final one, believed by most commentators to be the Roman Empire, was a fierce persecuting beast. It waged war against the saints, and for a time it prevailed against them, and Rome provided a picture of what was to come.

The great persecutions that have come to the Christian church down through the centuries have come from government. One government after another, from Egypt to Assyria to Babylonia to the Roman Empire to the time of Hitler to the Soviets, all have fought against the saints of God.

Remember that the saints in the early times of this era had to face the actual beasts in the Coliseum. In America, I think initially we had a government that looked upward to God. But more and more progressively, because of the sinfulness of Christians, because of our unwillingness to witness for Jesus Christ and get involved in the culture, we are seeing more and more discrimination against things Christian. If you are truly a Christian, then expect anti-Christian persecution. Jesus said that if they persecuted Him, the Master, how much more will they persecute us, His followers? But we can rejoice because one day, in His sovereignty, He will show us why He allowed it all.

Lord, give us strength today to face any persecution for Your name's sake. Strengthen our faith so that we will persevere to the end and receive the Crown of Life. Let us be faithful in prayer for all who suffer for Your sake...

BY GOD'S STRENGTH, WE ARE MORE CONCERNED WITH GOD'S APPROVAL, NOT MAN'S.

On Liberal Churches That Deny the Basics

"My brothers, not many of you should become teachers, knowing that we shall receive the greater judgment."

— James 3:1

Some of the liberal denominations have taken the resurrection of Jesus away from their statements of faith (if they have one), and their churches are withering away—for their congregations instinctively know that there is nothing there but froth, and they will not tolerate being deceived. If Christ was not bodily raised from the dead in human history, Christianity would cease to exist.

Over time, these liberal churches are dying. Their seminaries turn out ministers who do not believe the Bible—they do not believe Jesus is divine, that He died for our sins, and, as noted, that He rose from the dead. One could ask why they are even in the ministry, but they will have to answer that for themselves. They should beware of what James says, that teachers will incur stricter judgment.

Sometimes, the person in the pew in these churches actually does believe. But the leadership does not believe the things of Christ. This is a blight upon the church at large. These churches, once in the main line, are beginning to fade away.

A survey from about twenty years ago showed that by the middle of the next century, there will be two great religious forces in America and far and away the largest one, will be evangelical Christianity. Alister E. McGrath writes, "In a 1990 survey of the 500 fastest growing Protestant congregations in the U.S., 89 percent were found to be evangelical." That trend continues. The other force will be Roman Catholicism—maybe a third or a half that size.

Lord, give us strength to stand against false teaching and hold fast Your Word. Thank You for preserving Your church all these centuries, even when there are Pharisees and Sadducees in our midst...

BY GOD'S STRENGTH, WE CAN EMBRACE THE FAITH ONCE AND FOR ALL HANDED TO THE SAINTS.

NOVEMBER 30

"Can't We All Get Along?"

"Behold, how good and how pleasant it is for brothers to dwell together in unity!"
— Psalm 133:1

I remember when I was newly converted I was invited by a friend to attend a country church. As I pulled up in front of the church, I could see that there was a big conflict brewing between the church members outside. There was a man at the front of one group and another man in front of the other group, and they were yelling at each other. I had no idea what they were talking about.

Here I am, six or eight weeks old in the Lord, and I've been invited to learn about Christianity from my friend, and they are just about to go at it with fisticuffs, and I thought any moment this is going to turn into a huge brawl. I was so astonished, and I remember wondering is this what Christianity is all about?

I remember how repulsed I was by that, and I thank God for His persevering grace that held on to me in spite of that. Of course, that's no excuse for us to us to say something like, "If so and so is a Christian, I don't want to have any part of Christianity." That's like saying, "If he's going to go to hell, then I'm going to go to hell too."

Problems of pride and desire for preeminence often cause Christians to not act Christianly sometimes toward each other. How pleasant it is when Christians work well together in unity.

Lord, give us strength to live at peace with all men, especially our fellow Christians. Forgive us for the pride in our hearts that too often prevents us from getting along with our fellow believers...

BY GOD'S STRENGTH, WE CAN EXPERIENCE UNITY IN THE BODY OF CHRIST.

DECEMBER 1

The Beginning of Advent

"Listen, you will conceive in your womb and bear a Son and shall call His name JESUS."

— Luke 1:31

The church calendar begins the first Sunday of December, which marks the beginning of the Advent season. Advent comes from Latin and simply means "coming." Jesus came into the world the first time that first Christmas some 2000 years ago.

We remember that the entire Advent season climaxes on December 25, when the Western church (Protestant and Catholic) celebrate His birth. The Eastern church (Orthodox, Coptic, etc.) celebrate His birth on January 6, along with the coming of the wise men. A church council to reconcile these two dates came up with the notion of the 12 Days of Christmas. Regardless of the particular day celebrated, what counts is that we remember Christ's coming into the world. In one sense, we could celebrate Christmas every day of the year because every day we should celebrate the salvation the Savior has brought to us.

Advent and the whole Christmas season is marked by light. Lots of lights. Why is that? Because suddenly into the darkness of the world of woe there shone a great light, as the Son of God first manifested His light and His glory. Incredible! Jesus is the Light of the World, and wherever He has gone He has brought His light. He has enlightened the minds of countless millions of people. The Bible tells us that God is light, and Jesus is God the Son, and so He brought that light of heaven with Him into this world.

Lord Jesus, Light of the World, shine in our darkness. Help us this Advent season to prepare properly for Your coming again. Renew our hearts with Your light and peace…

BY GOD'S STRENGTH, WE CAN SHINE OUR LIGHT IN THIS DARK WORLD.

DECEMBER 2

It All Belongs to God

"You are cursed with a curse, your whole nation, for you are robbing Me."

— Malachi 3:9

Some people avoid church because they think it's all about money. But it is really more about the concept of stewardship. The first principle of stewardship is very simply stated by the psalmist: *"The earth belongs to the Lord, and its fullness, the world, and those who dwell in it"* (Psalm 24:1). It all belongs to God. He created it, and He allows us to use it. We are mere stewards of these resources. He blesses us with good seasons and rain and all of the things that are needful. However, He does say one thing: we are to return a tenth of that to Him, just as a test of our faith and obedience to Him.

This brings us to the second principle of stewardship, namely, that the tithe belongs to the Lord. It is His, He claims it, and therefore if we do not return it, we are, He says, robbing Him. *"Will a man rob God? Yet you have robbed Me. But you say, 'How have we robbed You?' In tithes and offerings"* (Malachi 3:8).

It is not ours. One writer says, "When we keep it, it is simply an act of theft. We may have put it in our bank account…we may have a new car that we have driven in to church, we may be watching football games on a new TV, but it is not ours." At minimum, give to the Lord ten percent of what you have, and watch how He blesses you for it.

Dear God, give us the strength today to set aside that which is Yours. Forgive us for any stinginess on our part. Please, make us generous, as You are generous…

BY GOD'S STRENGTH, WE CAN
GIVE FREELY AND GENEROUSLY.

DECEMBER 3

Did Jesus Exist?

"The king, before whom I also speak freely, knows about these things. For I am persuaded that none of this is hidden from him, for this was not done in a corner."

— Acts 26:26

There continue to be some skeptics, not of a learned sort I may say, who deny the historicity of Jesus. But there is no true historian in all of the world who would dare place his reputation on the line by saying that Jesus never lived. However, there are those amateur skeptics that like to come up with such statements from time to time that Christ was a fable, He never really existed, and the Bible is a collection of myths. But there is a great deal of attestation for both.

It is like a tumor of the brain, to use a not very happy metaphor, which cannot be removed by surgery without killing the patient. To remove the Scriptures and to remove Christ from history is indeed to destroy the body of history completely.

There is more evidence for the fact that Jesus Christ lived than that Julius Caesar lived. To deny the basic historicity of the New Testament is to deny all of ancient history together. Not only do we have the witness of the New Testament writers, Matthew, Mark, Luke, John, Paul, Peter, James, and Jude, but we have many other Christian writers of the first and second centuries, including Barnabas, Ignatius, Clement, Irenaeus, Hermes, and Tertullian. And then there are many non-Christian sources testifying to the existence of Jesus and the Christians. These include Josephus, Tacitus, Thallus, Phlegon, Suetonius, Pliny the Younger, Emperor Hadrian, Emperor Trajan, Lucian of Samosata, Mara bar Serapion, The Talmud, and Toledoth Jeschu. By first century historical standards, Jesus was well-established historically.

Dear Lord, give us the strength and opportunity to share with somebody the incredibly strong proof of Your life and work...

BY GOD'S STRENGTH, WE CAN RECOGNIZE THAT HISTORY IS HIS STORY.

DECEMBER 4

"Thou Hast Conquered, Oh Thou Galilean"

"But if it is of God, you will not be able to overthrow them, lest perhaps you be found even fighting against God."

— Acts 5:39

After the conversion of Constantine, he allowed for the freedom of the Christian church for the first time in its existence. The Christians could crawl out of the catacombs and actually build buildings where they could publicly worship Jesus. It was a glorious time for the church after 300 years of persecution.

But a few decades after Emperor Constantine's death, there arose a ruler from his own family who tried to turn his back on Christianity and make the Roman empire solidly pagan. His name was Julian the Apostate.

By rejecting Jesus, Julian the Apostate made a wreck of his life, but thankfully his reign was short-lived. It is said that he was wounded in battle, and as he lay dying, sinking into the sand, he picked up a handful of sand filled with his own blood and threw it into the sky and said, "Thou hast conquered, Oh Thou Galilean" and thus, Julian's work perished with him. Attempting to overthrow the Christian religion by writing a book against it, he inadvertently ended up confirming most of its basic historic tenants.

Our faith is built upon a solid rock that neither pagan nor demon can overthrow. Yes, there have been small clouds that have come and obscured the sun for a moment. "Julian was such a cloud," said Athanasius, the great defender of the faith. But the cloud, as he said, "…it is a little cloud, it passes away." The sun, however, continues to shine in its brightness in the sky, and so it is with Christ.

Lord, give me strength to endure the godless cry of pagans and persecutors, knowing that they are but clouds before the sun…

BY GOD'S STRENGTH, WE CAN PERSIST, KNOWING JESUS WILL PREVAIL.

You Can't Outgive God

"Bring all the tithes into the storehouse, that there may be food in My house, and test Me now in this, says the Lord of Hosts, if I will not open for you the windows of heaven and pour out for you a blessing, that there will not be room enough to receive it."

— Malachi 3:10

God wants us to be generous, and He blesses us for it. You can't out-give God, and the windows of heaven will be opened unto you. It isn't a matter of finance—it's a matter of faith and acting on God's promise found here in Malachi. You cannot possibly lose. If you believe that promise, you will inevitably be a tither—or more. I think about a young boy in his very early teens. He wasn't very strong and he was small for his age, but he had to make a living. He got a big cart and pushed it down the streets of Chicago, crying out, "Cheese for sale. Cheese for sale." This little scrawny kid managed to make enough money to live when he had no other help.

His daughter (or niece, I am not sure which) came to our church years ago and wanted to meet with me in my office. I had the pleasure of listening to his story through her. God blessed this young man because he gave his life to Christ and determined that he would tithe on all he made. First thing you know he had somebody else pushing another cart. Then he had somebody else pushing another cart for him, and then another one, and another one. It wasn't too many years later when children in school were in a spelling bee, and one of the children was asked, "How do you spell cheese?" and one little boy said, with a bright smile, "Kraft"—because the television had told him "that's how you spell cheese." J. L. Kraft's name had become synonymous with cheese.

Father God, give to us the strength to be faithful in our giving to Your kingdom. Thank You that You are so generous, You just give and give and give. Let us be like You…

BY GOD'S STRENGTH, WE CAN GIVE TO THE LORD, KNOWING HE OWNS IT ALL.

Wherever You Are, Be There

"So teach us to number our days, that we may apply our hearts to wisdom."

— Psalm 90:12

Sometimes somebody can be present with you, but they are actually far away. We should strive to "be there" in the midst of conversations we are often half absent from—that we might "be there" in the moments that we have to spend with spouse or child or parent or friend.

Those who do not live in the present are like the man in the following poem:

He was going to be all that mortal should be—Tomorrow;
No one should be kinder nor braver than he—Tomorrow.
A friend who was troubled and weary he knew,
Who'd be glad of a life and who needed it, too,
On him he would call and see what he could do—Tomorrow.

Each morning he stacked up the letters he'd write—Tomorrow;
More time he'd have to give others, he'd say—Tomorrow.

The greatest of workers this man would have been—Tomorrow.
The world would have known him had he ever seen—Tomorrow,
But the fact is he died and he faded from view,
And all that he left here when living was through
Was a mountain of things he intended to do—Tomorrow.

Wherever you are, be there…today, if possible. Ask God to teach you to live fully in the present that you may take advantage of every opportunity He gives you to serve Jesus Christ.

Lord Jesus, give us the strength to live in the present and fulfill all our duties of the day…

BY GOD'S STRENGTH, WE CAN SERVE HIM TODAY AND TOMORROW.

Amazing Stories of Amazing Grace

"But we have this treasure in earthen vessels, the excellency of the power being from God and not from ourselves."

— 2 Corinthians 4:7

The Bible has resulted in the conversion of hundreds of millions of people—"earthen vessels"—by God's grace. There are amazing stories of God's amazing grace.

An interesting one is the conversion of Sgt. Jacob DeShazar, who flew with Doolittle's squadron in World War II. His plane went down over Japan after they had bombed Nagoya. He was captured and placed in a five-foot cell in Japan. There he was treated cruelly. At first his heart was filled with hatred for his tormentors.

Then a small New Testament was placed in his hands by a visitor, and he began to read it. As a result, DeShazar accepted Jesus Christ into his heart as Savior and Lord of his life. He said that his heart was so filled with joy in that tiny five-foot cell that he would not have changed places with any person in the world. He came to forgive his enemies.

When the war ended and he was released and brought home, he determined to go back to Japan as a missionary, to take the love of God to those who had been his mortal enemies.

The story of his capture, his imprisonment, and his conversion was placed in a tract. That tract fell into the hands of Mitsuo Fuchida, the Japanese pilot who led the attack on Pearl Harbor. He was converted. He later found Sgt. Jacob DeShazar, and the two of them conspired to bring the Gospel of the love of God to the people of Japan. God can transform the human heart.

Lord God, thank You for the transforming power of the Gospel. Thank You for transforming my heart and daily forming me into Your own image. Thank You for making us part of Your story…

BY GOD'S STRENGTH, OUR HEARTS CAN BE TRANSFORMED.

DECEMBER 8

Fear of Failure

"Do not fear, for you shall not be ashamed nor be humiliated; for you shall not be put to shame..."

— Isaiah 54:4

We all have to grapple with the fear of failure which immobilizes so many of us. I am sure there is not a person alive who has not had to wrestle in some dark night with that archfiend, the fear of failure. How many of us have started out and gone but a little way, until we felt the icy fingers of fear gripping our hearts and turning our blood to cold, jellied soup? The poet put it like this:

Lord, I'm afraid of ridicule.
So many things I'd like to attempt
But failure invites embarrassment.
Have you a promise for sensitive souls?

Does it sometimes seem to you that the whole world is against you? Why do the cosmic forces seem to be pressing against you? If you have ever felt that way, you have known the dread, the fear, the anxiety that has given rise to all the primitive religions of this world. Many of these religions were established because men thought the universe and the cosmic forces of the world were arrayed against them. Consequently, they created gods that they imagine live within the forces of thunder and lightning, tree and river, snake and alligator, and they have tried to propitiate them.

But thankfully the God of the universe, who has revealed Himself in Christ, tells us to not fear, nor be ashamed. Regardless of how we feel at the moment, we can be confident, knowing that God is at work in our lives. Let faith replace fear.

Lord, thank You for what You said through Your servant Isaiah, "Do not fear, for you will not be ashamed." Give us strength today to bring our fears to You. When we are afraid, let us trust in You...

BY GOD'S STRENGTH, WE ARE
NOT BOUND BY OUR FEARS.

Finding the Power of God

"For I am not ashamed of the Gospel of Christ.
For it is the power of God for salvation to everyone
who believes, to the Jew first, and also to the Greek."

— Romans 1:16

Too many of us have an unusual problem. We have too many powers. We have powers of intellect, physical prowess, academic accomplishment, athletic trophies, business success, professional advancement, and social standing. The problem with all these superfluous powers is that they can prevent us from finding the power of God—which alone can bring ultimate success in life. As Jesus asked, What if you gain the whole world and lose your soul?

But power does not originate with us, does it? The physical strength that we have is derived from the food we eat. We have intellectual abilities. From whence did they come but from God? Even the power station does not make power. It simply finds it in one form and converts it to another. It may find it in a river and change it into electricity. It may find it in coal, and change it into steam. Or in the atom and change it into nuclear power.

That power is outside of us and all around us. The power of God is out there, around us like radio and television waves. But it is not until we turn on the dial that we can take hold of those powers and appropriate them and receive them for ourselves. The power of God is available to you and me. We need to receive power through Christ, who strengthens us. Then we will be able to achieve, to do all things. That is the secret.

Oh, God, Source of all strength, grant us today Your power and cleanse away all things that hinder Your power from flowing in our lives…

BY GOD'S STRENGTH, WE CAN LET THE
POWER OF THE GOSPEL CHANGE US.

DECEMBER 10

The Meat of the Word

"Brothers, I could not speak to you as to spiritual men… I have fed you with milk and not with solid food. For to this day you were not able to endure it…"

— 1 Corinthians 3:1a-2

The late Dr. Donald Gray Barnhouse pastored Tenth Presbyterian Church in Philadelphia. Barnhouse was the gentleman through whom I first heard the Gospel on the radio and through whom Christ was pleased to reveal Himself in me. And so he has been a person whom I have always appreciated, though I only met him one time. At that time, I told him who I was and that I had been converted about 4 years prior to that through one of his radio broadcasts.

He had preached for 16 years on the book of Romans and he got me at Romans 3:19 and 20. He generally preached on one or two texts at a time and went into them with a great deal of depth. Obviously the more texts that you try to preach on in a sermon the shallower will be the digging that you do. He believed in trying to go deeper and dig a deeper hole over a smaller area. So one or two texts a week took him 16 years to get through the book of Romans and so he had a great love and delight for the Apostle Paul.

There are different preaching styles. Dr. Barnhouse's style may be too slow for some, but it does show that we can deeply plumb the depths of God's Word and still come up with treasures. The meat is there for those who want to find it.

Lord, give us strength, insight, and wisdom to dig deep into Your Word. Let the Holy Spirit feed us the meat of Your Word…

BY GOD'S STRENGTH, WE CAN FIND THE TREASURES IN GOD'S WORD.

DECEMBER 11

Positive Thinking

"Finally, brothers, whatever things are true, whatever things are honest, whatever things are just, whatever things are pure, whatever things are lovely, whatever things are of good report, if there is any virtue, and if there is any praise, think on these things."

— Philippians 4:8

Norman Vincent Peale is best known for his famous book *The Power of Positive Thinking*. Now he has been criticized by evangelical Christians for simply playing on one string of a harp, and there is perhaps a little truthfulness to this in that he left many of the great doctrines of the Christian faith not denied, but more or less ignored, while he played on the string of the power of positive thinking. But let me say this, he played better on that string than anybody else has, and he certainly helped many people.

I remember a young man who worked on our custodial staff here at the church who was one of the most negative, downcast, self-reproaching individuals that I have ever met. So I took out of my library my copy of Peale's book and I told him that if anybody ever needed to read this book he did, and I gave it to him with the hope that he profited from it.

But long before Peale stressed positive thinking, the Apostle Paul was sounding the very same note. Perhaps the note from which Peale got his inspiration for his book, I don't know that for certain, but the text that we read today is certainly one of the most positive thinking kinds of texts that there is. So certainly Paul was a man who knew the importance of positive thinking. You could not have a greater text for a message or book on true positive thinking than Philippians 4:8.

Beautiful Savior, give us the strength to take every thought captive and to think of the good and the lovely…

BY GOD'S STRENGTH, WE CAN
WALK BY FAITH NOT BY SIGHT.

DECEMBER 12

Deciding to Hope In God

"And hope does not disappoint, because the love of God is shed abroad in our hearts by the Holy Spirit who has been given to us."

— Romans 5:5

The Bible has a good bit to say about the matter of our thinking. The Bible teaches that we have the power to govern our thoughts and, therefore, we are responsible for our thinking. Now most people don't think that we are. They believe that thinking is just something that goes on all of the time and is almost beyond our control.

And there certainly is a steady stream of thinking that goes on and I suppose it goes on in everyone. It goes on in my head—I can't see what is going on in yours. I trust you are not like the young farm boy who came to work at a farm and the owner was a little concerned about this young fella and he said to him, "John, what do you do in your spare time?" "Well," he said, "sometimes I sits and thinks, and sometimes I just sits."

But we can control our thinking. We can just let the chips fall where they may or we can choose to hope in God. As the prayer states: "God is good, all the time. All the time, God is good. Prayers go up. Blessings come down. Believe it, receive it, one day closer to home."

The Bible tells us that whatever comes our way, we should put our hope in God. As has been said, we should not doubt in the dark what God has shown us in the light. This is hope anchored in reality. It is a hope based on the very character and revelation of God, who confirmed His Word, and who raised Jesus from the dead. By God's grace, we need not think of things that cause us to be despondent, but to instead, hope in God.

Give us the strength today so that our thoughts and the meditations of our hearts will be acceptable in Your sight, O Lord our strength and our Redeemer…

BY GOD'S STRENGTH, WE
CAN HOPE IN THE LORD.

DECEMBER 13

Every Thought Captive

"...casting down imaginations and every high thing that exalts itself against the knowledge of God, bringing every thought into captivity to the obedience of Christ."

— 2 Corinthians 10:5

Christianity involves our actions, our words. Every thought is to be brought into captivity to the obedience of Jesus Christ. This is a tremendous statement.

This kind of thought is reiterated, even the wise Solomon said many centuries before, *"...for as he thinks in his heart so is he"* (Proverbs 23:7). What you really are is what you think in your heart. *"For out of the heart proceed evil thoughts, murders, adulteries, sexual immorality, thefts, false witness, and blasphemies,"* and so on, said Christ (Matthew 15:19).

If people continue to think negative thoughts, those channels seem to be worn down as it were in the mind, and the thoughts like streams running down the side of a mountain find a channel to run in and so our thoughts will run more and more in those kinds of channels. If they are spiritual and heavenly and positive and loving, they will tend to flow more in those directions.

Therefore, it is so important that we learn to control our thoughts because it is out of the thoughts, the heart, and the mind that our lives proceed. You have no doubt heard the old maxim: Sow a thought, reap an action. Sow an action, reap a habit. Sow a habit, reap a character. Sow a character, reap a destiny. Ultimately your destiny will be determined by what you think. There is no way you can escape that. You are what you think.

Lord, give us strength today to think Your thoughts and not sin against You in our mind today. Please break the bad habits of wrong-thinking within us...

BY GOD'S STRENGTH, WE CAN LOVE THE LORD WITH OUR MIND.

DECEMBER 14

Living According to the Truth

"...whatever things are true...think on these things."
— Philippians 4:8

In Philippians 4:8, Paul tells us to think on good and noble things. The first one he mentions is to think on what is true. That means true as opposed to false and true as opposed to unreal—the real as opposed to the unreal. Now we live in a day when many people echo Pilate, saying, "What is truth?" And they believe that there is no real truth.

Mark Twain said that the problem with most people is not what they don't know, but what they know for certain that isn't true. I think that statement is applicable to this discussion. Many think there is nothing real. But we know that Christ is true. We know that His Word is true. We know that God is true.

We should think on those things and whatever thoughts we should think on should be thoughts that are true, thoughts that are genuine and not phony. Many people live lives which are just not genuine, they are phony.

What they really try to be and to appear to people on the outside is not what they really are at all, and ultimately that is discovered. That's why people so often today don't last long in marriages because finally what they really are becomes apparent. They don't last long in business, and many of them don't last long in the ministry because finally the truth of what they are becomes manifest and that all leads back to their thinking. Whatever things are true and real—those we ought to think about.

God of Truth, grant us the strength to see and discern between truth and falsehood. Help us to be true in all our ways...

BY GOD'S STRENGTH, WE CAN
BE MEN AND WOMEN OF TRUTH.

DECEMBER 15

You Are What You Think

"...whatever things are honest, whatever things are just, whatever things are pure, whatever things are lovely, whatever things are of good report...think on these things."

— Philippians 4:8

As we continue with devotional messages on this beautiful verse, we see that Paul tells the Philippians to think on good and positive things. They include:

- Whatever things are honest. Those things which are respectful, these are the kinds of things that he is saying we should think about.
- Whatever things are just. Though we as Christians are not of this world, we do live in it. We must live our lives justly and fairly, above reproach.
- Whatever things are pure. The Bible exhorts us frequently to purity of heart and mind. The Bible says that the pure in heart shall see God. If God seems distant, it could be because of impure thoughts (and actions).
- Whatever things are lovely. Now this means not only amiable, lovely, but also amicable as well, as opposed to discordant, loveable. The lovely and the beautiful draws us to God.
- Whatever is of good report. We ought to be thinking good things of people, and we ought to be speaking well of people because these are the kinds of things that build people up instead of tearing them down. Indeed, we can be not only good finders but good tellers as well, and as we share good reports we build up the body of Christ, instead of ripping it apart.

We choose our thoughts. Let us choose wisely.

Oh Lord, You who are the Altogether Lovely One, give me the strength to think wholesome thoughts. As the hymn says, May Your mind, Oh, Christ my Savior, live in me from day to day...

BY GOD'S STRENGTH, WE CAN DWELL ON WHAT IS WHOLESOME AND GOOD.

DECEMBER 16

A Christless Christmas

"And she gave birth to her firstborn Son, and wrapped Him in strips of cloth, and laid Him in a manger, because there was no room for them in the inn."

— Luke 2:7

There are probably few, if any, words more poignant than these: "*...because there was no room for them in the inn.*" How sad, indeed, that when the supreme Potentate of paradise condescended to make a visit to this sin-cursed world, there was no room to be found for Him in the inn.

Infinitely lesser kings of infinitely lesser domains visit this nation and there are dignitaries waiting at the airport, there are bands playing, there are whole suites of rooms reserved for them at the finest hotels. I remember reading of one visit when three floors at one of the finest hotels in New York was reserved for the retinue of some potentate of some pipsqueak country somewhere that most people never even heard of.

But when the King of heaven was born, there were no dignitaries waiting to receive Him. Oh, yes, there was a band sent by the king—but it was a band of soldiers sent to kill Him, not to welcome Him. How tragic that when Jesus was born into this world, there was no room for Him here on earth.

Jump ahead to our time, and even though He rules on high and will one day call each of us to give an account to Him, there is still no room for Him—in our schools, our government, our malls (which ironically cash in on His birthday, no less), or the public square. Blessed are those who make room for Him in their lives.

Lord Jesus, give me strength for today to unashamedly embrace You as my own. Forgive me for any inkling of denying You, Savior, before people because it's not the "in" thing to embrace You...

BY GOD'S STRENGTH, WE ARE HONORED TO BE CALLED CHRISTIANS.

DECEMBER 17

The Homeless Savior

"Jesus replied, 'The foxes have holes and the birds of the air have nests, but the Son of Man has no place to lay His head.'"

— Matthew 8:20

There are two very touching texts found in the Bible that are touching only when they are touched together. Most people never see the connection because they are separated by a chapter heading. These are John 8:1 and John 7:53. In 8:1 we are told that Jesus went unto the Mount of Olives, and in 7:53 we read, *"Then everyone went to his own house."*

Jesus had been teaching the multitude, and when evening came they all went to their own homes. He had no place to go. Not even the homes of the foxes or the nests of the birds.

Someone put it very well when he said that Jesus was born in another man's stable, laid in another man's manger, preached from another man's boat, rode on another man's colt, ate the final supper in another man's room, died on another man's cross for other men's sin, and He was laid in another man's tomb. There was just not any place for Him in this world—not at His birth (no room in the inn), not during His life, not even at His death. We never even provided for Him a place to die. We lifted Him up off the earth and between heaven and earth He hung and He died. There was no room for Him here on this earth—an earth that He created, an earth that He gave life—but there was no room for Him. He became poor for us that we might become rich. What a Savior!

Lord, give us the strength to be ever thankful and mindful of what You did for us when You lived and died in this world...

BY GOD'S STRENGTH, WE HAVE A HOME IN HEAVEN WITH JESUS.

Missing Christ at Christmas

"He said to them, 'But who do you say that I am?'"
— Matthew 16:15

A Christless Christmas is what many will have again this year. Perhaps the first person listed, at least indirectly, who had a Christless Christmas would be the innkeeper. The Bible says there was no room for Mary and Joseph at the inn.

The innkeeper probably said, "Oh, folks, I am so sorry. I can see you are in a bad way, but this is enrollment time. Caesar has issued an edict, and we are just jam-packed. That is true of every hostel in town. I only wish you would have let me know you were coming." Why did the innkeeper have a Christless Christmas that day? It was because he just didn't know.

There are millions in this country today who will have a Christless Christmas this year because of spiritual ignorance.

Some of our TV staff took our cameras out on the street and interviewed people. They asked all sorts of people the question: "Who would you say that Jesus is?" We got some of the most incredible statements you have ever heard.

There are millions of people in America who do not know that He is the incarnate God, the Creator of the universe, the second Person of the Trinity, the Maker of all things, the Judge of heaven and earth—that He is God Almighty, incarnate in human flesh. They don't know why He came.

This Christmas, let us pray for opportunities to tell others about Jesus, so they will no longer have a Christless Christmas.

Lord, give us strength today so that we may share Who You are with someone who does not know You...

BY GOD'S STRENGTH, WE CAN KNOW THE REAL MEANING OF CHRISTMAS.

Born in Bethlehem, As Foretold 700 Years Earlier

"But you, Bethlehem Ephrathah, although you are small among the tribes of Judah, from you will come forth for Me one who will be ruler over Israel. His origins are from of old, from ancient days."

— Micah 5:2

Before Jesus was born, there were hundreds of texts found in the Old Testament describing His birth and life and ministry and passion and death and resurrection. There is nothing vaguely like this anywhere else in the world.

We find many of these prophecies in Isaiah; so much so, that some have called it the Gospel of Isaiah. And yet it was written seven hundred and some years before Jesus Christ was born. Absolutely phenomenal! This is proof positive the Scriptures were inspired by Almighty God, who alone knows the end from the beginning and all things that will come to pass.

The Bible tells us the name of the very town where Jesus would be born, as we see in Micah 5:2. There were two Bethlehems. This particular one is spelled out: Ephrathah.

Some might say, "Jesus lived there for only a couple of years, at most. What about the fact that He grew up in Nazareth, and, furthermore, that He did most of His ministry out of Capernaum on the coast of the Sea of Galilee, and not in Bethlehem? Why doesn't the Old Testament say anything about Nazareth?" There is one good reason: No such city existed when Isaiah lived and didn't for several hundred more years.

God of heaven and earth, we thank You for the prophecies that show us so clearly Your foreknowledge and omniscience. Thank You for sending Your only Son, and telling us about it, hundreds of years before it came to pass...

BY GOD'S STRENGTH, WE CAN SEE AND KNOW THE TRUTH.

DECEMBER 20

The Real Hope of the World

"...and every tongue should confess that Jesus Christ is Lord, to the glory of God the Father."

— Philippians 2:11

Times do change don't they? 100 years ago the voices of the apostles of human perfectibility were heard throughout the land, loud and clear. Millions of Americans got up in the morning and stood before their windows and recited ten times, "Every day, in every way, we're getting better, and better, and better." And so, this philosophy was rampant in America.

But times do change, don't they? It was about the same time that a British lord stood up in Parliament and declared, "Gentlemen, we are about to usher in the Golden Age." And then it came—the Argonne, the Marne, Flanders Field, where blood was mingled with mud, and the apocalyptic horseman on the pale horse rode across the continent of Europe and left a carnage in his wake. But still the voices of some continued, "Every day we're getting better and better," for this was a war to end all wars, and then, Pearl Harbor, Dunkirk, and D-Day, the Bataan death march, Hiroshima—and the voices grew weaker, "Every day, in every way, we're getting..."

Today wars continue, though not worldwide. How wrong they were—the Golden Years didn't come, the bloody years came. Now, even some psychiatrists have come to realize that man is far from perfectible. But it is in just such darkness as this, in just such a black night as this, that we must see that first star that shone over Bethlehem. Jesus is the real hope of the world.

Lord, give me strength for today to follow after You and Your ways in a world that is largely following after the evil one. We praise You that one day all mankind will bow down before You...

BY HIS STRENGTH, WE BOW THE KNEE TO JESUS CHRIST.

DECEMBER 21

What We Celebrate at Christmas

"...who, being in the form of God, did not consider equality with God something to be grasped."
— Philippians 2:6

Jesus Christ was not merely a man, and Christmas doesn't celebrate the birth of a man. Christmas is a celebration of the birth of the God-man. This is not some apotheosis like that of the Caesars in which a man was elevated to "God" status. This is the great condescension of the Trinity when almighty God deigned to become one of us and to be born among men.

This fact, however, of the supernatural origin and essence of Christianity is often denied today in our world. For example, consider the remnant Communist countries where the idea is inculcated daily into people's minds, both young and old, that Christianity is a myth and an opiate of the people.

But these denials are not restricted to other lands—in our own midst on many campuses parents have found that children have come back from school and have been divested of their earlier beliefs.

The essential supernatural character that Christmas is a birth of God into the world is often denied. But the fact is that Christmas cannot be successfully denied, though it has been tried for twenty centuries. No, the victories are too many.

The historical record is clear that Jesus Christ lived a remarkable life, and He changed all of history through His death and resurrection. In a sense you could say: At Christmas time, we also celebrate Good Friday and Easter.

Lord, give me strength for today to live on the supernatural plane, as we praise You for the grand miracle of Your incarnation. Help me to be Christ-like to those around me...

BY HIS STRENGTH, WE CAN DAILY RELY ON HIS MIRACULOUS POWER.

DECEMBER 22

A Small Sampling of Jesus' Impact

"But He emptied Himself, taking upon Himself the form of a servant, and was made in the likeness of men."

— Philippians 2:7

As Christmas approaches, it is interesting to reflect on the impact of Jesus. Consider a sampling:

- Suppose we would gather a group of literary men together and ask them what is the greatest masterpiece of literature ever written by man, and many will tell, perhaps the majority, the greatest work ever penned by merely human hands was *Paradise Lost*, written by John Milton—a believer of what some would call "the delusion of the Christian faith"—a believer in the Bible.
- Even the sagacious Ben Franklin, not known for his piety in his life, in his later years wrote to Thomas Paine and implored him not to release the manuscript, of his *Age of Reason*. Of Jesus of Nazareth, Franklin said, "I have this to say, that the system of morals that He left us, and the religion that He has given to the world is the greatest thing that it has ever seen, or is ever likely to see."
- How about men like Patrick Henry, that great speaker who championed freedom? He said, "The book worth all other books in the world is the Bible."
- And then there was Dr. Benjamin Rush, anatomist and physiologist, who said that the only true and perfect religion that man has ever seen is the religion of Jesus Christ.
- And Isaac Newton, the scientist and philosopher, said that the only perfect philosophy in the world is the philosophy of the Gospel.

We are all infinitely better off for Jesus Christ's having been born.

Lord Jesus, thank You for coming and thank You for the Christmas celebration. Thank You for changing our world in so many positive ways. Give us strength to live out the Christian life so we, too, may be a source for good...

BY GOD'S STRENGTH, WE CAN IMPACT THE WORLD AROUND US.

DECEMBER 23

Don't Miss the True Message of Christmas

"And being found in the form of a man, He humbled Himself and became obedient to death, even death on a cross."

— Philippians 2:8

A strategic way to oppose Christmas is by distorting its meaning. Tragically, this has been done very successfully by millions of Americans who would never think of denying the facts of Christmas, and yet, they haven't the foggiest idea of what Christmas is really all about.

There is the method of commercialization. They keep their eyes on Santa Claus and they never see the cross that stands in the shadows behind a manger. And if not commercialization, then pure, unadulterated sentimentality. Christmas is so sweet, and light, and loving they say with vague generalities and a foggy haze.

Christmas, of course, is all about the gift of the Son of God. When we come to experientially know the saving power of Jesus Christ, He transforms our lives. He was not only born in a filthy stable some 2,000 years ago, but when we come to know Him, He is born in our sinful heart and He cleanses us. He died in our place, paying for a gift that we could never buy, and He offers it to us freely when we trust in His saving work. This is the meaning of Christmas and of One who was born to die, and pay the wages of sin, who came into this slimy world and took all of the slime upon Himself and endured the penalty for it.

Do not let the true message of Christmas be crowded out by the *celebration* of Christmas.

Thank You, God, for the gift of Your Son, as we give gifts this season, help us to be truly generous, reflecting Your heart and love. Give us the strength to celebrate this Christmas right…

BY GOD'S STRENGTH, WE CAN REFLECT GOD'S GENEROSITY.

DECEMBER 24

What If Jesus Had Never Been Born?

"He who was seated on the throne said, 'Look! I am making all things new.'"

— Revelation 21:5

Some people have made transformational changes in one department of human learning or in one aspect of human life, and their names are forever enshrined in the annals of human history. But Jesus Christ, the greatest man who ever lived, changed virtually every aspect of human life—and most people don't know it. The greatest tragedy of the Christmas holiday each year is not so much its commercialization (gross as that is), but its trivialization. How tragic it is that people have forgotten Him to whom they owe so very much.

Because of Jesus and the church, we see historically all sorts of positive ways in which life on earth had been transformed for the better. This includes transforming the value of human life, the creation of the hospital, education for the masses, and giving birth to modern science. All the early pioneers of science believed that a rational God had a made a rational universe and it was their job to "think God's thoughts after Him," as astronomer Johannes Kepler put it.

More than a century ago, poet James Russell Lowell, author of the hymn "Once to man and every nation" said this: "I challenge any skeptic to find a ten square mile spot on this planet where they can live their lives in peace and safety and decency, where womanhood is honored, where infancy and old age are revered, where they can educate their children, where the Gospel of Jesus Christ has not gone first to prepare the way."

Jesus Christ, we thank You today for coming into our world and transforming it. Help us to transform our particular sphere of influence where You have placed us…

BY GOD'S STRENGTH, WE
CAN CHANGE THE WORLD.

The Uniqueness of Christmas

"Therefore God highly exalted Him and gave Him the name which is above every name..."

— Philippians 2:9

There is a certain exclusiveness about Christmas. There is a uniqueness to it. Jesus Christ stands alone—the unique God-man in the world. He cannot be put in a row with other so-called founders of religion. Jesus Christ claims to be God, who has come into the world to save the lost. One day every knee shall bow and every tongue confess that He is Lord of all.

I talked to a woman at a dinner not so long ago who was a member of some Christian church and she endeavored to defend to me her belief that, "Of course I'm a Christian, but I believe that anyone who lives a sincere life and tries to do good will eventually get to heaven." She missed the point entirely.

By saying this, she is simply saying she's not a Christian. She doesn't understand what Christmas means and what Christianity is. If it were true that Christianity were a religion that said, "Try to do the best you can. Do what God has said in His word. Try to live by the teachings of Jesus Christ, who is a great prophet. Follow the Sermon on the Mount. Do what your conscience tells you. Be kind to your neighbor, and perhaps you'll get to Heaven,"—if Christianity were a religion that said that, then I maintain that any other religion would be equally as good, because they all have their ethics. They all have their principles. They all have their rules. But none of them has a Savior except Christianity.

Jesus, my Savior, thank You for humbling Yourself and opening the way to heaven for us, who cannot get there on our own. Give us the strength to live humble lives and follow in Your footsteps...

BY GOD'S STRENGTH, WE CAN ACQUIRE HUMILITY.

I Was Blind, Now I See

"…we declare to you that which we have seen and heard, that you also may have fellowship with us…"

— 1 John 1:3

Some Christians hold back from being witnesses for Christ because they don't feel qualified somehow. But you are not called to be an expert witness—just a witness, and there is a great deal of difference. The preacher is supposed to be an expert witness, but the layman is not.

You recall that in the Bible there was a man who was a witness, and they tried continually to change him into an expert witness and he would not be changed. Remember him, the man born blind described in John 9? They said to him, "Now tell us the truth. We know that God does not hear sinners and this man (Jesus) is a sinner and, therefore, God wouldn't hear His prayers, so how can you see?" And he said, "That's systematic theology 302, and I haven't even been to seminary. I don't know. But one thing I know: Whereas I was blind, now I see."

You don't have to be a walking biblical encyclopedia to be a witness for Christ; you simply have to know the Gospel and know what has happened in your life. Of course, then there is the excuse, "Well, that's the preacher's job. He's the one who knows the answers to all of those questions."

In Evangelism Explosion, we teach you the answers to a few basic objections, which are heard over and over again. In answering about a dozen questions, we take care of about 99 percent of the objections raised in evangelism. If you are in Christ, you were once blind, but now you see.

Jesus, give me strength for today that I might share Your love with someone who needs to hear how You have touched my life. Let me be a faithful witness and thank You for the opportunities You give me…

BY HIS STRENGTH, WE CAN HAVE SPIRITUAL SIGHT.

DECEMBER 27

Speaking for the Lord

"Then Moses said to the Lord, 'O my Lord, I am not eloquent, neither before nor since You have spoken to Your servant. But I am slow of speech, and of a slow tongue.'"

— Exodus 4:10

When God commissioned Moses, the latter gave excuse after excuse to try and wriggle out of it. One was that he was a poor speaker. Well, in trying to recruit Christians to try and share their faith, I've heard that excuse myself. "Lord, I'm not articulate." "Well, I can't express myself like you can." How clearly I've heard that said many, many times.

There are similar excuses that are given many times. "I just can't talk to others." "I'm too shy." "I can't speak in other people's homes to strangers," and so on. Well, I remember clearly feeling the very same way myself. And yet God said to Moses, *"Who has made man's mouth? Or who made the dumb, or deaf, or the seeing, or the blind? Have not I, the Lord?"* God has made our mouths and if we are slow of speech, God can help that.

We certainly know that many times in the Scriptures in those days God made the blind to see and the deaf to hear and the dumb to speak. Surely He can make the slow of speech more eloquent than they are, and yet how many times we limit the power of God in saying that He cannot change us. Nevertheless, I have seen and I know of many people in our church, and people around the world, who have been transformed by this experience.

If you have trouble sharing your faith, ask God for His help. This is a prayer He is delighted to answer.

Oh, Lord God, help me to share my faith and to teach others Your words. Thank You for Your words, which are both eloquent and true. You who made my mouth, teach me to speak rightfully...

BY HIS STRENGTH, HE CAN USE MY LIFE AND MY MOUTH FOR HIS CAUSE.

To Forget or to Remember?

"Do this in remembrance of Me." Luke 22:19
"…forgetting those things which are behind…"
— Philippians 3:13

I am sure that Christians must get confused when they read a verse like this. Paul says, "This is what I do, I forget those things which are behind." And yet I have preached sermons on a number of occasions on "remember." Jesus said, "Remember Me." We are told over and over again in the Bible to remember.

Are we to forget or are we to remember? Well, obviously we are to do both, and the question is: What are the objects of the verbs, remember and forget? There are certainly things that we are to remember. We are to remember what Jesus Christ has done for us upon the Cross.

The things that Paul is talking about forgetting would be of two classes. Just like a runner or skater skating for 1500 yards, they have to forget their successes or failures in a hurry and not sit back and rest upon those laurels.

I think it is particularly true that as they get older people begin to rest more and more on their laurels and stretch less and less toward the prize, the mark of the high calling of God. We need to forget about our victories and not simply float on them, but to reach out to the things that yet remain to be done. Nor should our past failures weigh us down.

Let us thank God for what He has done in the past, as we strive to serve Him in the present and future.

My Lord and Savior, thank You for what you have done for me. Help me to not be a prisoner of the past with its failures or its victories…

BY GOD'S STRENGTH, WE ARE
ABLE TO STRETCH FORWARD.

FIDO

"...forgetting those things which are behind..."
— Philippians 3:13

Years ago we had a guest speaker at our church who made the point so well that we need to forget the things that are behind and press forward in Christ.

Lt. Clebe McClary is a veteran of the Viet Nam War. He unfortunately experienced the blast of dynamite which blew off his arm, which he only discovered when he couldn't reach his rifle because there was nothing on his shoulder any longer. It also blew out his eye and half of his face, his teeth, his nose, and did all sorts of other damage. I think he has had over 35 major surgical operations. Despite all these hardships, he reminds himself regularly to forget.

He has a license plate on the front of his car which says "FIDO." That's F-I-D-O. No, that's not the name of his dog. It stands, he says, for "Forget It, Drive On." And let me tell you he has a lot to forget. Have you been hurt? Is your eye gone, your teeth, your arm? How many surgical operations has it taken to correct your injuries, and, of course, it is still not corrected—the damage from the hurt that you or I have experienced? Forget it, drive on. "*...Forgetting those things which are behind and reaching forward to those things which are ahead, I press toward the goal...*" (Philippians 3:13-14a).

Too many people allow the past to destroy their present and their future. FIDO is a message like that of the Apostle Paul—to consciously not drag the baggage of the past forward.

Lord God of Justice, we ask that You help us to forget what is behind. Help us to not let past hurts define and hinder us. Thank You that one day You will right all wrongs...

BY HIS STRENGTH, WE CAN
LEAVE THE PAST BEHIND.

Finish Well

"He who has an ear, let him hear what the Spirit says to the churches. He who overcomes shall not be hurt by the second death."

— Revelation 2:11

In Greek mythology, Orpheus, the golden voiced, loses his beautiful wife, Eurydice, and so with lyre in hand he makes his way down through the darkness of the infernal regions in quest of the lost Eurydice, singing his plaintive melodies.

As he goes forth and fills the chambers of that nether world with the rich sonorous tones of his plaintive cry, Tantalus stops his futile bending after the receding waters and listens for a while. Even the cheeks of the furies are wet with tears as they hear the poignant plea of Orpheus for his lost wife.

At last, Orpheus reaches Pluto, the god of this nether world, who finally condescends to allow him to take his wife back on one condition: that he will not set his eyes upon her until they fully reach the land of light above. They set off, Orpheus before, and his beautiful wife, Eurydice, behind.

They pass one obstacle and one danger after another. All hell holds its breath as they make their way tortuously upward, ever closer, until finally they can see the light. So elated is Orpheus, he turns to tell his wife that soon they will be there—and in that moment, all his labor is lost and Eurydice vanishes.

That ancient and familiar myth teaches us a great truth: that it is only he who perseveres until the end who shall be saved. It does not really matter how well we start. It is the finish that counts. As the Apostle Paul said: *"You ran well. Who hindered you…"* (Galatians 5:7).

Lord, give me the strength to finish well. If I have previously allowed obstacles to hinder my race, as happened to the Galatians, please forgive me and then give me the grace to get up again and continue with the race you have marked out for me…

BY GOD'S STRENGTH, WE CAN MAKE IT OVER THE FINISH LINE.

The Spirits of New Year's Eve

"Who has woe? Who has sorrow? Who has contentions? Who has babbling? Who has wounds without cause? Who has redness of eyes? Those who tarry long at the wine, those who go to seek mixed wine."

— Proverbs 23:29-30

Some today call alcoholism merely a "disease." The Bible calls it *drunkenness*. But you know, it is an interesting "disease" because the only way you can become an alcoholic is to get drunk. The Bible says that no drunkard will enter into the kingdom of heaven (see I Cor. 6:10).

Someone has said that *if* alcoholism is a disease (and certainly when a person becomes addicted and enslaved by it, it takes on many aspects of a disease):

It is the only disease that is contracted by an act of the will...

It is the only disease that is bottled and sold...

It is the only disease that provokes crime...

It is the only disease that bars the patient from heaven.

It is a tragic "disease" in America, and it is found among many young people today. Many who are turning away from drugs are turning to alcohol. This is even true of churched young people. Having a drink is one thing, but we should not do anything—including having a drink—if it causes our brother to fall away from the faith.

The Bible says that we should not be drunk with wine but instead be filled with the Holy Spirit. Having the joy of the Lord inside takes away the empty hole that some try to fill with drunkenness.

Lord, on this New Year's Eve, we know that many will turn to the bottle for solace. We ask, Dear Father, that instead they would turn to You. Thank You for this past year. We lay the new one at Your feet...

BY GOD'S STRENGTH, OUR HEARTS CAN BE AT REST.

DAILY BIBLE READING GUIDE

January

1	Genesis	1-2:17	Matthew	1	Psalm	1
2	Genesis	2:18-4:16	Matthew	2:1-18	Psalm	2
3	Genesis	4:17-6:22	Matthew	2:19-3	Psalm	3
4	Genesis	7-9:17	Matthew	4:1-22	Proverbs	1:1-17
5	Genesis	9:18-11:9	Matthew	4:23-5:20	Psalm	4
6	Genesis	11:10-13:18	Matthew	5:21-42	Psalm	5
7	Genesis	14-16	Matthew	5:43-6:24	Psalm	6
8	Genesis	17-18	Matthew	6:25-7:23	Proverbs	1:8-19
9	Genesis	19-20:18	Matthew	7:24-8:22	Psalm	7:1-9
10	Genesis	21-23	Matthew	8:23-9:13	Psalm	7:10-17
11	Genesis	24	Matthew	9:14-38	Psalm	8:1-9
12	Genesis	25-26	Matthew	10:1-31	Proverbs	1:20-33
13	Genesis	27-28	Matthew	10:32-11:15	Psalm	9:1-6
14	Genesis	29-30	Matthew	11:16-30	Psalm	9:7-12
15	Genesis	31	Matthew	12:1-21	Psalm	9:13-20
16	Genesis	32-33	Matthew	12:22-45	Proverbs	2:1-11
17	Genesis	34-35	Matthew	12:46-13:17	Psalm	10:1-11
18	Genesis	36-37	Matthew	13:18-35	Psalm	10:12-18
19	Genesis	38-39	Matthew	13:36-58	Psalm	11
20	Genesis	40-41:40	Matthew	14:1-21	Proverbs	2:12-22
21	Genesis	41:41-42:38	Matthew	14:22-15:9	Psalm	12
22	Genesis	43-44	Matthew	15:10-39	Psalm	13
23	Genesis	45-47:12	Matthew	16:1-20	Psalm	14
24	Genesis	47:13-48:22	Matthew	16:21-17:23	Proverbs	3:1-10
25	Genesis	49-50	Matthew	17:14-18:9	Psalm	15
26	Job	1-3	Matthew	18:10-35	Psalm	16
27	Job	4-7	Matthew	19:1-15	Psalm	17:1-5
28	Job	8-10	Matthew	19:16-30	Proverbs	3:11-20
29	Job	11-14	Matthew	20:1-19	Psalm	17:6-12
30	Job	15-18	Matthew	20:20-34	Psalm	17:13-15
31	Job	19-21	Matthew	21:1-17	Psalm	18:1-6

February

1	Job	22-24	Matthew	21:18-32	Proverbs	3:21-35
2	Job	25-29	Matthew	21:33-22:14	Psalm	18:7-15
3	Job	30-32	Matthew	22:15-46	Psalm	18:16-24
4	Job	33-34	Matthew	23	Psalm	18:25-36
5	Job	35-37	Matthew	24:1-31	Proverbs	4:1-9
6	Job	38-40:2	Matthew	24:32-25:13	Psalm	18:37-42
7	Job	40:3-42:17	Matthew	25:14-46	Psalm	18:43-50
8	Exodus	1-3	Matthew	26:1-30	Psalm	19:1-6
9	Exodus	4-6:12	Matthew	26:31-46	Proverbs	4:10-19
10	Exodus	6:13-8:32	Matthew	26:47-68	Psalm	19:7-14
11	Exodus	9-10	Matthew	26:69-27:10	Psalm	20
12	Exodus	11-12	Matthew	27:11-44	Psalm	21:1-7
13	Exodus	13-14	Matthew	27:45-66	Proverbs	4:20-27
14	Exodus	15-16	Matthew	28	Psalm	21:8-13
15	Exodus	17-18	Mark	1:1-28	Psalm	22:1-11
16	Exodus	19-20	Mark	1:29-2:17	Psalm	22:12-21
17	Exodus	21-22	Mark	2:18-3:30	Proverbs	5:1-14
18	Exodus	23-24	Mark	3:31-4:29	Psalm	22:22-31
19	Exodus	25-26	Mark	4:30-5:20	Psalm	23
20	Exodus	27-28	Mark	5:21-6:6	Psalm	24
21	Exodus	29-30	Mark	6:7-29	Proverbs	5:15-23
22	Exodus	31-33:6	Mark	6:30-56	Psalm	25:1-7
23	Exodus	33:7-34:35	Mark	7:1-30	Psalm	25:8-15
24	Exodus	35-36	Mark	7:31-8:13	Psalm	25:16-22
25	Exodus	37-38	Mark	8:14-9:1	Proverbs	6:1-11
26	Exodus	39-40	Mark	9:2-32	Psalm	26
27	Leviticus	1-3	Mark	9:33-10:12	Psalm	27:1-6
28	Leviticus	4-5:13	Mark	10:13-31	Psalm	27:7-14
29	Leviticus	5:14-7:10	Mark	10:32-52	Proverbs	6:12-19

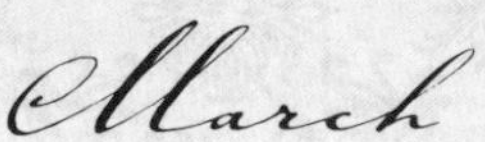

1	Leviticus	7:11-8:36	Mark	11:1-27	Psalm	28
2	Leviticus	9-10	Mark	11:28-12:12	Psalm	29
3	Leviticus	11-12	Mark	12:13-27	Psalm	30:1-7
4	Leviticus	13	Mark	12:28-44	Proverbs	6:20-29
5	Leviticus	14	Mark	13:1-31	Psalm	30:8-12
6	Leviticus	15-16	Mark	13:32-14:16	Psalm	31:1-8
7	Leviticus	17-18	Mark	14:17-42	Psalm	31:9-18
8	Leviticus	19-20	Mark	14:43-72	Proverbs	6:30-35
9	Leviticus	21-22	Mark	15:1-32	Psalm	31:19-24
10	Leviticus	23-24	Mark	15:33-47	Psalm	32
11	Leviticus	25-26:13	Mark	16	Psalm	33:1-11
12	Leviticus	26:14-27:34	Luke	1:1-25	Proverbs	7:1-5
13	Numbers	1-2:9	Luke	1:26-38	Psalm	33:12-22
14	Numbers	2:10-3:51	Luke	1:39-56	Psalm	34:1-10
15	Numbers	4:1-5:10	Luke	1:57-80	Psalm	34:11-22
16	Numbers	5:11-6:27	Luke	2:1-20	Proverbs	7:6-20
17	Numbers	7:1-65	Luke	2:21-40	Psalm	35:1-10
18	Numbers	7:66-9:14	Luke	2:41-52	Psalm	35:11-18
19	Numbers	9:15-11:3	Luke	3:1-22	Psalm	35:19-28
20	Numbers	11:4-13:25	Luke	3:23-4:13	Proverbs	7:21-27
21	Numbers	13:26-14:45	Luke	4:14-37	Psalm	36
22	Numbers	15-16:35	Luke	4:38-5:16	Psalm	37:1-9
23	Numbers	16:36-18:32	Luke	5:17-32	Psalm	37:10-20
24	Numbers	19:1-21:1-3	Luke	5:33-6:11	Proverbs	8:1-11
25	Numbers	21:4-22:20	Luke	6:12-36	Psalm	37:21-31
26	Numbers	22:21-23:26	Luke	6:37-7:10	Psalm	37:32-40
27	Numbers	23:27-25:17	Luke	7:11-35	Psalm	38:1-11
28	Numbers	26-27:11	Luke	7:36-50	Proverbs	8:12-21
29	Numbers	27:12-29:11	Luke	8:1-18	Psalm	38:12-22
30	Numbers	29:12-31:24	Luke	8:19-39	Psalm	39
31	Numbers	31:25-32:42	Luke	8:40-9:9	Psalm	40:1-8

April

1	Numbers	33-34	Luke	9:10-27	Proverbs	8:22-31
2	Numbers	35-36	Luke	9:28-56	Psalm	40:9-17
3	Deuteronomy	1-2:23	Luke	9:57-10:24	Psalm	41:1-6
4	Deuteronomy	2:24-4:14	Luke	10:25-11:4	Psalm	41:7-13
5	Deuteronomy	4:15-5:33	Luke	11:5-32	Proverbs	8:32-36
6	Deuteronomy	6-8	Luke	11:33-54	Psalm	42:1-6
7	Deuteronomy	9-10	Luke	12:1-34	Psalm	42:7-11
8	Deuteronomy	11-12	Luke	12:35-59	Psalm	43
9	Deuteronomy	13-14	Luke	13:1-30	Proverbs	9:1-12
10	Deuteronomy	15-16:20	Luke	13:31-14:14	Psalm	44:1-12
11	Deuteronomy	16:21-18:22	Luke	14:14-35	Psalm	44:13-26
12	Deuteronomy	19-20	Luke	15:1-32	Psalm	45:1-9
13	Deuteronomy	21-22	Luke	16:1-18	Proverbs	9:13-18
14	Deuteronomy	23-25	Luke	16:19-17:10	Psalm	45:10-17
15	Deuteronomy	26-28:14	Luke	17:11-37	Psalm	46
16	Deuteronomy	28:15-68	Luke	18:1-30	Psalm	47:1-9
17	Deuteronomy	29-30:10	Luke	18:31-19:10	Proverbs	10:1-10
18	Deuteronomy	30:11-31:29	Luke	19:11-44	Psalm	48:1-8
19	Deuteronomy	31:30-32:52	Luke	19:45-20:26	Psalm	48:9-14
20	Deuteronomy	33-34	Luke	20:27-21:4	Psalm	49
21	Joshua	1-2	Luke	21:5-38	Proverbs	10:11-20
22	Joshua	3-5:12	Luke	22:1-38	Psalm	50:1-15
23	Joshua	5:13-7:26	Luke	22:39-62	Psalm	50:16-23
24	Joshua	8-9:15	Luke	22:63-23:25	Psalm	51:1-9
25	Joshua	9:16-10:43	Luke	23:26-56	Proverbs	10:21-30
26	Joshua	11-12	Luke	24:1-35	Psalm	51:10-19
27	Joshua	13-14	Luke	24:36-53	Psalm	52
28	Joshua	15-16	John	1:1-28	Psalm	53
29	Joshua	17-18	John	1:29-51	Proverbs	10:31-11:8
30	Joshua	19-21:19	John	2	Psalm	54

May

1	Joshua	21:20-22:34	John	3:1-21	Psalm	55:1-11
2	Joshua	23-24	John	3:22-36	Psalm	55:12-23
3	Judges	1-2:5	John	4:1-26	Proverbs	11:9-18
4	Judges	2:6-3:31	John	4:27-42	Psalm	56
5	Judges	4-5	John	4:43-5:15	Psalm	57:1-6
6	Judges	6-7:8	John	5:16-30	Psalm	57:7-11
7	Judges	7:9-8:35	John	5:31-47	Proverbs	11:19-28
8	Judges	9	John	6:1-24	Psalm	58
9	Judges	10-11	John	6:25-59	Psalm	59:1-8
10	Judges	12-13	John	6:60-7:13	Psalm	59:9-19
11	Judges	14-15	John	7:14-44	Proverbs	11:29-12:7
12	Judges	16-17	John	7:45-8:11	Psalm	60:1-4
13	Judges	18-19	John	8:12-30	Psalm	60:5-12
14	Judges	20-21	John	8:31-59	Psalm	61
15	Ruth	1-2	John	9:1-34	Proverbs	12:8-17
16	Ruth	3-4	John	9:35-10:21	Psalm	62
17	1 Samuel	1-2:26	John	10:22-42	Psalm	63
18	1 Samuel	2:27-4:22	John	11:1-44	Psalm	64
19	1 Samuel	5-7	John	11:45-12:11	Proverbs	12:18-27
20	1 Samuel	8-10:8	John	12:12-26	Psalm	65
21	1 Samuel	10:9-12:25	John	12:37-13:17	Psalm	66:1-12
22	1 Samuel	13-14:23	John	13:18-38	Psalm	66:13-20
23	1 Samuel	14:24-15:34	John	14	Proverbs	12:28-13:9
24	1 Samuel	16-17:37	John	15-16:4	Psalm	67
25	1 Samuel	17:38-18:30	John	16:5-17:5	Psalm	68:1-6
26	1 Samuel	19-20	John	17:6-26	Psalm	68:7-14
27	1 Samuel	21-23	John	18:1-24	Proverbs	13:10-19
28	1 Samuel	24-25	John	18:25-40	Psalm	68:15-20
29	1 Samuel	26-28	John	19:1-27	Psalm	68:21-27
30	1 Samuel	29-31	John	19:28-20:9	Psalm	68:28-35
31	2 Samuel	1-2:7	John	20:10-31	Proverbs	13:20-14:4

June

1	2 Samuel	2:8-3:21	John	21	Psalm	69:1-12
2	2 Samuel	3:22-5:5	Acts	1:1-22	Psalm	69:13-28
3	2 Samuel	5:6-6:23	Acts	1:23-2:21	Psalm	69:29-36
4	2 Samuel	7-8	Acts	2:22-47	Proverbs	14:5-14
5	2 Samuel	9-10	Acts	3	Psalm	70
6	2 Samuel	11-12	Acts	4:1-22	Psalm	71:1-8
7	2 Samuel	13-14	Acts	4:23-5:11	Psalm	71:9-18
8	2 Samuel	15:1-12	Acts	5:12-42	Proverbs	14:15-24
9	2 Samuel	15:13-16:14	Acts	6-7:19	Psalm	71:19-24
10	2 Samuel	16:15-18:18	Acts	7:20-43	Psalm	72
11	2 Samuel	18:19-19:43	Acts	7:44-8:3	Psalm	73:1-14
12	2 Samuel	20-21	Acts	8:4-40	Proverbs	14:25-35
13	2 Samuel	22-23:7	Acts	9:1-31	Psalm	73:15-28
14	2 Samuel	23:8-24:25	Acts	9:32-10:23	Psalm	74:1-9
15	1 Kings	1-2:12	Acts	10:24-11:18	Psalm	74:10-17
16	1 Kings	2:13-3:15	Acts	11:19-12:19	Proverbs	15:1-10
17	1 Kings	3:16-5:18	Acts	12:20-13:12	Psalm	74:18-23
18	1 Kings	6-7:22	Acts	13:13-41	Psalm	75
19	1 Kings	7:23-8:21	Acts	13:42-14:7	Psalm	76
20	1 Kings	8:22-9:9	Acts	14:8-28	Proverbs	15:11-20
21	1 Kings	9:10-11:13	Acts	15:1-21	Psalm	77:1-9
22	1 Kings	11:14-12:24	Acts	15:22-41	Psalm	77:10-20
23	1 Kings	12:25-14:20	Acts	16:1-15	Psalm	78:1-8
24	1 Kings	14:21-16:7	Acts	16:16-40	Proverbs	15:21-30
25	1 Kings	16:8-18:15	Acts	17:1-21	Psalm	78:9-16
26	1 Kings	18:16-19:21	Acts	17:22-18:8	Psalm	78:17-31
27	1 Kings	20-21	Acts	18:9-19:13	Psalm	78:32-39
28	1 Kings	22	Acts	19:14-41	Proverbs	15:31-16:7
29	2 Kings	1-2	Acts	20	Psalm	78:40-55
30	2 Kings	3-4:37	Acts	21:1-26	Psalm	78:56-72

July

1	2 Kings	4:38-6:23	Acts	21:27-22:22	Psalm	79
2	2 Kings	6:24-8:15	Acts	22:22-23:11	Proverbs	16:8-17
3	2 Kings	8:16-9:37	Acts	23:12-35	Psalm	80:1-7
4	2 Kings	10-11	Acts	24	Psalm	80:8-19
5	2 Kings	12-14:22	Acts	25:1-22	Psalm	81:1-7
6	2 Kings	14:23-15:38	Acts	25:23-26:23	Proverbs	16:18-27
7	2 Kings	16-17	Acts	26:24-27:12	Psalm	81:8-16
8	2 Kings	18-19:13	Acts	27:13-44	Psalm	82:1-8
9	2 Kings	19:14-20:21	Acts	28:1-16	Psalm	83:1-18
10	2 Kings	21-22	Acts	28:17-31	Proverbs	16:28-17:4
11	2 Kings	23-24:7	Romans	1:1-17	Psalm	84:1-7
12	2 Kings	24:8-25:30	Romans	1:18-32	Psalm	84:8-12
13	Jonah	1-4	Romans	2:1-16	Psalm	85:1-7
14	Amos	1-2	Romans	2:17-3:8	Proverbs	17:5-14
15	Amos	3-4	Romans	3:9-31	Psalm	85:8-13
16	Amos	5	Romans	4:1-15	Psalm	86:1-10
17	Amos	6-7	Romans	4:16-5:11	Psalm	86:11-17
18	Amos	8-9	Romans	5:12-21	Proverbs	17:15-24
19	Hosea	1-2	Romans	6:1-14	Psalm	87
20	Hosea	3-5	Romans	6:15-7:6	Psalm	88:1-9
21	Hosea	6-7	Romans	7:7-25	Psalm	88:10-19
22	Hosea	8-9	Romans	8:1-17	Proverbs	17:25-18:6
23	Hosea	10-11	Romans	8:18-39	Psalm	89:1-8
24	Hosea	12-14	Romans	9:1-21	Psalm	89:9-13
25	1 Chronicles	1-2:17	Romans	9:22-10:4	Psalm	89:14-18
26	1 Chronicles	2:18-4:8	Romans	10:5-11:10	Proverbs	18:7-16
27	1 Chronicles	4:9-5:26	Romans	11:11-32	Psalm	89:19-29
28	1 Chronicles	6	Romans	11:33-12:21	Psalm	89:30-37
29	1 Chronicles	7-8	Romans	13	Psalm	89:38-45
30	1 Chronicles	9-10:14	Romans	14:1-18	Proverbs	18:17-19:2
31	1 Chronicles	11-12:22	Romans	14:19-15:13	Psalm	89:46-52

August

1	1 Chronicles	12:23-14:29	Romans	15:14-33	Psalm	90:1-10
2	1 Chronicles	15-16:36	Romans	16	Psalm	90:11-17
3	1 Chronicles	16:37-18:17	1 Corinthians	1:1-17	Proverbs	19:3-12
4	1 Chronicles	19-21	1 Corinthians	1:18-2:5	Psalm	91:1-8
5	1 Chronicles	22-23	1 Corinthians	2:6-16	Psalm	91:9-16
6	1 Chronicles	24-26:19	1 Corinthians	3	Psalm	92
7	1 Chronicles	26:20-27:34	1 Corinthians	4	Proverbs	19:13-22
8	1 Chronicles	28-29	1 Corinthians	5	Psalm	93
9	2 Chronicles	1	1 Corinthians	6	Psalm	94:1-11
10	Ecclesiastes	1-3:22	1 Corinthians	7:1-16	Psalm	94:12-23
11	Ecclesiastes	4-6	1 Corinthians	7:17-35	Proverbs	19:23-20:4
12	Ecclesiastes	7-9:12	1 Corinthians	7:36-8:13	Psalm	95
13	Ecclesiastes	9:13-12:14	1 Corinthians	9:1-18	Psalm	96
14	2 Chronicles	2-5:1	1 Corinthians	9:19-10:13	Psalm	97
15	2 Chronicles	5:2-7:10	1 Corinthians	10:14-11:1	Proverbs	20:5-14
16	2 Chronicles	7:11-9:31	1 Corinthians	11:2-34	Psalm	98
17	Song of Songs	1-4	1 Corinthians	12:1-26	Psalm	99
18	Song of Songs	5-8	1 Corinthians	12:27-13:13	Psalm	100
19	2 Chronicles	10-12	1 Corinthians	14:1-19	Proverbs	20:15-24
20	2 Chronicles	13-15	1 Corinthians	14:20-40	Psalm	101
21	2 Chronicles	16-18:27	1 Corinthians	15:1-34	Psalm	102:1-11
22	2 Chronicles	18:28-20:37	1 Corinthians	15:35-49	Psalm	102:12-17
23	2 Chronicles	21-23	1 Corinthians	15:50-16:4	Proverbs	20:25-21:4
24	2 Chronicles	24-25	1 Corinthians	16:5-24	Psalm	102:18-28
25	2 Chronicles	26-28	2 Corinthians	1:1-11	Psalm	103:1-12
26	2 Chronicles	29-31:1	2 Corinthians	1:12-22	Psalm	103:13-22
27	2 Chronicles	31:2-33:20	2 Corinthians	1:23-2:11	Proverbs	21:5-16
28	2 Chronicles	33:21-35:19	2 Corinthians	2:12-3:6	Psalm	104:1-18
29	2 Chronicles	35:20-36:23	2 Corinthians	3:7-18	Psalm	104:19-30
30	Micah	1-4	2 Corinthians	4	Psalm	104:31-35
31	Micah	5-7	2 Corinthians	5:1-10	Proverbs	21:17-26

September

1	Isaiah	1-2	2 Corinthians	5:11-6:2	Psalm	105:1-11
2	Isaiah	3:1-5:7	2 Corinthians	6:3-7:1	Psalm	105:12-22
3	Isaiah	5:8-8:10	2 Corinthians	7:2-16	Psalm	105:23-36
4	Isaiah	8:11-10:19	2 Corinthians	8:1-15	Proverbs	21:27-22:6
5	Isaiah	10:20-13:22	2 Corinthians	8:16-9:5	Psalm	105:37-45
6	Isaiah	14-16	2 Corinthians	9:6-15	Psalm	106:1-15
7	Isaiah	17-19	2 Corinthians	10	Psalm	106:16-31
8	Isaiah	20-23	2 Corinthians	11:1-15	Proverbs	22:7-16
9	Isaiah	24-26	2 Corinthians	11:16-33	Psalm	106:32-39
10	Isaiah	27-28	2 Corinthians	12:1-10	Psalm	106:40-48
11	Isaiah	29-30:18	2 Corinthians	12:11-21	Psalm	107:1-9
12	Isaiah	30:19-32:20	2 Corinthians	13	Proverbs	22:17-27
13	Isaiah	33-35	Galatians	1	Psalm	107:10-22
14	Isaiah	36-37	Galatians	2:1-10	Psalm	107:23-32
15	Isaiah	38-40	Galatians	2:11-3:9	Psalm	107:33-43
16	Isaiah	41-42	Galatians	3:10-25	Proverbs	22:28-23:9
17	Isaiah	43-44:23	Galatians	3:26-4:20	Psalm	108:1-5
18	Isaiah	44:24-46:13	Galatians	4:21-5:6	Psalm	108:6-13
19	Isaiah	47-49:7	Galatians	5:7-26	Psalm	109:1-20
20	Isaiah	49:8-51:16	Galatians	6	Proverbs	23:10-18
21	Isaiah	51:17-54:17	Ephesians	1	Psalm	109:21-31
22	Isaiah	55-57:13	Ephesians	2	Psalm	110
23	Isaiah	57:14-59:21	Ephesians	3	Psalm	111
24	Isaiah	60-62	Ephesians	4:1-16	Proverbs	23:19-28
25	Isaiah	63:1-65:16	Ephesians	4:17-5:7	Psalm	112
26	Isaiah	65:17-66:24	Ephesians	5:8-33	Psalm	113
27	Nahum	1-3	Ephesians	6	Psalm	114
28	Zephaniah	1-3	Philippians	1:1-26	Proverbs	23:29-24:4
29	Jeremiah	1-2:30	Philippians	1:27-2:11	Psalm	115:1-11
30	Jeremiah	2:31-4:9	Philippians	2:12-30	Psalm	115:12-18

October

1	Jeremiah	4:10-5:31	Philippians	3-4:1	Psalm	116:1-11
2	Jeremiah	6-7:29	Philippians	4:2-23	Proverbs	24:5-14
3	Jeremiah	7:30-9:16	Colossians	1:1-23	Psalm	116:12-19
4	Jeremiah	9:17-11:17	Colossians	1:24-2:5	Psalm	117
5	Jeremiah	11:18-13:27	Colossians	2:6-23	Psalm	118:1-16
6	Jeremiah	14-15	Colossians	3-4:1	Proverbs	24:15-22
7	Jeremiah	16-17	Colossians	4:2-18	Psalm	118:17-29
8	Jeremiah	18-20	1 Thessalonians	1-2:16	Psalm	119:1-8
9	Jeremiah	21-23:8	1 Thessalonians	2:17-3:13	Psalm	119:9-16
10	Jeremiah	23:9-25:14	1 Thessalonians	4	Proverbs	24:23-34
11	Jeremiah	25:15-26:24	1 Thessalonians	5	Psalm	119:17-24
12	Jeremiah	27-29:23	2 Thessalonians	1	Psalm	119:25-32
13	Jeremiah	29:24-31:14	2 Thessalonians	2	Psalm	119:33-40
14	Jeremiah	31:15-32:25	2 Thessalonians	3	Proverbs	25:1-10
15	Jeremiah	32:26-34:22	1 Timothy	1	Psalm	119:41-48
16	Jeremiah	35-37	1 Timothy	2	Psalm	119:49-56
17	Jeremiah	38:1-40:6	1 Timothy	3	Psalm	119:57-64
18	Jeremiah	40:7-42:22	1 Timothy	4	Proverbs	25:11-20
19	Jeremiah	43-45	1 Timothy	5-6:2	Psalm	119:65-72
20	Jeremiah	46-47	1 Timothy	6:3-21	Psalm	119:73-80
21	Jeremiah	48-49:6	2 Timothy	1	Psalm	119:81-88
22	Jeremiah	49:7-50:10	2 Timothy	2	Proverbs	25:21-26:2
23	Jeremiah	50:11-51:14	2 Timothy	3	Psalm	119:89-96
24	Jeremiah	51:15-64	2 Timothy	4	Psalm	119:97-104
25	Jeremiah	52	Titus	1	Psalm	119:105-112
26	Habakkuk	1-3	Titus	2	Proverbs	26:3-12
27	Lamentations	1-2:6	Titus	3	Psalm	119:113-120
28	Lamentations	2:7-3:39	Philemon	1	Psalm	119:121-128
29	Lamentations	3:40-5:22	Hebrews	1	Psalm	119:129-136
30	Obadiah	1	Hebrews	2	Proverbs	26:13-22
31	Joel	1-2:17	Hebrews	3	Psalm	119:137-144

November

1	Joel	2:18-3:21	Hebrews	4:1-13	Psalm	119:145-152
2	Ezekiel	1-3	Hebrews	4:14-5:10	Psalm	119:153-160
3	Ezekiel	4-6	Hebrews	5:11-6:12	Proverbs	26:23-27:4
4	Ezekiel	7-9	Hebrews	6:13-7:10	Psalm	119:161-168
5	Ezekiel	10-12	Hebrews	7:11-28	Psalm	119:169-176
6	Ezekiel	13-15	Hebrews	8	Psalm	120
7	Ezekiel	16	Hebrews	9:1-15	Proverbs	27:5-14
8	Ezekiel	17-18	Hebrews	9:16-28	Psalm	121
9	Ezekiel	19-20:44	Hebrews	10:1-18	Psalm	122
10	Ezekiel	20:45-22:22	Hebrews	10:19-39	Psalm	123
11	Ezekiel	22:23-23:49	Hebrews	11:1-16	Proverbs	27:15-22
12	Ezekiel	24-25	Hebrews	11:17-40	Psalm	124
13	Ezekiel	26-27	Hebrews	12:1-13	Psalm	125
14	Ezekiel	28-29	Hebrews	12:14-29	Psalm	126
15	Ezekiel	30-31	Hebrews	13	Proverbs	27:23-28:6
16	Ezekiel	32-33:32	James	1	Psalm	127
17	Ezekiel	33:33-35:15	James	2	Psalm	128
18	Ezekiel	36-37	James	3	Psalm	129
19	Ezekiel	38-39	James	4	Proverbs	28:7-17
20	Ezekiel	40	James	5	Psalm	130
21	Ezekiel	41-42	1 Peter	1-2:3	Psalm	131
22	Ezekiel	43-44	1 Peter	2:4-45	Psalm	132
23	Ezekiel	45-46	1 Peter	3	Proverbs	28:18-28
24	Ezekiel	47-48	1 Peter	4	Psalm	133
25	Daniel	1-2:23	1 Peter	5	Psalm	134
26	Daniel	2:24-3:12	2 Peter	1	Psalm	135:1-12
27	Daniel	3:13-4:18	2 Peter	2	Proverbs	29:1-9
28	Daniel	4:19-5:16	2 Peter	3	Psalm	135:13-21
29	Daniel	5:17-6:28	1 John	1-2:11	Psalm	136:1-12
30	Daniel	7:1-8:14	1 John	2:12-27	Psalm	136:13-26

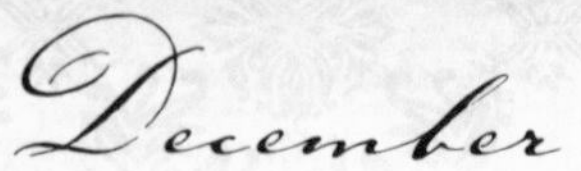

1	Daniel	8:15-9:19	1 John	2:28-3:10	Proverbs	29:10-18
2	Daniel	9:20-11:1	1 John	3:11-4:6	Psalm	137
3	Daniel	11:2-35	1 John	4:7-21	Psalm	138
4	Daniel	11:36-12:13	1 John	5	Psalm	139:1-10
5	Haggai	1-2	2 John	1	Proverbs	29:19-27
6	Zechariah	1-4	3 John	1	Psalm	139:11-16
7	Zechariah	5-8	Jude	1	Psalm	139:17-24
8	Zechariah	9-11	Revelation	1	Psalm	140:1-5
9	Zechariah	12-14	Revelation	2:1-17	Proverbs	30:1-10
10	Esther	1-2:18	Revelation	2:18-3:6	Psalm	140:6-13
11	Esther	2:19-5:14	Revelation	3:7-22	Psalm	141
12	Esther	6-8	Revelation	4	Psalm	142
13	Esther	9-10	Revelation	5	Proverbs	30:11-23
14	Malachi	1-2:16	Revelation	6	Psalm	143
15	Malachi	2:17-4:6	Revelation	7	Psalm	144:1-8
16	Ezra	1-2:67	Revelation	8-9:12	Psalm	144:9-15
17	Ezra	2:68-4:5	Revelation	9:13-10:11	Proverbs	30:24-33
18	Ezra	4:6-5:17	Revelation	11	Psalm	145:1-7
19	Ezra	6-7:10	Revelation	12	Psalm	145:8-13
20	Ezra	7:11-8:14	Revelation	13	Psalm	145:14-21
21	Ezra	8:15-9:15	Revelation	14:1-13	Proverbs	31:1-9
22	Ezra	10	Revelation	14:14-15:8	Psalm	146
23	Nehemiah	1-2	Revelation	16	Psalm	147:1-11
24	Nehemiah	3-4	Revelation	17	Psalm	147:12-20
25	Nehemiah	5-6:14	Revelation	18:1-10	Proverbs	31:10-17
26	Nehemiah	6:15-7:65	Revelation	18:11-24	Psalm	148:1-3
27	Nehemiah	7:66-8:18	Revelation	19:1-10	Psalm	148:4-6
28	Nehemiah	9:1-31	Revelation	19:11-21	Psalm	148:7-14
29	Nehemiah	9:32-10:39	Revelation	20	Psalm	149
30	Nehemiah	11-12:26	Revelation	21	Proverbs	31:18-31
31	Nehemiah	12:27-13:31	Revelation	22	Psalm	150